My Mother's Keeper

My Mother's Keeper

B. D. Hyman

William Morrow and Company, Inc.
New York

Library of Congress Cataloging in Publication Data

Hyman, B. D. (Barbara Davis)
My mother's keeper.

1. Davis, Bette, 1908–   . 2. Hyman, B.D. (Barbara
Davis) 3. Moving-picture actors and actresses—United
States—Biography.   4. Mothers and daughters.   I. Title.
PN2287.D32H9 1985   791.43′028′0924 [B]   85-250
ISBN 0-688-04798-X

Printed in the United States of America

First Edition

1 2 3 4 5 6 7 8 9 10

BOOK DESIGN BY JAMES UDELL

My Mother's Keeper

PART I

1

On May 1, 1947, I was born in Santa Ana, California, to Ruth Elizabeth Sherry (Bette Davis) and was christened Barbara Davis. I was named after my Aunt Bobby (Barbara) who was Mother's only sister. Aunt Bobby had entered a strong plea for a namesake and although Mother detested the name Barbara, she decided to oblige her sister. As soon as she had named me, Mother decreed that I was never, under any circumstances whatsoever, to be referred to as Barbara. "Christ, what a horrible name! Those dreadful nicknames are even worse. Babsy. *Shit!* No one in their right mind would call their daughter Barbara. We'll call her B.D." And so it has always been.

Mother and Sherry, the way she always referred to my father, had a lovely Tudor-style house in Laguna Beach which was perched atop a giant cliff overlooking a rock-strewn cove below. I remember it well, for we were to return there several years later. My first three years were spent there and my best friend was my father's dog, a large boxer called Schatzie. Schatzie was my devoted and constant companion. He used to position himself between me and the open-hearth fireplace when I was crawling or toddling near it and always stayed between the water and me when I was on the beach. He appears in most of my early photographs.

From the moment I was born, Mother took me everywhere and I have fleeting memories of towns and cities all over the United States. Mostly, however, my early memories center around Butternut, the estate in New Hampshire Mother had purchased sometime between her first and second marriages, to Ham Nelson and Arthur Farnsworth. She did not sell Butternut until 1961 and we went there frequently. The original house on the estate was occupied by the caretaker and his family since Mother had built two other houses. The "white" house had been the first and was a charming Colonial nestled in the woods and surrounded by stone terraces and English-style formal gardens. Mother had lived in the white house in the beginning but by my time it was occupied by Grandmother Ruthie and Mother had built the "barn." The barn was just that, a huge weathered gray barn which Mother had moved, timber by timber, silo included, to the top of the Butternut hillside and had converted into a sort of giant lodge that was quite magnificent. A wrought-iron spiral staircase was built into the silo to give access to the second floor, previously the loft, and another interior staircase was situated at the opposite end. Everything was huge, the bay window, the central chimney with fireplaces facing each end of the ground floor and the innumerable picture windows. Although converting it into an abode, Mother did not insulate the lodge or build any cupboards or shelves except for a few bookcases and a couple of kitchen cabinets. The walls remained the original barnboards with all the necessities of life hanging on them.

In 1949, at the ripe old age of two, I made my first, also my last until fourteen years later, movie appearance in *Payment on Demand*. The script called for Mother to have a young daughter and, just in case I should later decide to take up acting, she slid me into the cast in order to get my list of credits off to an early start. During those early years I came to know every studio and back lot in Hollywood.

During that same year, Mother's marriage to Sherry came unglued. Sherry, who was fortyish, had fallen in love with my nineteen-year-old nurse, Marion. They ran away together and tried to take me with them but were foiled in the attempt by

Dell, the cook, who refused to let me leave since she ". . . didn't have any such instructions from Miss Bette." By such slender threads hang our destinies. Dell phoned Mother at the studio but, by the time she got home, my father and Marion had fled. I was to see them again, still happily married with two children, fourteen years later when we had lunch together in New York. Mother was particularly distressed for, separate and apart from having her third marriage come to an abrupt and inglorious end, she was then involved in making *All About Eve,* the story of a forty-year-old stage actress whose career and husband are usurped by a woman half her age. Mother never again permitted Sherry's name to be mentioned in her presence.

During the making of *All About Eve,* Mother met Gary Merrill and their film relationship spilled over into their personal lives. They were married on the heels of Mother's divorce from Sherry, with Mother paying alimony in exchange for sole custody of me. I was later adopted by Gary. They honeymooned in Maine, Gary's home ground, and then, while Gary was off in the Virgin Islands making a picture, Mother bought a house in Malibu and began her dutiful-wife period.

Since Mother was unable to have any more children, she and Gary entered an adoption application and, upon Gary's return from the Virgin Islands, Margot, named after Margot Channing, came into our lives. Gary was home for a month or two before leaving for Germany to do another picture. Mother was hanging in with dutiful wife but had not really contemplated dutiful wife with absentee husband. When *Another Man's Poison* was offered, to star both of them, Mother jumped at it and off we went to England, servants and all.

We spent six months in England, returned to Malibu for a month or two and then moved to old Hollywood in order to be closer to the mainstream. Gary worked for Twentieth Century-Fox for a year and Mother made *The Star* as a respite from her domestic duties. Also during that year my brother, Michael, was adopted. He, like Margot, had been found through a doctor who arranged private adoptions. For Mother, God was in His heaven and all was right with the world. Gary was getting home at night, the marriage was going smoothly, I had a brother and sister to keep me amused and we were all living together in one house. Stability, in our lives at least, was just as fleeting as fame and it was no more than a couple of months before Gary stopped being quite so loyal and dependable and the marriage was in serious trouble.

I was too young to understand anything but the fact that my mother and father had taken to fighting. The sounds of violence were frequent, unmistakable and terrifying. The crashing and shouting and screaming were bad but the sound of my mother crying was the worst. When I asked her about it, though, she told me not to worry, that I was too young to understand. "Daddy sometimes gets very upset and says things he doesn't mean." It wasn't too bad when the sounds were far away at the other end of the house but, when they were loud and close by, I clutched my favorite doll and hid my head under my pillow. Humming to myself was a help. It drowned out the other noises.

Since both she and Gary were from the East, Mother felt that things might get better if we all returned there. She agreed to star in the stage production of *Two's Company* and back we went to the East Coast, this time taking up residence in New York in a duplex apartment overlooking the East River. Mother went to work and Gary took a shot at dutiful husband.

During the out-of-town previews of *Two's Company,* Mother didn't feel well. Her normal high level of energy was lacking and she was beset with fainting spells. By the time the show came to Broadway, she was very poorly and, on the night of dress rehearsal, her entire face swelled up. A doctor applied a poultice, which did a little good, and, on opening night, Mother determinedly went on. She was fine for a while, but toward the end of the first act she passed out cold. The curtain dropped and the audience was asked to stay seated. I was present for my first Broadway opening and became panic-stricken, but Aunt Bobby refused to let me go rushing off backstage. Sure enough, a few minutes later the curtain went up and Mother came to the footlights to deliver the much-reported line "You can't say I didn't fall for you," whereupon she finished the performance and was immediately rushed to the hospital. A tooth was pulled, osteomyelitis of the jaw diagnosed and an operation performed. Mother convalesced for six weeks in the hospital and I frequently spent the night with her in a spare bed which she had had set up in her room.

When Mother was well enough, we moved out of the New York apartment and stayed in a cottage at the Homeward Inn in Maine while Mother and Gary went house-hunting. I was five and thoroughly enjoyed the change of scenery. After a summer-long search, they found the house of their dreams in Cape Elizabeth. To reach the enormous old Colonial-style house one had to drive down a long dirt road, through an apple orchard and past a pond before arriving at a circular driveway. The whole property constituted a peninsula jutting out into the ocean with its own cove and a lovely private beach. So often was "Which way?" asked by prospective guests that Mother came to name the place "Witch-Way", the change in spelling seeming appropriate in view of her then reputation.

In due course a substantial stableyard was created by fencing in the center of the circular driveway and a red barn was built. There promptly accumulated one donkey, two goats, four sheep, two pigs, uncountable chickens and dozens of cats. Mother assumed the enlarged role of dutiful *country* wife and abandoned her career altogether. She spent her time covered in dirt, weeding out old flower beds and lily banks, resurrecting a lovely old rock garden, creating a vegetable garden and digging years of neglect out of the asparagus beds and berry patches. A greenhouse was built, I was enrolled at Waynefleet School in Portland and Mother joined the PTA.

Amid this frenzy of domesticity and relative peace with Gary, it dawned on Mother that dutiful country wives knew how to cook, something she had never undertaken before. She pursued the matter with her usual dedication and zeal, whereupon a further realization came. We could live off the land if we wanted to. The sheep and pigs were butchered in the fall and replaced with baby ones in the spring. Gary set out lobster pots, collecting his catch from a kayak, we all gathered mussels from the rocks right in front of the house and we made clamming trips to Prouts Neck and elsewhere to harvest steamers. We had our own fruit trees and blueberries abounded.

"Christ!" exclaimed Mother one day. "You can't waste all this. It would be a crime."

We hadn't thought that we were wasting anything in particular and were puzzled by her remark until she came home one day with an armful of nature books on survival in the wild.

Fresh produce and seafood were one thing, but survival in the wild had an ominous ring to it. Mother would have none of our forebodings, however, and as she read her naturalist works she discovered wonders such as seaweed pudding. I still shudder just thinking about it. She was in a positive lather over this particular item and made us all comb the shoreline for the "best" type of seaweed. It seemed that this scrumptious stuff came in varying degrees of desirability and Mother insisted that we pay attention. One type had more nutrients while another cooked into a softer custard. While we enjoyed clambering around the rocks and tide pools searching for Mother's raw ingredients, we tried not to dwell on the next phase of the adventure.

Once she was satisfied with the harvest, Mother set about the creation of her first naturalist culinary masterpiece. She worked for days, cooking her pile of seaweed down to mush and then turning it into a watery custard that had absolutely no flavor. Mother was in seventh heaven and consumed pounds of the stuff while the rest of us strained to choke down one small bowl. She uttered occasional cries like *"God!* Can you believe it was once only seaweed?" and "It's incredible. Who wants more?" while remaining blithely unaware that every one else at the table was choking on every mouthful. The reappearance of this item on the menu from time to time did nothing to alleviate its lack of appeal.

Unfortunately, strange concoctions were not enough to satisfy Mother's newly found naturalist urges and she became something of an all-round health nut. Gary took to sucking raw eggs out of their shells. I dreaded the possibility that Mother might require me to follow suit but she passed that one up. Perhaps she, too, found the idea repulsive. Swimming naked in the ocean every morning sounds wonderful until one becomes aware that the water temperature in Maine does not get much above 50 degrees until July or August and that, even then, it tends to hover around the 60-degree mark. Most people settle for wading at the water's edge until midsummer and only the hardy types stay in for long even then. Our mad dashes into the surf early each morning definitely placed us among the "hardy customers" in Mother's opinion and so, at the onset of winter, what could have been more logical than our partaking of a Scandinavian custom? Instead of rushing naked into the surf, Mother made us all rush naked into the nearest snowbank. She went into raptures and insisted that we roll around until we turned blue. She was convinced that she had found the prevention of the common cold and snow baths loomed large in her Maine legend. The servants were exempt but house guests, to their horror, were not. There were, of course, some guests who were completely unmoved by Mother's blandishments. Claude Rains, for instance, visited often but staunchly refused to partake of either the surf or the snowbanks.

At two, Margot had begun to have serious behavioral problems. She was erratic and frequently violent and had her own nurse who did nothing but care for and restrain her. Margot lived on the third floor and at night was tied up in her bed in a straitjacket for her own protection. Michael and I seldom saw her and were told later that Margot's extraordinary, almost superhuman strength was a common compensation for her mental limitations. It was not unusual for Margot, at the tender age of two, to hurl furniture around the room and, on one occasion, she managed to push a bureau across her room and through the window. Mother and I were sitting in the dining room when we saw the bureau fall and crash on the lawn. After that, Margot was never left alone except when tied in her bed.

Mother wanted to put Margot in a hospital but Gary wouldn't hear of it. "You do what you please with *your* daughter but not with *mine*! Margot will not be shut away in a mental home!" Things got worse and worse but Gary, despite his continual protestations of dislike for children in general, felt very paternal toward Margot. There finally came a time when Mother was unable to keep a nurse for more than a week or two at a time and the strain became enormous. Mother and Gary began to have vicious fights over who was to blame for Margot's condition, and although Michael and I saw little of our sister, we constantly felt the effect of her presence.

Eventually Mother took Margot to New York for psychological testing. Her condition was diagnosed as mental retardation as a result of brain damage. The cause was thought to be either the result of a difficult forceps delivery or of having been dropped on her head by a baby nurse whom Mother had then fired for drunkenness. Gary, of course, blamed the nurse, whom Mother had hired, and Mother blamed the delivery. Whatever the truth of the matter, whatever the heartbreak, it was an irrefutable fact and had to be dealt with.

Against Gary's angry protests, Mother found a small private school for retarded children in New York State which accepted Margot as a lifetime student, her brain damage having been deemed irreversible. It was quite some time before my sister was able to come home for visits, but when she did, she showed marked improvement and eventually the alternating moods of violence and lethargy waned. It was a very sad situation but Margot did come to love the school and regard it as her real home.

Dutiful country wife was a good role and health nut a good sideline, but cooking for more than a week at a time was out of the question for Mother. Cape Elizabeth was not exactly on the beaten track and servants turned out to be a little thin on the ground. The closest source Mother was able to find was an employment agency in Boston but was hard pressed to come up with some sort of incentive to induce anyone to accept a job in Cape Elizabeth, Maine. After some debate, it was decided to look for a couple who would live in for three-week periods and then go home for a week. This produced a surprising number of applicants and Mother finally settled on a Swedish couple called Nils and Elsa who shortly took up residence in the servants' wing. The wing was actually rather nice. It consisted of two bedrooms, a bathroom, a sitting room and a kitchenette. Nils and Elsa were very pleased with their prospects and Mother was delighted with her choice. Elsa was a superb cook and fastidious housekeeper, while Nils drove well, buttled to perfection and loved to work in the garden. It seemed as though all of Mother's interviewing time had been well spent and, since they were both quite young and energetic, there was a good chance that they would be with us for a long time. Wrong.

A short while after the couple had moved in, the entire household was awakened early one morning by hysterical shrieking, which seemed to be emanating from the vicinity of the kitchen. We hurried to the scene and found Nils shaking his fist at Gary and bellowing in Swedish while Elsa was crashing about upstairs and crying loudly. Gary stood there, stark naked, leaning on the counter, calmly drinking his customary morning martini. Mother also became hysterical and, after she had cried and shouted for a while, Gary wandered off to seek other amusement or get dressed, whichever came first. The upshot was that our ideal couple beat a hasty retreat, Nils expressing sorrow at leaving the rest of us but explaining that he just couldn't subject his wife to any more of Gary's bizarre conduct.

As the couples came and went, Mother became less concerned with the efficiency of the next prospect than with how easily upset the wife was and how jealous the husband, explaining that Mr. Merrill was really quite harmless despite his disconcerting habit of roaming around naked from time to time. The breakfast streaker had an extraordinarily long run of success at causing maids of all creeds and colors to run screaming into the morning mist, but his reign of terror eventually came to an end. Mother found servants made of sterner stuff. They somehow managed to totally ignore Gary and go peacefully about their duties as though naked men swilling martinis at dawn were among life's commonplaces.

The first of these rare gems was Leroy Thomas, butler, gardener, chauffeur, handyman and constant friend to small children. He was to be with us throughout our Maine period and beyond. Mother introduced him to us when he served his first dinner. "We have a new houseman and I think we will all like him. His name is Leroy and—"

"No it's not!" Gary interrupted. "He told me he hates being called Leroy . . . he prefers Thomas."

"What do you mean he prefers Thomas?" Mother bellowed.

"Just that!" Gary bellowed back. "He told me about it when I was talking to him in the kitchen before dinner." Mother purpled with fury at this encroachment upon her domain and shrieked, "What the hell were you doing talking to the butler behind my back? What the hell were you doing in the kitchen? Of course . . . you wouldn't tell *me* he prefers being called Thomas! You love to see me embarrassed in front of servants, don't you?"

"To hell with that shit," Gary retorted. "Just call the man Thomas and shut up!"

17

Thomas had heard every word of this interchange without turning a visible hair. It was quite some time before a maid-cook stayed put but she was worth waiting for. Ogleetha was her name and, fortunately, she liked to be called by it. She, too, was with us for many, many years.

Our outdoor activities in the winter were numerous and included sledding, games of fox and hounds on snowshoes, cross-country skiing and skating. Our pond was about an acre in size and had a large stone barbecue beside it. Electricity had been run out there, so we had music and lights to skate by. Many a skating party lasted way into the night with an unending supply of hot dogs, hot cocoa and hot punch. Gary was a first-class skater and it wasn't long before he started pick-up hockey games. As soon as there were enough regulars Gary decreed that his team, of which he was the captain, would adopt tams and kilts as their uniform. On their first outing thus clad, we learned why Gary was so thrilled with his idea. As if he were a true Scot, Gary was wearing nothing under his kilt and every time he stretched for a shot or took a spill, one had the added drama of Gary mooning Maine. He had struck again.

My birthday is on May 1 because, to a certain extent, Mother planned it that way. When she reached the eighth month of her pregnancy, she knew that the delivery would have to be by cesarean section and, therefore, scheduled. She hadn't a doubt in her mind that she was carrying a girl and wanted her to have her birthday on May Day. Mother had images of May-poles and ribbons fluttering in the breeze and of organdy and lace dresses. I'm grateful to have been a girl.

Every year my birthday was marked with a Maypole dance on the lawn, with all my friends being instructed in the dance, weaving and braiding the pastel-colored ribbons around the pole. For Mother it was a regular Rite of Spring and nothing was allowed to get in its way. In California it worked out splendidly because the weather is reliably hot in May and outdoor parties are a safe concept. In Maine, however, the weather on May 1 is far from reliably hot. There are years when the sun is shining, the birds are singing, the grass is greening-up and the tulips are in bloom. Then there are the other years when the last gasp of winter asserts itself. It never lasts long, but one day is all that's needed to put a real crimp into a Maypole dance. I can recall some very brisk ones when we all had to run to keep warm and one in particular when Mother had to bundle us all up in boots, leggings, snow coats, hats and mittens before we could face the stormy blast. The snow was deep and the ribbons were frozen stiff but Mother would not forgo the Rite, even for one year. "My daughter is a May Day girl and she will have a Maypole dance and baskets will be filled with spring flowers. *God!* Why do you suppose I planned her birthday this way?"

2

When I was eight we returned to California for Mother to make *The Virgin Queen* and Gary stayed behind in Maine. Things had again been going badly in their marriage and the fact that Gary hadn't seen fit to go to work in a long time and money was in short supply didn't help matters. My memories of those next few months are a blur of friends' houses lived in until the friends returned and of cheap rentals, all for the purpose of cutting down on expenses. The best thing was that we had got away from Gary.

While we were in our duplex on East River Drive in New York, our household had been comparatively peaceful. Aside, that is, from the occasional faint sounds of strife which filtered down from Mother and Gary's second-floor suite. It was most likely that things were as bad as ever without my knowing it. It wasn't until the hectic months of searching for and then settling into Witch-Way had given over to the regular routine of everyday life that I was again assaulted by the inescapable sounds of violence. At first Mother seemed to be able to spare the rest of us the worst of it by containing the raging battles behind the closed doors of their suite, but, as the struggles became fiercer and the anger more intense, it must have been that only her own survival was on her mind.

My room at Witch-Way was at the top of the staircase at one end of the hallway while the master suite was a long way away at the other end. As the fights got louder and louder and their door was left open, it became impossible for me to pretend that nothing was happening, impossible to ignore it by hiding my head under my pillow. The noises penetrated and I couldn't stop myself from listening, from straining to understand what was happening. As long as I could hear Mother shouting back at Gary, I knew she was all right. But when I couldn't hear her anymore, I would open my door and listen for her. When there was only the sound of her weeping and pleading among Gary's threats and name calling, my fear for Mother would overcome my terror of Gary and I would find myself irresistibly drawn down the hall to protect my mother. Once in their presence, I wouldn't be able to talk. Mother would look at me, usually from the floor at Gary's feet, and scream, "Get out! Go away!" as she rocked and moaned. Looking back, I'm sure that she only wanted to protect me from Gary but, at the time, it seemed as though she were rejecting my help and it hurt. Gary would glare at me, face contorted into a vicious mask, and shout, "Get away from me and mind your own business, you little slut, or I'll give you the same as your mother! Would you like that . . . . huh?" Then he would lurch a step or two in my direction while Mother shouted, "Gary, no! Don't! God, please no! B.D., run! Get out! Now!" I would scream, "Don't hurt Mommy anymore! Don't hit her again!" and Gary would slap me across the face or knock me down and Mother would scream louder that I was making it worse.

Whatever Gary's treatment of Mother and me, he was always careful to shield Michael, whom he adored, from the worst of it. Before beginning one of his rampages, Gary invariably took my brother to his room and locked him in. Then, when the battles were over, Gary would often go to Michael and tell him that he didn't think he would be able to put up with Mommy much longer, that the two of them might have to run away soon. Gary was also likely to burst into tears and fall asleep curled up on Michael's bed with his arms around his little son.

One night I went to bed while a party was going on. It was

very noisy and, with guests milling on the lawn beneath my windows, it was impossible for me to fall asleep. As I lay there listening to the conversations below, a heated argument broke out between Gary and another man. The man was accusing Gary of having an affair with his wife and I recalled the few times I had walked into the living room early in the morning only to freeze in my tracks and quietly back out upon seeing Gary sprawled on the couch with his best friend's wife. I wondered if that was the wife now in question and found it rather pleasing to listen to this man raging at Gary. There was lots of arguing and then the sounds of doors slamming and people leaving. All was quiet for a while and then I heard Mother shouting at Gary in the entry hall at the bottom of the stairs. "You make me sick! You think you're such a hotshot with all the broads? *Ha!* You haven't laid *me* in years. The only time you touch me is when you beat me up. *Bastard!* That's all you're good at." Then came Gary's evil laugh and sneering tones. "What are you bitching about? Getting slapped around is the only thing you enjoy, you stupid cunt! If it doesn't do anything for you, why do you beg for it all the time?"

"Oh, my God! That's what you always say and you know it isn't true. You know that violence terrifies me. All I want is to be loved like a woman."

"*Bullshit!* You're no woman . . . you're a frigging ice queen. Without an audience you're not worth a shit! Maybe if I knocked you on your frigid ass on the stage of the London Palladium and then jumped you, you'd perform. Outside of that, a knothole in a tree is more exciting than you."

"*Jesus!* You really are something! I suppose all the other men in my life didn't know what they were talking about? One of them even—"

"*Jesus Christ!* Are you going to hand me that crap about Howard Hughes screwing you on a bed of gardenias again? He fucked every two-bit twat in Hollywood and you're proud of holding out for ten bucks worth of gardenias! Poor dumb son of a bitch wasted a lot of flowers. The only people who can be around you for long without wanting to kill you are faggots, so don't waste your time telling me about all the men—"

"So my other three husbands were fags, were they? Well let me tell *you* something . . . . at least *they* were men! They—"

"They nothing! They all kicked the shit out of you. You've told everybody who would listen to you about it. The first was a nothing, the second was a drunk who never left his mommy's titty and the third ran away with your slut daughter's nurse. The only thing I'll say for them is that they got airplanes out of you. You didn't have anything left when I came along."

Mother screamed, "Stop it! Stop it! I can't take any more" and I heard their feet pounding up the stairs. When she reached the top Mother shrieked, "Get away from me! Go to your whore! I don't want you." A stream of curses and threats filled the night and I realized that I had moved from my bed to the door, just a few feet from where they were standing. Mother suddenly whispered a plea that he not ". . . frighten the children." But Gary shouted, apparently directly at my door, "Maybe the little slut should come out and see what you get for starting a fight."

"Gary, get out of my house!" Mother yelled, panic in her voice. "Leave this instant! Leave B.D. out of this for God's sake!" I ran and jumped back into bed, but too late. The door flew open and Gary roared, "You want to listen? You might as well have a clear view as well!" He laughed at me and Mother threw herself at him like a crazed cat. Gary turned and knocked her to the floor. She tried to get up and he knocked her down again. She tried to run back down the stairs, I think in an attempt to steer Gary away from me, but he caught her at the top of the stairs. I could see her flailing at him, trying to get loose. He had her by the neck and, as she got down a couple of steps, he moved to the other side of the railing and jerked her along until her feet could no longer touch ground and she dangled by her neck while he bellowed about teaching her a real lesson. Mother was making gurgling, choking noises and I couldn't stand it anymore. I flung myself at Gary's back, pummeling him with my fists, trying to make him let go of her. I screamed hysterically, "You're killing her, you're killing her!" He kicked me away a couple of times. Mother was just hanging there, thrashing wildly and choking. I couldn't just give up. This time he was going to kill her. Oh, how I wished somebody would hear and come to help, but there wasn't a soul stirring anywhere despite all the noise. Suddenly Gary let go of Mother and she fell halfway down the stairs, to the landing directly below her.

I wanted to run to help her but Gary spun around, hit me and flattened me against the wall. I must have passed out because I don't remember anything more until I woke up on my bed.

There were voices coming from the front hall and to my overwhelming relief I heard Mother's. Then I heard Gary's laughter and amiable tones, then strange male voices. I got up and, feeling sore all over, made my way to the top of the stairs where I crouched to hear what was going on. Mother was pacing wildly and flapping her arms. Gary was sitting on the hall bench with his legs crossed, drink in hand, swirling the ice cubes casually around in his glass and smiling benignly at two uniformed policemen. Mother was shrieking half incoherently at the policemen, showing them her neck and accusing Gary of trying to strangle her. One of the policemen tried to explain, evidently not for the first time, that unless she were willing to press charges, which would necessitate them taking Gary off to jail, there was nothing else they could do. Mother said that she didn't want it in the newspapers but that they should do something informally. The policeman said his hands were tied and turned his attention to Gary when Mother became increasingly hysterical. Gary explained that it had been a simple domestic argument, winked knowingly and said that he was sure they knew how that was. He said that it was really nothing for them to concern themselves with and that his wife was prone to overreaction and hysteria, as he was sure they could see for themselves. Then he offered them a drink. I wanted to run downstairs, but then Gary would clobber me again after the policemen left. I stayed where I was and when it was all over I scurried back to my room. My toy poodle, Tinker-Bell, was curled up on my bed. I snuggled close to her, glad of something warm and friendly to love and by whom to be loved. I could understand *her*.

One of the houses we camped in for a few weeks was a charming stone cottage in Brentwood, a suburb of Los Angeles. The garden was English in style and contained a secluded gazebo. I mention it because an unusual thing happened one day.

I was wandering in the garden and came upon Mother sitting alone in the gazebo and crying quietly. She hadn't heard me approach and I stood for a few moments, listening to her weeping and wondering whether to withdraw in silence or go to her and try to be of some comfort. I couldn't ignore her unhappiness and continued the last few steps to the gazebo. "What's the matter, Mom?" I asked gently, putting a hand on her shoulder. "Is there anything I can do to help?"

"No," she replied, starting slightly and looking up at me, "it's nothing for you to worry about." She forced a little smile through her tears. "Sweet of you to care, though."

"It's Daddy, isn't it?" I suggested, sitting down opposite her.

"Yes, but don't worry. It'll all work out somehow."

"But it won't, Mom," I protested. "It never does . . . it just gets worse."

"You don't understand."

"Then tell me about it. I was there when Daddy tried to choke you. I saw it all. If I hadn't stopped him he might really have killed you."

"Oh, B.D.!" she suddenly wailed. "Just love and trust me. I love you more than anything. You know that I wouldn't let any harm come to you. It's just that you're too young to understand. I have to stick it out for you kids."

"I'm *not* too young!" I protested again. "I know everything that goes on, I really do. I just don't understand why you go on living with him."

Mother pulled herself together a little. She wiped her eyes, blew her nose, lit a cigarette and stared directly at me. "You may know what goes on with Daddy and me but what you can't know, darling, is that it doesn't make any difference. All men are the same in the long run."

"What do you mean?" I asked, completely baffled by her response.

"Well . . . you might as well know it all. The others beat me up too. Men think it's their great power over us. God help you, you'll find out soon enough, my darling daughter. The bastards can't stand a bright, strong woman." I sat quietly while Mother puffed on her cigarette a few times and got a distant expression in her eyes. "Ham . . . his great weakness was money. He forced me to have two abortions because I was paying all the bills and he wouldn't have children unless he could pay for them. He was a brilliant trumpet player. Somehow he never got a break and he took it out on me. It broke my heart but I had to leave him. He was my first love." Another pause and still the distant look. "Then there was Farney. A real charmer but an alcoholic who was tied to his mother's apron strings . . . and what a mother! *Christ*, what a cold bitch. It was a tragedy when he died even though our marriage was headed for disaster anyway. *He* used me too . . . he got violent at times to take out his frustrations. *Ha!* Then came your real father. *Brother!* Sherry was a real pip . . . all muscle and no brain. He boxed in the Olympics and swam in the Pan-Am Games. All he cared about was his damn physique! It *was* pretty beautiful, I'll tell you that much. He *loathed* my brightness. It drove him mad trying to prove his manly superiority." She gave me a wan smile. "You, my dear, were an immaculate conception."

"What's that?" I asked, not having the least notion.

"You're too young to understand, but I don't recall ever being laid by your father. You had to be an immaculate conception."

I still had no idea what she meant but, all these years later, I have a hunch that it was not so much another swipe at my father as an expression of her wish that she could have conceived me without undergoing the degradation of the sexual act. She wrote in her autobiography that sex was God's joke on humanity, a grotesque anachronism and an outdated testament to man's waning power, whatever that may mean.

I had heard everything that Mother said. The stuff about her husbands wasn't new and I was still puzzled. How could she say that it didn't make any difference whether or not she left Gary? Why did she say that all men were the same? It didn't make any sense. We knew all kinds of people who were happily married.

"I don't know what you mean, Mom," I finally confessed. "It can't be that everybody's miserable. We know lots of people who are happy together. Look at the Henreids . . . you don't mean to tell me they're pretending, do you?"

"Gawd, yes!" she exploded. "It's all part of life's greatest farce. Paul would go for me in a minute if I gave him the chance . . . but I'm too good a dame to do that to Lisl." This wasn't helping. I'd only seen Paul behave as a perfect gentleman, so I came back to the point.

"But why stay with Daddy? Wouldn't we be better off with just us?"

"That's enough, B.D.!" she said in a sharp rebuke. "I won't take any more from you. I can't! I won't face being alone again. I've been alone since my father walked out on me when I was a little girl like you. Nothing I did pleased *him* either. He was a brilliant lawyer and had I been a boy he'd have recognized his brains in me . . . but I was a girl . . . so he wrote me off. I don't blame him for despairing of Ruthie; my mother just wasn't up to him. She was a flibbertigibbet without a brain in her head. She still is. My sister, Bobby, was sweet but a bore and Daddy didn't care about any of us. Had I been a son, things would have been different. Boy, is that the truth! There's only one way for a female to be recognized in this man's world, as you'll all too soon discover, and that's to fight every inch of the way. You can *never* stop fighting. I fought and I'm still fighting and I'll go on fighting until my dying day.

"You see, since my daddy deserted us, I've been the father and it seems I always will be. I was the strong one. It fell to me to hold our little band together. Sure, Ruthie was a crusader and I'll always be grateful to her for her dedication. She saved my life . . . but in the end *she* fed off my strength too. Even Ruthie became a taker, and I became father not only to Bobby but to Ruthie and then Bobby's daughter, Fay, when Bobby's marriage inevitably crumbled. *Brother!* Even my husbands expected me to be father. Sometimes I would *die* not to be strong, not to have to fight . . . it will always be my curse. You see, B.D., to survive you must learn to fight. You're bright too so you're also cursed as I was. Never relax, sweetheart, or the Lilliputians will climb up your legs and devour your soul. Be a fighter or be swallowed up with the weaklings. Never let your guard down . . . *never*!" She suddenly stood up, took my hand and, with a deep breath, straightened like a soldier and said, "Come on, daughter, let's go in. We'll fight the world together, you and I."

Mother was thrilled to be doing *The Virgin Queen*. She had always said that she was too young to play Queen Elizabeth when she did *The Private Lives of Elizabeth and Essex* and, now that she was playing her again, she would have the chance to really do her justice. She felt a great affinity for Queen Elizabeth, envied her her power and believed that she and the queen were very much of a kind. Additionally, this time she would not have to fight the costume battle she usually did over each character she portrayed. When she had made *Elizabeth and Essex* back in 1939, she and Orry Kelly, the costume designer, had conspired against the director, Michael Curtiz, to get authentic costumes into the picture. Curtiz had contended that realistically huge skirts and neck ruffs were far too cumbersome to be handled well or photographed satisfactorily. Mother had Kelly make an entire set of scaled-down costumes which she wore for costume tests and rehearsals. She also had him make a set of historically accurate ones which she wore for shooting and refused to remove. She won her point and it was a matter of great satisfaction and glee to her for years thereafter.

Errol Flynn had played Essex the first time and Mother's longtime friend, Olivia De Havilland, had played Elizabeth's rival for his affections, Lady Penelope. Olivia and Errol had had a mad affair during the making of the film and Mother was quick to point out that "although Errol is undeniably sexy, Bette Davis will never be a notch on his belt. No siree, bub! I'd scratch his eyes out and he knows it." She did, however, like his portrayal of Essex despite her opinion of him as a man.

Mother again shaved her hairline back to show an authentically bald head, which Queen Elizabeth had suffered as a consequence of diphtheria, and in *The Virgin Queen* she removed her wig in a scene with Lady Penelope, this time played by Joan Collins, to reveal a specially made rubber cap with some bits of fuzzy gray hair stuck here and there. It was absolutely awful-looking, which was precisely what Mother wanted.

I was on the set with Mother during filming and for the first time I began to pay attention to the details of her professional life and what was going on around me. It was fun. It was nice having people tell me what a great actress my mother was and how fortunate I was to be her daughter. I began to see her through the eyes of the world instead of merely from my little girl's viewpoint. I had always loved her, of course, but now I began to admire her and her determination. At home life was so confusing and often frightening. Even when Gary wasn't around, the havoc he wreaked when he was around was dominant in my mind. Mother didn't present a clear image to me; she didn't seem to know what she wanted. Here, in her element, I was seeing her at her best, being herself, doing what she did well and doing it with absolute conviction. She was in control of herself and events around her and even when she was fighting with someone, there seemed to be a purpose to it.

Mother didn't think much of Richard Todd as Essex and said, "Compared to Errol he's a milquetoast. Elizabeth would have dumped him in five minutes flat." Other than that she was pleased with the picture and prevailed upon Twentieth Century-Fox to open it in Portland, Maine, as a benefit for a local children's hospital. We returned to Maine early in the summer so Mother could be on hand for the opening. There was an enormous cocktail party at Witch-Way and everyone wanted Mother to demonstrate her "queen's walk" which was so talked about in the movie. It looked to me as though she had a rash between her legs and had to keep them apart when she walked but, fortunately for moviegoers everywhere, I was the only one who saw it that way. Mother shone and was far more alive and animated than she had been at any time in the past few years.

3

In the fall of 1955, Michael and I stayed in Maine while Mother returned to California to make *Storm Center,* a film about a defiant librarian, a character who appealed greatly to her. She applauded her spirit and liked the New England setting. Shortly thereafter she signed to do *The Catered Affair* with Ernest Borgnine as her husband and Debbie Reynolds as her daughter. The character she played was Aggie Hurley, a frowsy Bronx woman, so Mother padded her costumes to look as frumpy and sloppy as possible. Aggie Hurley was another character to whom Mother became dedicated.

Mother never seemed in the least concerned about going off and leaving Michael and me with Gary. Although my fear of him was never far from the forefront of my mind, things were actually a lot easier when Mother wasn't around. That she left me alone with Gary at all was a puzzlement; it was as though she truly believed there was no violence . . . an argument once in a while, perhaps, but certainly nothing to get upset about.

Gary took Michael and me to California at Thanksgiving for a visit. We stayed in a posh rental at Malibu, not too far from the studio where Mother was working. One weekend we were all invited for the day to the home of Debbie Reynolds and Eddie Fisher. I recall how idyllically happy they seemed together and it amazed me when, not long after, Eddie Fisher ran off with Elizabeth Taylor. Oh, Hollywood! The Fishers and their children were extremely nice and it was a lovely day. Mother didn't think much of Eddie Fisher, but Debbie Reynolds rated well with her as ". . . a promising young actress who's a tough customer."

When *The Catered Affair* was completed, Michael and I returned to Maine with Aunt Bobby while Mother and Gary set off on a holiday together in their new black Mercedes sports car with a red leather interior. Mother was aglow with excitement and told me all about their plans to drive to Florida, spend two weeks on a big sailboat that Gary had chartered and then drive up to Maine to join the rest of us for the summer. They planned to be away together for about two months and it was obvious that Mother thought the trip was going to smooth things out between Gary and her. She even had red leather luggage made to fit exactly behind the bucket seats and seemed to believe that the pieces of her life could as easily be fitted back together. When they rejoined us in Maine two months later, however, the only thing that had changed was that the happy glow with which Mother had departed Malibu was gone.

Mother had no satisfactory movie lined up and decided that if she wanted to get her career back into full swing she would have to be in California to pursue it. She told me that since *The Catered Affair* had fizzled and she had played a frump to boot, Hollywood had decided that she was all washed up and had turned its back on her; she would have to be there to change their minds.

She persuaded Gary's brother, Jerry, and his family, who also lived in Cape Elizabeth, to close up their house and move into Witch-Way for the time she would be away since she wanted Michael and me to stay in Maine rather than be dragged to California again with all the uncertainty that faced her out there. There was plenty of room for all of us at Witch-Way and living with Uncle Jerry, Aunt Marguerite, Susan, Chris and baby Mark was my first experience of normal family life. The contrast was overwhelming; no shouting, no screaming, no beatings and no fear, just kindness and love. I had found heaven.

That period turned out to be one of disappointment and

frustration for Mother. She was unable to get a movie of any kind and ended up doing a bunch of television shows just to survive. She did *Playhouse 90* and *Ford Theatre* as well as a handful of others I don't recall. Even the first pilot she ever did for a TV series failed to pan out. Whenever she talked about that time in her life, it was with great bitterness and resentment toward the film industry for trying to "dump" her.

The greatest delight for me was the discovery of cooking. Aunt Marguerite was wonderful and we developed a deep and permanent affection for one another while I puttered in the kitchen learning how to cook and also how to bake. The Jerry Merrills and Michael and I became one big family, with Mother calling frequently to make sure that we were doing everything her way. The redoubtable Thomas was still with us but his week off was getting longer and longer. He tended to stay away for ten days to three weeks at a time and then turn up to say that he had been "terrible sick." He would resume work for a month or so before doing it again. Gary's Rottweiler, Klaus, was also with us and he too disappeared for days at a time and worried everyone to death. Whenever Mother called she would receive a bulletin from me on the status of the household which usually ended in one of two ways: "Thomas is missing but Klaus is back" or "Klaus is missing but Thomas is back."

Shortly before the end of that year, Aunt Marguerite took me aside one evening and said, "I want you to know, B.D., that Uncle Jerry and I have become very fond of you. We were expecting a spoiled, snotty child but you aren't that at all. I know how difficult things must be for you with your parents but you must never despair. You're sweet and generous and kind. Don't ever lose those qualities or allow yourself to become convinced that you don't have them." It was a nice compliment at the time but nothing more. Later, however, Aunt Marguerite's words were to come back to me often and I clung to them in my moments of self-doubt. As Mother's daughter I was to have many such moments.

The day that Mother rejoined us in Maine the following summer, I was not at the door to greet her. I had heard her arrive and run to my room to hide but, when Aunt Marguerite came to coax me downstairs, I fled to the barn in tears. Mother's return meant that Aunt Marguerite and Uncle Jerry would be gone forever. I didn't want to lose them and I cried and cried. In the end I cried myself out, dried my eyes and returned to the house to hug my mother. She carried on at length about how much she had missed me and then enthused about a forthcoming movie called *Look Homeward Angel*. Since Mother couldn't bear to be without Michael and me anymore, we were off to California in time for the next school year.

Mother had rented a ranch house in Brentwood and, on the day we moved in, she fell down the cellar stairs and fractured a vertebra. It would be many months before her back was fully mended, so *Look Homeward Angel* was lost to her. About two weeks later I was thrown from my horse during a riding lesson and broke my arm. Now Mother and I each had a hospital bed. We relocated to a house in the Emerald Bay Beach Club in Laguna Beach. Then, two weeks later, we moved to a house across the way which Mother had seen from her window and liked better. We stayed there through the winter and, when Mother was fully recovered in the early spring of 1958, she was offered parts in two movies to be filmed in Europe. They were cameo roles but it was the only movie work available to her. She decided to accept the roles, send Michael to stay with Gary in Maine and take me with her. She felt that it was a terrible comedown but she was fed up with doing television.

The first part was as Catherine the Great in *John Paul Jones* with Robert Stack, to be shot in Spain, the other was in *The Scapegoat* with Alec Guiness, to be made in England. Aunt Bobby would come with us to help Mother and look after me and the trip would include lots of sightseeing. We would visit Italy and France as well as Spain and England. I was thrilled to bits and could hardly wait.

Shortly after my eleventh birthday we went to New York and boarded the *Independence* bound for Gibraltar. The voyage took four days and, although it was rough at times, I loved every minute of it. Mother enjoyed herself and socialized quite a bit, which was unusual since she generally avoided parties. One of the events I remember from the voyage was a funny-hat contest. To my surprise Mother threw herself into it with abandon. Aunt Bobby, she and I set about the use of all the materials issued by the ship for the competition. There were paper plates, fruit baskets, plastic forks and spoons, crepe paper, artificial flowers and so on. We spent hours concocting our entries and ended up with some crazy creations. The Paris milliners had nothing to fear from us but we were tickled pink and won all the prizes. Mother was fully convinced that we won strictly on the merits and wouldn't hear of the possibility that her being Bette Davis had anything to do with it.

Mother always had a blind belief that people were not influenced by her fame and that she was loved by "honest" people who cared only about her as a person, not her fame. She was unshakable in this conviction, even extending it to tradesmen who grossly overcharged her and doctors who made productions out of small things in order to do the same. It happened throughout her life and she maintained an extraordinary naïveté about it. Thus I learned to live with all the sycophants who worshipped the "real" Bette Davis. They never did convince me and most of them were aware of it, even while showering me with gifts in order to please her. She considered me very hard and often asked, "How can you be so cynical? These people love your mother and you too. I don't understand you." There were, of course, some true friends among the crowd, but very few. Sometimes it hurt me to see her so deceived. More often, though, it was downright infuriating to watch her stubborn blindness.

After we docked at Gibraltar, we motored to Seville for the night and on for Madrid the next morning, stopping at points of interest along the way. I think we drove through every village in Spain; I know we walked through every cathedral and historical building. Mother was riveted by every detail and in the same way that she attacked acting or gardening in Maine, she applied her energy and enthusiasm to being a tourist. No stone was left unturned, her feet never tired and she missed nothing. We even had to try to learn the flamenco. By the time we arrived in Madrid, we had seen so much of Spain that we felt like natives.

We took up residence in the same hotel where all the other Americans involved in the movie were staying. Since it was to be a long shooting schedule, many of the participants had brought their families with them. There were even a couple of girls my own age. John Farrow was the director and his daughter, Mia, and I became fast friends. Part of the filming of *John Paul Jones* was done in the throne room of the Royal Palace in Madrid. It was cluttered with all the paraphernalia of filmmaking but it was still the throne room. At the foot of the steps to the throne there was a pair of larger-than-life marble lions. They were absolutely gorgeous and during one of the lunch breaks Mia and I decided that it would be great fun to sit astride them. We climbed up on their backs and promptly precipitated an international crisis. After we had been rudely snatched down, the alarums and excursions had subsided and the shouting had stopped, we were informed that the Spanish people, who had kindly consented to their throne room being used for the movie, did in no way appreciate their sacred lions being abused. It seemed that there was a representative of the government on the set at all times to ensure the safety and care of the palace. He was appalled by our irreverence and it took a fair amount of talking to convince him that we were really unaware of the significance of the lions and that we meant and did no harm. It all blew over but, whereas Mia and I had been allowed to roam about the palace at will, we were now strictly confined to the filming area. Mother was furious that I should have been treated like a vandal and had quite a few words to say about it. The restriction, however, remained. Her final words on the subject were *"Brother!* These damned foreigners!"

When Mother's scenes were completed, amid much grumbling by her that Robert Stack was ". . . the dullest actor who ever lived and as much like John Paul Jones as a cat in hell," there was time to spare before she was due in England and off we went to Rome. I loved the Appian Way, the Colosseum and the restaurants but I was tiring of cathedrals. They had all begun to look alike.

Ben Hur was being filmed while we were in Rome and since it was being directed by Willie Wyler, who had long been an important man in Mother's life, I got to hang around while the chariot race was being set up in the specially constructed arena. Mother was terrified during the racing sequences but all I could see were the magnificent horses. It was a thrill to watch and we spent several days on the set. I got to know each of the two teams of four horses intimately. I realize that I should have been traipsing around after Charlton Heston but that was part of my normal life. Being around that caliber of horseflesh wasn't. The highlight of my week was getting a ride around the racetrack in a chariot. It was very exciting and a vast improvement on cathedrals. Mother's parting comment was "Charlton Heston is such a pompous ass. He's lousy as Ben Hur. If Stephen Boyd had played the lead the movie might at least have had some guts."

On leaving Rome we headed north and saw much of Italy. Mother decided that she was meant to be Italian and that she had come home. We stayed in Venice for a few days and I was enthralled. I dragged Aunt Bobby all over the place because I adored the footpaths with no traffic, the bridges over the canals and the gondolas. The whole city was rather like a fairy tale and every time I see a film or read about Venice sinking it saddens me terribly. We stayed at the Gritti Palace on the Grand Canal and tried to take in everything. I fed the pigeons in St. Mark's Square and we visited the glassworks. They made a vase for Mother while we watched. We saw the ladies making lace, took a skinny-dip in the Adriatic off a little island outside Venice and then headed for France.

The island of Mont-Saint-Michel is actually a hill rising out of the sea about half a mile offshore. The only modes of transportation are goatcarts and burros and the roads are paths, many of them cobblestoned. The town is constructed in snake-like fashion along the main path to the top of the hill and the inevitable cathedral and it is a breathtakingly beautiful spot. I have since learned that the cathedral is in fact an abbey, not a cathedral, however, the error was probably not my fault. In Mother's life everything and everybody was always the biggest, the best, the most famous or all three. Each lobster she ate was better than any before, any doctor who ministered to her was the best in the world and probably the most famous as well. It stands to reason that we would have visited the odd abbey, village church or even chapel, with Mother proclaiming it to be a cathedral. It might have lacked a bishop, but Mother had been there and that was sufficient unto the day.

Although the cathedral at Chartres is rendered uniquely beautiful by its world-famous blue stained-glass window, it is memorable to me because of an incident that occurred while we were there. No one is allowed to take photographs inside the cathedral, it being explained that this injunction is sacred law. The cynical tourist suspects that it has more to do with enhancing the sale of picture postcards than sacred law, however, a tall thin lady, dressed all in black, wearing sunglasses and carrying a camera had dogged our footsteps since our arrival in Chartres and continued after us when we entered the cathedral. When we had seen all and absorbed the eerie blue lighting of the interior Mother, as usual, went to light a candle. The lady in black, who had been skulking in the shadows meanwhile, suddenly burst forth from behind a column and tried to take Mother's picture. Unfortunately for the woman, the flashbulb exploded in her face, causing many lacerations and a lot of blood. Mother at first was petrified, believing that she had been subjected to a terrorist attack, but when we had calmed her down by explaining what had happened, she took all the blame upon herself and began tearfully apologizing to anyone who would listen. By the time an ambulance arrived, it seemed as though the entire population of Chartres had also. Through the chattering and arm waving we finally understood that the event was being regarded as a miracle. The explosion of the flashbulb was God's vengeance on one who would break the sacred law, and Mother was God's representative in the teaching of this lesson. We departed quickly through a cheering and waving multitude lest Mother assume for them the proportions of Joan of Arc.

Next stop England, but first the boat train. When the train rolled onto the boat there was so much creaking and groaning that we thought we were done for, but it crossed the Channel safely, as it had been doing for many years. I had not been to England since I was three, right after Mother and Gary were married, but I felt at home. We stayed at an inn called Ye Olde Bell on the Thames in Hurley. I was entranced by it and spent hours watching the river locks. Mother was forever having to walk into the woods to find me. We visited all the royal palaces within reach, were particularly taken with Windsor Castle, visited the Tower of London and Hyde Park, saw the changing of the guard at Buckingham Palace and rode on top of as many double-decker buses as we possibly could. Harrods, a store to end all stores, which has everything from a fishmonger to couturier fashions, consumed days of our time. I decided that, while Mother thought she was Italian, I was English. I stated at the time, and with absolute certainty, "Someday I shall marry an Englishman . . . I know it." Needless to say, Mother lit a candle in St. Paul's Cathedral.

All too soon for me—and after Mother had said of Alec Guiness, "He's overbearing, egotistical, haughty, snotty, insensitive to play opposite and a dreadful actor"—*The Scapegoat* was finished and it was time to go home. Mother wanted to take Michael something special from our trip abroad so, just before we were due to sail, she purchased a Yorkshire terrier puppy and named him Lord Pip Mountbatten. He had to be kenneled on the ship but we managed to have him smuggled into our cabin at night and whisked away again each morning. We sailed on the *Queen Mary* this time and the crossing was much smoother. When we arrived in New York it was straight on to Maine for the rest of the summer. Michael was, at first, thrilled with Pip but he really wasn't suited to a little boy. He was just too yappy and nervous and, despite his adorable appearance, Michael quickly lost interest in him. A bigger dog would have been a better choice but Mother was enchanted with Yorkies.

At summer's end we moved back to California and rented a house on Hanover Drive in Beverly Hills. We had a huge pool with an elaborate pool house. The pool was a great conversation piece because it had a mermaid painted the full length of the bottom. There were also a tennis court and a formal garden. A gardener came with the house and we were a source of considerable annoyance to him. He was such a tyrant, in fact, that Mother was afraid to pick flowers from "his" garden. We used to do it at night.

Picking flowers was one of Mother's favorite pastimes. Wild flowers or orchids, she loved them all. Give her the chance and she would strip a garden naked in no time, gathering arrangements. She didn't believe in scissors or gardening shears . . . she liked to rip the unsuspecting blooms off without a thought to the damage she might be doing to the plant itself. She tore away with carefree abandon, to the dismay of gardeners everywhere. It also gave her a big kick to reach over the fence and pluck anything she fancied from the neighbor's garden, like a kid stealing apples from the farmer's orchard.

Apart from tearing flowers from their roots, there were other things that gave Mother satisfaction. It was as if she gave vent to her emotions by attacking inanimate objects. Gutting fish was another passion. She used to say, "I love to rip the guts out of fish. I like to feel the goo and blood and think of all the people who've done me dirt. *Christ!* Would I like to do this to a few people I could name." After playing Queen Elizabeth she fancied the idea of having the power to behead people. Just the thought of it could put her in a good mood for days.

Thomas and Ogleetha had come to California with us and on one of Ogleetha's days off Mother was in the kitchen cooking. I decided to surprise her with my new baking skills and make one of her favorites, apple bread, for dinner. As I set about finding the ingredients, Mother looked up and asked what I was doing in the kitchen. I beamed enthusiastically. "I'm going to make one of your favorite desserts."

"That's marvelous," she replied, "but not while I'm cooking. *God!* You can't have two people in the kitchen at once."

"I promise not to get in your way," I said plaintively. "It's a big kitchen and I only need this spare counter, way over here. I thought that we could do something together. Aunt Marguerite and I always cooked at the same time. She said she enjoyed my company."

Mother spun on me and snarled, "I'm so happy for you and your precious Marguerite! *Brother!* I guess you wish you were still with her. *Well,* let me tell you something, young lady, Marguerite was only with you because I paid her to be. You really break my heart. *Jesus!* I'm the one who loves you . . . not Marguerite." Never before had I felt so crushed and I couldn't understand why Mother would say such cruel things. I ran from the kitchen, holding back the tears until I reached the security of my room.

While we were at Hanover Drive I began to take riding seriously. Mother had calmed down concerning the hazards involved and it quickly became the most important thing in my life. I not only rode constantly and began to really learn horsemanship, but worked in the stables and learned about the care and feeding of horses. I enjoyed the stable work almost as much as the riding.

There were still no movie offers, so Mother did an episode of *Wagon Train*. She had known Ward Bond, star of the series, from earlier years at Warner Bros. and enjoyed working with him. I was on the set and was allowed to ride the horses. I also got a lesson from one of the stunt men on how to drive a Conestoga wagon with a team of four. Mother was getting nervous about my interest in driving wagons and chariots, so I had to assure her that it was only the horses that attracted me, not the idea of becoming a stunt woman. A little while later she did another episode of *Wagon Train* in a different role but, aside from that, she was without work for some eight months.

We stayed in Beverly Hills throughout that school year and it was my first experience of a public school. Because the school was in Beverly Hills, I didn't think I would have a problem with it. Whenever I had changed schools in the past, being a film star's daughter had brought me a lot of grief. Some of the children thought I was someone of whom to be jealous while others thought I was different and should be shunned. It always seemed to have been decided before I ever appeared that a film star's daughter had horns. This was the principal factor in my preference for friends who not only had nothing to do with my school life, but were also much older than I. Beverly Hills notwithstanding, I was the only person in the whole school with any relationship to the film industry and I was again regarded as having horns. It was very disappointing.

Jim Burke, my riding instructor and owner of the ranch where I rode, announced one day that I was sufficiently accomplished to own my own horse if I wanted to. Mother bought me a lovely Quarterhorse mare named Sally, whereafter Sally saw a great deal more of me than Mother did.

In March I contracted bronchial pneumonia and was confined to bed. By the third week I was feeling much better but was not allowed up due to the residual fluid in my lungs. I grew very bored. During the past winter I had collected a vast quantity of minuscule seashells while combing the tide pools of Laguna Beach with some cousins (the Favors) who lived near the beach. To break the tedium of my convalescence, I took out the box of shells and began to create designs on sheets of notepaper by gluing sand and shells to the top left-hand corners. I had been doing this for a few days when Perc Westmore, the head makeup man at Warner Bros., was visiting Mother and came upstairs to say hello to me. When he saw my "custom" notepaper he got very excited and told me that if I could make enough sheets he would sell them in the boutique of his beauty salon. I asked what he meant by enough. He told me not to worry, he would send over the supplies and I should just give it my best shot. Sure enough, late that afternoon a messenger arrived with fifty boxes, each containing eight sheets of very expensive-looking notepaper. I was rather awed at the prospect of trying to do four hundred individual shell designs, but amazed myself by actually finishing all fifty boxes by the end of the week. Perc came to get them himself, said that he was delighted and handed me seventy-five dollars.

I was tickled pink with my sudden wealth and enlisted Aunt Bobby's aid in the spending of it. "I'm going to buy a birthday present for Mother," I confided. "The one thing I know she wants badly is a new set of luggage and now I have the money to buy it for her." Aunt Bobby produced the name of a discount luggage dealer in Los Angeles. As soon as I was well enough to be up and about, I went to the store and found exactly what I wanted: a matched set of lightweight luggage, good quality, robin's egg blue (Mother's favorite color) and consisting of a large suitcase, a medium suitcase and a makeup kit.

Just before dawn on Mother's birthday, I took the three pieces of luggage with big red bows tied to the handles of each, tiptoed into her bedroom and placed them in the center of the room where she would see them when she first woke up. On top of the largest suitcase I put a large cardboard birthday card, which I had made and painted myself, that said, "HAPPY BIRTHDAY. I LOVE YOU, MOM. FROM B.D."

When Mother awoke I heard her whoop from my room across the hall. By the time I got there she was sitting on her bed crying, with the makeup kit on her lap. She held out her arms to me and wailed, "Oh, B.D.! It's *just* what I wanted. How did you know? You must have spent all your money on it. The color is divine and the sizes are perfect. Oh, darling, it's the best birthday present I've ever had. Ever." I cried too.

4

Gary continued to come and go at random intervals and was drunk far more often than he was sober. I didn't make a conscious decision about my plight, but it slowly dawned on me that if Mother had minded Gary's attacks and all the violence, she would have done something about it. I was sick not only of being slapped around by Gary, but even more of the constant fear and uncertainty his mere presence engendered in me. I began to stay out of their fights as much as I could, no matter how much it seemed as though he were about to kill Mother. Sometimes he came straight at me without first attacking Mother and I gradually developed the ability to detect a change in the tone of his voice. When that change came and I was quick enough, I got out of the house before the fighting began. I had several hiding places, two of which he never found, one behind some bushes on the hillside overlooking the pool, the other behind the vine-covered chain-link fence that surrounded the tennis court. He rarely failed to search for me but, more often than not, I evaded him. It entailed my sleeping out of doors in my secret places and creeping to my bed at dawn but it was worth it. By that time, Gary had forgotten.

In June we packed up again and went to Maine for the

summer. Sally came too and continued to be my best friend. I got up every morning at dawn and rode endlessly. I was constantly in trouble for missing meals. By this time I was very good at horse and stable management, and the housekeeper was heard to bewail the fact that "Miss B.D. keeps her stable far better than she keeps her room." It took a while but, when Mother discovered how early I was taking to horse, she promptly banned it, announcing that she did not approve of a young girl being up and out at dawn. Eight o'clock and later, it seemed, met with her approval but not earlier. Arguing the matter brought me nothing but "It isn't the proper thing for my daughter to do. *Brother!* Just get off my back about it."

Mother always had tacit lists of things of which she did and did not "approve." Her highest compliment, in her view, was to tell me that she approved of me. I never nailed down exactly what she meant by this but she always glowed when saying it. She did not approve of asking what was for dinner, talking baby talk to babies (it warped their future speech patterns), artificial flowers, improperly dressed children (properly being the way she dressed *her* children) or houseguests doing anything for themselves without permission or assistance. The things she approved of varied and were never known in advance. She had lists of things she approved of for herself, but different ones for everyone else. She neither realized nor cared that the lists were different and inconsistent, but whether or not she approved of things loomed very large in her legend. She often spoke of her father's disapproval of her and felt the need either to approve or disapprove of everything herself.

My practice of hiding whenever I detected the telltale edge to Gary's voice had become second nature to me. One night, while I was sleeping in the apple orchard, I was awakened by the sound of a horse's high-pitched screaming, a sound they only make when they are terrified. Thinking that a fire must somehow have broken out in the stable, I sprinted the hundred yards from the orchard and flung myself through the door. The lights were on and Gary was in Sally's stall with a length of barbed wire in his hand. The mare was plunging hysterically around the stall, banging her knees into the walls and screaming in terror. Gary was holding the wire in a loop above his head and making lunging moves at Sally, quite obviously

bent on getting the loop over her head and around her neck.
His back was to the stall door. I leaped across the intervening
twelve feet, threw the bolt and flung open the door. Sally
plunged through the opening, knocking Gary backward into
the wall as she did so, and took off at a mad gallop with me
hard on her heels. I went back into hiding, knowing that Sally
wouldn't go far, and waited to see what Gary would do next.
It wasn't long before he stumbled out of the stable and went
to the house. I waited five more minutes, to be on the safe side,
then found Sally and led her back to the stable. Her neck,
shoulders and face were badly lacerated, her knees were banged
up and she was lame. I spent the rest of the night treating her
wounds and poulticing her knees. In the morning Gary drove
off and I went in search of Mother. I told her what had happened and insisted that she come to see Sally. She resisted
strenuously, arguing that she didn't ". . . have to walk all the
way to the stable just to see a couple of scratches on a horse,"
but I eventually prevailed and got her down there. She glanced
at Sally and said, "Gary's an idiot. He was roaring drunk and
probably decided to go for a ride in the middle of the night."

"If that were the case, Mother," I demanded angrily, "why
was he in her stall slashing at her with barbed wire?"

"He probably mistook it for a lead rope," she replied and
walked away.

Summer came to an end. Mother and Gary got ready for
their tour of the country with *The World of Carl Sandburg,* a
dramatic reading of Sandburg's works which was to receive great
acclaim. Mother enrolled Michael and me at Chadwick School
in southern California, in second and seventh grades, respectively. This was Michael's first time at boarding school and I
was all set to play mother; however, within a couple of weeks
he, as well as I, had a whole set of buddies and the last thing
he wanted was a big sister breathing down his neck. At Chadwick, thank heavens, we weren't outcasts. There were all sorts
of film children there, including Liza Minnelli, and we were
just two more. Sally had again crossed the country since the
school provided boarding facilities for students who had their
own horses. The condition of boarding was that the students
care for their own stock. I arose at five each day, walked the

half mile to the stables, fed, watered and mucked out, then hotfooted it back to the dorm to shower, change and get to breakfast by seven-thirty. I rode most days after classes and taught Sally and myself to jump. There was plenty of room to ride on campus and the Chadwicks were very lenient, provided that we used good judgment.

During Christmas vacation Mother and Gary rented the house at Laguna Beach where I was born. Margot was flown in from her school in New York State and Mother, who was always very emotional about Christmas, believed that despite the almost total deterioration of her relationship with Gary, we would have one big happy reunion. All I can recall of that Christmas is we children tiptoeing around, trying not to be held responsible for starting the next shouting match; that and the fact that I pleaded with Mother to leave Gary. Whenever we were all in the same place at the same time, it was the same story: fights, beatings, curses and screaming. If Gary was there, the rest was sure to follow.

At Easter vacation Michael and I were flown up to San Francisco to join Mother and Gary who were there doing the final performances of the northern leg of the Sandburg tour. When we arrived we found a situation which so frightened us that we locked ourselves in our rooms for most of the time. The shouting and screaming, not to mention the crashings and bangings, were enough to frighten anyone, let alone the seven- and eleven-year-old children of the antagonists.

Tennessee Williams was in San Francisco for a meeting with Mother concerning the possibility of her doing *The Night of the Iguana* on Broadway. His go-between was a lady by the name of Viola Rubber. Viola was as aware of the situation between Gary and Mother as must have been everyone else in the hotel and she was nice enough to take Michael and me on outings to Fisherman's Wharf and Top of the Mark and on as many cable-car rides as we wanted. Just before we were to go back to school, Mother told us that she had finally come to terms with the fact that she had to divorce Gary. I was immensely relieved, but Michael took it very badly.

June arrived and another school year came to a close. Michael, Sally and I returned to Maine for what was to be our last summer there. After Mother's announcement in San

Francisco, and knowing that Gary had been replaced in the southern leg of the Sandburg tour by Barry Sullivan, the last person I expected to see when I got to Maine was Gary, but there he was and nothing had changed. Gary would argue that there was no real reason for them to get divorced and Mother would sometimes stand her ground and sometimes give in but, whatever her posture of the moment, either immediately or within a few hours they were once more shouting and throwing things. Gary would then leave, only to reappear unannounced and do it all again.

Mother was utterly miserable but was determined to put a good face on things. It was obvious to everyone who knew us that divorce was inevitable but she kept postponing the actuality. Her marriage to Gary was to have been the marriage to end all marriages and she simply could not bring herself to accept another failure.

Many friends came and went that summer, including the Batchelder family whom Mother had known for most of her life. She and Ellen Batchelder had been friends since their teens. Their daughter, Gay, was about my age and an avid horsewoman to boot. We hit it off immediately and formed what was to be a lifelong friendship. Mother, entirely of her own volition, had the idea that it would be nice if Gay and I could ride together and rented an extra horse for the duration of the Batchelders' stay. It made that last summer in Maine even more special for me.

Giving up her marriage to Gary was the most heartbreaking thing Mother ever had to do. It wasn't that there was any tenderness, let alone love, left between them. It was that she had to forsake her self-image of successful wife and mother, roles she had always held to be more important than any others. She was convinced that Gary was her last chance to maintain that image and, rather than accept the shattering of the image, she had hidden for a very long time behind an emotional smoke screen.

Upon her divorce, Mother sold Butternut and Witch-Way. We were sad about this phase of our lives coming to an end. Despite Gary, we had loved our childhood in Maine and Mother, to her credit, had accomplished her purpose of giving us some basis in reality with a New England rural upbringing.

She was convinced, with good reason, that growing up solely in Hollywood would make it impossible for us to have our feet on the ground in later life. The glitter and glamour of Hollywood were all right as a place but not as a philosophy.

The successful wife half of her image was destroyed and Mother determined never to marry again. There was ". . . no man worth a shit as a husband on the face of the earth. They all let you down . . . it's just a question of time." She focused all of her hopes for emotional fulfillment on me, proclaiming that I was the most talented, brilliant, beautiful being on earth. I came to pity anyone who failed to rave about me in her presence. According to her, there was nothing and no one good enough for B.D. B.D. was all that remained of her dream and, if nothing else in her life were certain, at least she could rely on that. B.D. was to be the fantasy daughter of the world's greatest mother and the presents lavished on her would know no bounds. "B.D. is the only thing I have ever really loved."

The fear and the hurt of the last five years were finally over. I had survived. Because Mother had been pulled too many ways at once and had not protected me, I had learned to protect myself. I never doubted that she loved me and I never had any reason to contemplate my own feelings. She was my mother and I loved her. She had always been generous with me and particularly so after Gary had hurt me. Now she loved me more than anything else and whatever I wanted was mine. I slipped into the new role without a thought. It seemed perfectly natural to equate gifts with love. Whenever I gave Mother a card or a present of any sort, I received an "Oh, thank you, B.D. I'm so happy that you love me so much."

It wasn't that Mother had no love for Michael. She did love him, but it wasn't clear whether she loved him for himself or just as the symbolic son. I had always been Mother's daughter and when Gary was angry with her he also vented his fury on me. Michael, on the other hand, was the apple of Gary's eye and, although Mother got custody of both of us, Michael remained loyal to Gary. Mother, despite protestations to the contrary, deeply resented my brother's inability to accept her as his one and only parent. Whenever Michael returned from visiting Gary, Mother subjected him to merciless cross-questioning. What had Gary said about Mother? What had Michael said about Mother? Whom did Michael love better? How could he love Gary at all when she was the only one who loved *him*? And on and on and on. Michael would sneak into my room at night to pour out his woes and have a good cry. We were probably closer as brother and sister during the next few years than at any other time in our lives.

5

It felt strange, knowing that we would not be returning to Maine, but stranger yet to be living in New York City. Although the entire entourage was in residence, Mother, Michael, me, Aunt Bobby, Thomas, Ogleetha, assorted pets and the omnipresent Sally (boarded at the Claremont Stables near Central Park), a town house on East Seventy-eighth Street took some getting used to. There was a pretty walled-in garden at the back and, with some of Mother's Early American furniture in it, the house took on something of the look of home. Michael went to a private boys' school in the city, but Mother was unable to find a school she considered suitable for me. She hired a tutor and I had my schooling each day in my suite on the third floor of the house. Mother's bedroom was the only other room on the third floor, the other bedrooms being on the fourth floor. The first floor consisted of a foyer, a kitchen and a dining room that opened onto the garden; the second floor contained the living room and the den. It was a typical layout for a town house where the space is vertical. My tutor, Mrs. Josephine Morris, was a super lady and I learned more from her than I had at any school. I loved the concentrated teaching and looked forward to my lessons. Since they only occupied the mornings I had the afternoons to myself.

I did a great deal of riding and began to get interested in modeling. I was a normal, healthy weight, which didn't cut it for photographic modeling, so I went on what Mother called the lettuce-leaf diet. She wasn't happy that at thirteen, I was deliberately getting skinny, but I was determined. I lost the weight and did some modeling for magazines and some live fashion shows. I had also begun to date. Mother was convinced that every man I met was overwhelmed by me, which proved embarrassing upon occasion. She began to live vicariously through me at this point and encouraged my dating. I was five feet ten inches tall, looked eighteen and always dated men much older than I. Mother usually approved of my choices and didn't mind how late I stayed out so long as I gave her a minute-by-minute account when I returned. If I saw the same man several times, she would become increasingly nervous and rules would come out of nowhere. She would want to know exactly where we were going and what time we expected to be home. On arriving at a specified destination I would find urgent messages that I phone her. When I called she would insist that I be home at an earlier time than had previously been agreed upon. If I failed to call, either deliberately or through not having received her message, she would greet me at the door in her nightdress and create an incredible scene in front of my date. She invariably succeeded in driving him off, sooner or later, one way or another.

The World of Carl Sandburg opened on Broadway, this time with Leif Erickson. The show had done very well on tour but didn't make it in New York and it closed. Mother then decided to write her autobiography, *The Lonely Life.* She collaborated with Sanford Dody and spent months in the den on Seventy-eighth Street working on it. It was torture for her to recall her past in detail and it upset her terribly. There were many times when she announced that she couldn't "make it." It was not just one thing that upset her, but the whole process of recall. She did not want to delve deeply into her strange love-hate relationship with Gary but it was drawn out of her. Although hardly any of it found its way into the book, Mother's blue pencil taking care of that, at least she had been forced to admit things to herself which she had theretofore sublimated. She had had her share of both triumphs and tragedies and she somewhat better understood her failed marriages by the end of the book. Mother certainly had greater peace of mind where Gary was concerned and she finally, at long last, shed her tears over his loss.

Gary still made the occasional appearance in our lives. He had visitation rights with Michael, but I had insisted on testifying at the divorce hearing that there was no reason for me to have to see him and that I did not wish to do so. The judge, hearing my reasons, agreed with me and excluded me from Gary's visitation rights. Nonetheless, Mother insisted that we all get together for Christmas that year, so Gary was with us. Her dream was dying hard.

It was 1961 and Jack Kennedy was about to be inaugurated. Mother was invited to do a reading of Carl Sandburg as part of the gala at the Washington Armory. There was great excitement. I had never attended anything so important before and Mother behaved like a kid herself. It was the first time she had looked forward to anything since the divorce and the fact that her "beautiful Jack" was about to be President made her world a little rosier. Not since Roosevelt had she felt so personally about a president. The first day or two was spent rehearsing for the gala and I wandered around an armory filled with practically nothing but famous names. It was a strange feeling. Usually the notable people in a crowd stand out. You say to yourself, "Oh, look, there's so-and-so." This time an unknown face was of interest. It might even be someone really important.

On the night of the gala there was a mighty blizzard in Washington. The snow was a foot deep and the city was one big traffic jam. The plows couldn't go to work until the streets were cleared of cars and the cars were stuck in the snow. We hadn't had the foresight to take our evening clothes to the last rehearsal as the other performers had and, since we were unable to get back to our hotel to change, Mother went onstage in the simple black dress she had worn since morning. The show was fabulous and Mr. Kennedy and all the other Kennedys attended the reception afterward for the performers. Because of the storm, I met the President-Elect of the United States in a wool skirt and blouse. I'm sure he didn't even notice, but I felt like a clod. Just before I was introduced to him, Mother whispered to me, "Now, when you shake hands with Mr. Kennedy, you just watch out. He's a notorious lady killer."

The next morning the snow had been cleared away and it was a beautiful day for an inauguration. Mother and I had on the right clothes this time. That night Frank Sinatra gave an enormous dinner party and was kind enough to put me at his table, which was where the President sat briefly when he joined us between inaugural balls. President Kennedy gave me a rose and said, "To youth. I wish I were nineteen again." I was tickled, but then Frank had to go and tell him that thirteen was more like it. It was a marvelous evening and an absolute tonic for Mother.

Sally came to the end of her time and I rode stable horses until a big bay hunter, Stoneybrook, captured my attention. We had a horse in the family again and I got to do a couple of modeling assignments in Central Park with him. I had begun to take jumping seriously, but because Stoney was twice the size of Sally, it frightened Mother to death. She regarded him as a potential killer and my jumping as a countdown to disaster. She didn't prevent me from pursuing my hunter classes since she didn't "approve of parents who forbid their children to participate in their chosen activities." So, always looking as though she expected the world to come to an abrupt end, she watched me ride, jump and compete in horse shows. Whenever I fell off, she flew into hysterics but, fortunately, I rarely blew it in her presence. Much though it frightened her, my pursuit of riding was inviolate. She had proclaimed so loudly and long that she didn't "approve" of preventing such things that she was hoist with her own petard.

The tutorial year ended and, leaving my horse behind for once, we went to California so Mother could play Apple Annie in *Pocketful of Miracles* with Glenn Ford. Mother rented a bungalow at the Chateau Marmont in Los Angeles and dispatched me to ride around with a real estate agent to look for a decent rental while she was working. It was the first time Mother had entrusted me with finding a suitable house to rent and I picked a lovely one on top of the hill behind the Chateau. It had a breathtaking view of the city and a swimming pool on stilts, sticking out into thin air like so many of the structures in the Hollywood Hills. Mother never did completely trust the pool and always stayed at the uphill end, believing herself thus to be on solid ground. The whole thing was a far cry from Mother's Yankee taste, being very modern with tons of glass—huge glass walls, glass tables—all pastels, with velvets and satin brocades and marble floors with Oriental carpets. It was a thoroughly California house and I loved it. Mother hated it but, to please me, she rented it. It set a precedent she was to regret from time to time.

While Mother was at Paramount doing *Pocketful of Miracles*, having almost walked off the picture because Glenn Ford insisted that Hope Lange have the dressing room next to his (the one Mother wanted), I found a new distraction. Elvis Presley was making *Blue Hawaii* on the same lot and I got a pass to his set which, naturally, was a closed one. A closed set permits no visitors except by special permission and no tours under any circumstances. This is a common restriction on any set where visitors can slow down production. On Elvis Presley's set, screaming, fainting girls would not have moved things along. I was not bitten by the Presley bug like most of the young people I knew. I loved his music but didn't particularly care for his hip-swiveling antics. It was more the boredom of watching Mother every day than curiosity about Elvis that prompted me to want to visit his set.

I quickly became a regular on the *Blue Hawaii* sound stage. The group was very congenial and all of Elvis's sidekicks were very nice to me. I discovered, much to my amazement, that Elvis was a thoroughly charming man; moody as all-get-out but sweet. He kind of took me under his wing and made me feel at home. It was a lot of fun.

Because I liked Elvis and was spending so much time on his set, Mother decided that I was in love with him. Further, since I was irresistible to the male of the species, it would only be a matter of time until he was head over heels for me. It became very trying, particularly when she began to speculate on what it would be like to have Elvis Presley as a son-in-law. The more I protested, the more convinced she became and I lived in constant terror of her going over to the Presley set and proclaiming to Elvis that it was all O.K., she approved of him. Luck was with me, however, and it didn't happen, but until we left Paramount the possibility hung over me like a dark cloud.

Mother living vicariously through me was all right within limits, and I was even getting used to some of her outlandish fantasies, but I wished that she would keep it to herself. I also wished, for her sake, that I looked like Marilyn Monroe to justify her opinion of me. When I looked in the mirror I saw a healthy-looking, California-beach-type blonde with green eyes, nothing spectacular; but to listen to Mother, Grace Kelly would have lost to me in a beauty contest. It was downright embarrassing when she shared this conviction, in my presence, with a roomful of people. It would have been nice if she'd permitted others to form their own opinions of me rather than discomfit them, and mortify me, with a speech like "I want to know if you all realize how damned good-looking my daughter is. I hope so because she's the best-looking female I've ever seen and you'd all better damn well appreciate her!" It was a real conversation stopper. She would stand there with her hands on her hips, looking triumphant, while fixing each person in the room with a meaningful stare as I tried to be swallowed up by the carpet.

That summer, 1961, Grandmother Ruthie died and Mother was devastated. She had turned her mother into a saintly legend and, in truth, suffered the loss of the image more than the loss of the actual woman.

When Harlow Davis had abandoned his wife and two daughters, Ruthie determined that Betty and Bobby would go to the best schools and be proper New England ladies regardless of her personal sacrifice or the lack of personal comfort or material things any of them might suffer. At first Ruthie did any sort of work that would provide an income; she was a laundress, cleaning woman and seamstress principally, but she had long aspired to being a photographer and one day got the break she needed, a job as a photographer's assistant. In due course she set up on her own as a free-lance photographer. Mother's recollections of Ruthie invariably centered on a picture of her slaving away over the endless retouching of negatives. Ruthie managed to negotiate reduced tuition fees for her girls by doing school yearbook photographs for free; and when Mother decided during her early teens that she wanted to be an actress, Ruthie allegedly convinced Mr. Anderson of the John Murray Anderson School of Acting to admit Mother on the cuff, promising to pay him whenever she could.

I know that in her book Mother wrote of Ruthie as a cross between a saint and a gladiator. There is no disputing that Ruthie did devote herself to her daughter, but only until her efforts bore fruit, when Mother began to earn money in the theater at age twenty-one, followed by her move to California and her first screen success, *The Man Who Played God,* at age twenty-three and the consequent lucrative Warner Bros. contract. The truth was that Ruthie had become as self-serving as any stage mother and had seen in her older daughter the chance to grab for the gold ring. The moment Mother was put under contract by Warner Bros., Ruthie bulldozed her into borrowing against the contract and buying a beautiful house that was far larger than they needed and an expensive luxury car. For the rest of Ruthie's life she not only expected but demanded to live as well as Mother or, preferably, better, and acted even more of a queen than Mother. She refused to live in the same house as Aunt Bobby, whom Mother also supported, but had to have a house all to herself. When Mother got a mink coat, Ruthie had to have a mink coat. Her wardrobe was far more extensive than Mother's and her thirst for jewelry and new cars was unquenchable. They fought like hellcats whenever they were together. It wouldn't be until years after Ruthie's death that my mother would come to see her in a more realistic light.

Mother always believed that Ruthie was entitled to everything she wanted because of her years of sacrifice. The trouble was that Ruthie went well beyond the bounds of reason in her wants and her deathbed request for a solid silver casket was a classic example. It came at a time in Mother's life when she was hurting for money. In the film industry one's fortunes can go up and down like a yo-yo and Mother was at the bottom of her string. Ruthie was fully aware of this when she left the deathbed request on her bedside table and, even though Mother seethed inwardly, she complied with the request by arranging for the casket on time payments. Ruthie had done an excellent job of making Mother feel guilty if her every wish were not Mother's command and she had, in a gesture of royal disdain, issued her last command.

6

It was time for school again and we returned to New York. This time I was enrolled at Grier, a girls' boarding school in Pennsylvania where the principal sport was riding. Stoneybrook and I moved onto campus in September and I went through the now-familiar routine of proving that I was a human being like everyone else before being accepted by the other girls. In addition to riding we played field hockey which I hated and was rotten at, skied which I loved and was good at, played tennis which I loved and was atrocious at and swam which I liked and was good at. I did better academically, thanks to my year of tutoring under Mrs. Morris, and made the honor roll. All things considered, it wasn't a bad year and definitely the most congenial since the early grades at Waynefleet.

Mother was playing Maxine Faulk in *The Night of the Iguana,* which had come successfully to Broadway after the customary out-of-town run. Mother was a hit and Patrick O'Neal as the male lead was marvelous. Mother really got her teeth into Maxine, even unto not wearing a wig. She had her hair dyed flame red, which was hideous but fit the part perfectly. Mother didn't mind in the least that she looked ridiculous . . . she was

Maxine. She visited me as often as she could at Grier, coming to school events and horse shows.

In June of 1962, Mother sent me out to California to look at rentals again. She wanted to get back to films after leaving *The Night of the Iguana* in April because of a personality conflict. Patrick O'Neal was brilliant in his role but had the habit of improvising bits of stage business and rephrasing lines. It didn't seem to bother anyone else in the cast, but Mother, a stickler for precise readings and hitting marks, was totally disconcerted. She railed at anyone who would listen but without success. Then she took on Patrick O'Neal, accusing him among other things of doing it on purpose to upstage her by throwing her timing off. He simply shrugged her off. To make matters worse, Margaret Leighton, who also got rave reviews, was a perfect lady and invariably polite. She got along with everyone, including Patrick O'Neal. Mother, naturally, labeled her a bitch and her parting speech to one and all who stood still to listen was "I'm sooooo happy that you're all such a congenial group! I'm sooooo happy that everyone thinks Maggie is so *charming* and Patrick so *brilliant*! I'm sorry I had to irritate you for so long with my professionalism. You obviously like doing it your way much better. *Well!* Now you can, my dears!"

Before leaving New York I had to sell Stoneybrook. Mother wanted me to be available to travel with her wherever she went and having a horse would be inconvenient and too consuming of my time. While Mother was packing up Seventy-eighth Street, I found another flashy Beverly Hills house, complete with projection room, volleyball court, a hillside of step-terraced gardens and a pool and pool house. All modern with huge bedroom suites, a sweeping curved staircase and sliding glass doors everywhere. I must have been going through a Hollywood phase. I closed the deal, the papers were sent to Mother for signature and, upon her arrival, she went straight there from the airport. Her comment was a plaintive "Oh, B.D., not another one?"

"You told me to please myself," I replied huffily, "and anyway, Early American houses aren't exactly thick on the ground in Beverly Hills." Mother stared at me squinty-eyed for a moment, then shrugged, gave vent to a sigh and said, "Well, I'll get used to it, I guess. At least it's private."

Mother immediately began work on *What Ever Happened to Baby Jane?* with Joan Crawford. The press was overflowing with expectations of the rivalry of the century and Mother, of course, was stating publicly that she and Joan were ". . . just two professional dames doing a job." Somehow, no one could accept that it was quite that simple. I knew a great deal about Joan, none of it good, and was curious myself to see how this was going to work out. It certainly was stirring lots of publicity even before shooting began. The producers were happy . . . publicity is the name of the game. Robert Aldrich directed and it was his lot to console both of his stars at all hours of the day and night and to try to keep the situation under control. There must have been times when he wondered if it was all worthwhile. Mother, as usual, decided that he was madly in love with her but couldn't stand Joan, ". . . but what can he do? He's stuck with Joan." I never doubted that Joan felt the same way but in reverse. Anyway, Bob Aldrich could not have got much sleep during filming, judging from the hours that Mother alone kept him on the phone at night.

I spent much of the shooting schedule on the set and my first contact with Joan Crawford went like this. Mother walked over to her and said, "Hello, Joan." Joan answered, "Hello, Bette." Mother said, "I'd like to introduce my daughter, B.D. B.D., Joan Crawford." I extended my hand and said, "Pleased to meet you, Miss Crawford." She pulled back from me, putting her hand behind her back as if I were diseased, and replied, "Hello, dear. One thing . . . my daughters, Cindy and Cathy, are going to be on the set with me a great deal. See them over there on the bench?" I looked in the direction in which she was pointing and saw two girls about my age, dressed in identical corduroy overalls and middy blouses, matching shoes and even the same hairstyle and color of hair ribbon. They were both knitting and, even though they were close enough to hear the conversation, neither of them looked up when their mother spoke about them. Joan continued, raking me up and down with a supercilious gaze. "I would appreciate it if you would not try to talk to them. They have been very carefully brought up and shielded from the wicked side of the world. You, obviously, have not. I don't want your influence to corrupt them. They are so sweet and innocent, you see? I know you will do as I wish. Thank you. Bless you, dear." With this, she smiled a saintly smile and walked away. Mother and I stared at each other, speechless. There really wasn't much one could say after that.

Joan, with much fanfare, provided the set with an enormous Pepsi cooler. Her own bottle of Pepsi, constantly at her elbow, was always half full of vodka. Joan thought this was an ironclad secret but everyone knew about it and Mother would rage in her dressing room. "That bitch is loaded half the time! How dare she pull this crap on a picture with me? I'll kill her!"

They maintained a strained politeness toward each other during shooting but in private Mother made it very clear what she thought of Joan. One thing that drove Mother crazy, aside from the vodka, was the varying sizes of Joan's falsies. In certain scenes Mother had to lean over Joan, who played an invalid, and she would complain, *"Christ!* You never know what size boobs that broad has strapped on! She must have a different set for each day of the week! I keep running into them like the Hollywood Hills! What does she think she's doing, for Christ's sake? She's supposed to be shriveling away while Baby Jane starves her to death, but her tits keep growing! Does she think the audiences are idiots? *Jesus!"*

I had a bit part as the girl who lived next door and Mother was delighted. Somehow the movie was finished and turned out to be a success. Mother felt rejuvenated and decided to buy a house. This was for keeps, so I gave her a break and found a beautiful Colonial-style house on Stone Canyon in Bel-Air. There aren't many Colonials in L.A., so Mother was thrilled and named it Honeysuckle Hill after the vine covering the chain-link fence that surrounded the property. Bougainvillaea sprawled over the front archway, hedges of hibiscus and camellia abounded and gardenias were growing everywhere. All Mother's energies went into decorating her new treasure with her Maine antiques. She announced that it felt just like Witch-Way and was happy. Unfortunately, the movie industry decided that the success of *Baby Jane* was a fluke and that Mother was a has-been. The only work she was able to find, once again, was in television. She did an episode of *The Virginian* and an episode of *Perry Mason.* She also made a singing and dancing appearance on *The Andy Williams Show.* Then, out of pure desperation, she ran her famous "Actress . . . wants steady employment in Hollywood . . ." ad in the trade papers and her career surged upward again.

While in Maine enjoying the role of wife, mother and PTA organizer, Mother had been the proud owner of the inevitable station wagon. Now, leaving all that behind her, she bought a metallic robin's egg blue Cadillac convertible with a white top and white leather upholstery. I was very happy about the improvement in her spirits, but distinctly hesitant about the thought of her driving a car again.

Gary, whatever his faults and despite any amount of alcohol, had never been less than an expert driver. Mother was not but thought she was, despite a record-breaking history of citations for running red lights, overshooting stop signs, speeding, illegal parking and a seemingly endless succession of fenderbenders. She even drove through the back wall of a friend's garage by putting the car in the wrong gear. She wasn't cited but she did have to rebuild the garage. On another occasion, when a friend and I were getting into the car from opposite sides, the friend got there first and Mother, hearing a door slam, drove off . . . right over my foot.

The most memorable car incident occurred after the whole family had been to a football game and was crammed into the station wagon. Gary took the quick way out of the parking lot by joining a fast-moving line of traffic in reverse, laughing all the way and bragging that he could drive just as well and just as fast backward as he could forward. Later, after we had stopped for gas, Mother took the wheel and, in due course, overshot our turnpike exit. Everyone, particularly Gary, shouted at her. She slammed on the brakes and slid to a stop on the shoulder of the highway. She then rammed the car into reverse, saying, "So you think reversing is a big deal. *Brother!* Watch this!" Wherewith, she stomped on the accelerator and traveled about fifty feet back straight into a highway drainage ditch. When the car had come to rest with screaming but uninjured children all over the place and luggage all over the children, Gary boomed out, "God, I'm impressed!" It took a wrecker to get the car out of the ditch and some minor repairs to the car before we were able to continue on our way.

All of this came to mind when Mother bought the Cadillac

but, fortunately, after making a U-turn on the Pacific Coast Highway and running smack into a station wagon going the other way, Mother decided that Californians were lousy drivers and hired a chauffeur.

Next, Mother bought a tomb. One day she told me that she had something to show me. We climbed into the Cadillac and were driven to Forest Lawn Cemetery. I was somewhat taken aback, but Mother looked like the proverbial cat who had swallowed the canary. Into the parklike grounds we swept, pulling up before an elaborate pink marble mausoleum with a statue of a girl in a floating gown standing before it. The girl looked familiar but I was unable to place her. The building itself was set in a little garden with stone benches and taped music, the whole surrounded by an iron fence. After a few moments of polite silence I turned to Mother and asked, "O.K. I give up. Why are we here?"

"Don't you like it?" She replied in a hurt voice. I said that it was beautiful for what it was, but that tombs really weren't my thing. Mother drew herself up, beamed at me and said, "We're all going to be buried here. I own it. No . . . don't look surprised. I really do own it. Isn't it magnificent?" When I asked why she had bought this marble pile, she looked crushed. "You don't understand," she wailed. "Look, B.D., we're all going to be buried here . . . together . . . there's room for all of us . . . *God* . . . I've taken care of all of it . . . no one has to worry about where they're going to be buried . . . I'm digging Ruthie up and moving her here." She spun around and waved at the surrounding panorama. "Look over there. You can see Warner Brothers Studios . . . and up there is the giant Hollywood sign. It's perfect. *Jesus!* I'll be able to see all of it when I'm here." And then, as an afterthought, "By the way, did you look carefully at the statue of the goddess in front? It's you . . . see?"

"That figures," I replied, suddenly realizing why the girl had looked familiar. Mother then told me the price of this monstrosity and I nearly fainted. She hastened to assure me that she had got a good deal. "The head salesman gave me a break because I'm a Yankee."

She had wanted to surprise me and she had succeeded, although not quite in the way intended. "I looked at lots of tombs before I chose this one," she added persuasively, perhaps noticing my marked lack of enthusiasm. "I'm sure you'll come to love it as much as I do." At my continuing look of skepticism, she went on to explain that her funeral wouldn't be anything elaborate; she just wanted a simple pine box to be slid into her slot like a true Yankee. "I will *not* fall into the trap of an expensive coffin and funeral like most people!"

No, sir! Keep it simple. That was Mother's credo.

At about this time Mother's housekeeper quit and no acceptable replacement was immediately available. Mother got into a terrible state because if Aunt Bobby were to take over the housekeeping chores, she would be left without her sister's services as lady's maid, companion and gofer. Since I enjoyed cooking and housekeeping was well within my competence, I volunteered to fill in until a new housekeeper could be found. Mother was overwhelming in her gratitude. For three weeks I cooked and polished and cleaned and laundered and it was very rewarding. Not only did I find that I enjoyed it, but Mother's nonstop praise for my efforts was exhilarating. The food I cooked was the best she had ever tasted, the brass and silver I polished had never shone so brightly, the floors had never had such a gleam and the house had never been so clean. Even her bed felt more comfortable because of the way I fluffed up the pillows. When I handed Mother her usual Scotch on the evening before the new housekeeper was to begin work, she exclaimed, "God, you're an incredible girl! I'm almost sorry that the new woman's starting tomorrow."

I became caught up in a mad whirl of parties, dates, horse shows, fox hunting, perpetuating my tan on Santa Monica Beach and more dates. Mother's tendency to question me on every little detail of my dating life back in New York took on a new dimension now that I was fifteen and going out with all sorts of interesting people of a remarkable range of ages. The more interesting Mother thought my date of the moment to be, the more she pumped me for every little detail of our relationship. I managed to fend off her intrusiveness quite well until I started going out with George Hamilton.

This was too much for Mother. She thought he was "a magnificent man" and if she had ever lived vicariously through me before, now she was in a positive lather of anticipation. She always had a gleam in her eye when I came home from a date with George but, one night when I stopped by her room to say good night as usual, her opening line was "Well? Did he lay you?" I was terribly embarrassed and more than a little disgusted by my own mother asking such a question.

"I beg your pardon," I foomfled.

"You know," she persisted. "Did he do it to you?"

"I never kiss and tell," I answered, trying to cover up my mortification with sarcasm. "Why don't you call George and ask *him?*"

"Oh, come on, B.D.," she wheedled, "you can tell me."

"But I'm not going to," I stated flatly.

"Well, he better have. I'll tell you that much," she said threateningly. I looked at her for just a moment more, then, still blushing to the roots of my hair, I fled to the privacy of my room.

Mother didn't give up after this attempt and, regrettably, the same scene played several more times. Despite the fact that I was ruder each time in my refusal either to confirm or deny the fulfillment of her fantasy, she kept right on trying and it never grew less embarrassing.

Mother became, for her, very social, and the bill at the florist's soared. She usually lit into someone during the course of an evening out and it generally resulted in an unpleasant scene. Even when I had not been with her, it was easy to tell when she had been at her nastiest. The next morning would go something like "What a night last night was. *Jesus!* So-and-so was a real bastard. *Brother!* Did he let me have it. *Weeps!* I'll never forget it. He went on and on. I thought he'd never let up on me. The hosts were shocked." She would deliver such a speech while pacing characteristically about the room and puffing madly on a cigarette. Then she would collapse into a chair, exhausted. I knew from experience that she had done an Academy-Award-caliber number on some poor soul. There was no stopping her when she got going. She thrived on being the center of attention and that was her way of doing it. It was most likely to occur when she was part of a large group and getting no special attention, even at her own house. If everyone present was having a good time but ". . . taking me for granted like I was the damned maid or something," meaning there was general conversation but not about her, off she would go.

To make matters worse, she had an uncanny knack for selecting either a vulnerable person who was in no way emotionally equipped to do public battle with Bette Davis or a relative who wouldn't answer back for the sake of good manners. In Mother's recollection of the event, a complete transference of roles occurred and no amount of arguing could persuade her that she had in any way been at fault.

She would then rush to the phone, the next morning, that is, and order some lavish floral arrangement to be sent to her host of the previous evening with a note to be hand-delivered within the hour. She would write something like "Dear so-and-so, I can't tell you how sorry I am for the wretched scene last night. I don't understand why people have to give it to me like that but I guess I'll run into it all my life. I'm only sorry that you had to listen to it. It was a lovely evening. Thank you. Bette." The chauffeur would be dispatched with the card to the florist and Mother would feel much better now that that was cleared up. The florists adored her.

The best thing to do when Mother went off on an unprovoked and utterly unwarranted tirade was to bite one's tongue until she was finished and then proceed as though nothing had happened. There were times when the victims, myself among them, were unwilling to sit back and be abused and had the temerity to defend themselves. This would lead to an immediate about-face on her part. "Don't do this to me! God! Not tonight! How can you do this to me tonight?" Whenever anyone made so bold as to defend himself against one of her tirades, he was met with some variation of this response and it was always the worst of times at which to distress her with *his* ill temper.

7

At dinner one night a typical donnybrook developed between Mother and Aunt Bobby. Mother habitually picked on Aunt Bobby for anything and everything and this time it was the roast beef. The standing rib which Bobby had cooked was a beautiful pale pink in the center, precisely the way everyone in the family, including Mother, liked it. Mother began by insisting that the pink wasn't rosy enough and that the edges were too gray. Aunt Bobby contended that it was just the same as it always was. I chimed in to say that it was delicious, then everyone ate in silence for a few minutes while Mother brooded. Suddenly she blurted, "Bobby has ruined this gorgeous piece of meat. None of you cares how I slave my guts out to buy you this fabulous food. It costs a fortune! The least I expect is to have it prepared the way I like it." She pushed her plate angrily away. "I can't eat any more . . . it's too horrible to swallow."

Mother had pushed her plate halfway off the table and Aunt Bobby, seated next to her, put her hand out to stop the plate from falling on the floor. At the same instant Mother started to get up from the table, leaning toward her sister. Aunt Bobby's hand, outstretched for the teetering plate, touched Mother's arm. The reaction was instantaneous. "How dare you strike me?" Mother screamed. "You ungrateful bitch!"

"I didn't," Aunt Bobby protested as she stood up with Mother's plate in her hand.

"You damned well did and you know it!" Mother bellowed. She gave Aunt Bobby a violent shove backward, which caused her to drop the plate of uneaten food all over the carpet before she lost her balance and fell heavily on her backside. As I sat there mute, having seen variations of this kind of thing before, I again wondered why Aunt Bobby put up with it, why she permitted Mother to treat her this way. I watched as she crawled across the carpet, picking up the debris, and felt positively heartened when she spat at Mother through tightly compressed lips, "Stop it, Bette! Stop it right this minute!" For an instant, as a vicious expression came over Mother's face, I thought she was actually going to kick Aunt Bobby. But then her expression changed as she planted her feet apart, put her hands on her hips, leaned forward and shouted down at her sister, "You have no idea what it's like to earn a living! You've sponged off me your whole life and you'll damn well take whatever I dish out. Don't you dare tell me to stop it. Don't you dare tell me anything." Aunt Bobby, saying nothing and avoiding Mother's gaze, got up from the floor and went to Michael, who had started crying shortly after this all began, and told him that he could leave the table.

"That's right!" Mother screamed. "Mollycoddle him. Let him be a damned crybaby. Jesus, Bobby! He has to learn to face up to life sometime, you know. It's a jungle and he better get used to it."

"That's not fair," I interjected; Michael was only ten years old. "Why do you have to bring Michael into this? He didn't do anything wrong."

"Oh, so you're against me too, eh, B.D.?" Mother asked scornfully. "Well, that's fine, my dear, just fine. *Brother!* You're all just great." She spun on her heel and stalked off through the door into the den.

I got up and began to help Aunt Bobby clear the table. I wasn't even halfway to the kitchen with the first armful of dishes before Mother burst back into the room. "B.D.! Put those dishes down this instant. That's Bobby's job. She has a *job* here, you know? It's something you all seem to forget. I pay her to do a *job*." As I went on to the kitchen, I snapped back at Mother angrily, "Aunt Bobby is also family and if I want to help her, I will." Mother grabbed Aunt Bobby roughly by the arm and started to shake her. "How dare you let B.D. do your job? I won't have you treat her like a maid." Aunt Bobby tried to pull away but Mother had a viselike grip on her arm and continued to shake her. Aunt Bobby cried out, "You're hurting me, Bette. Let go of me!" Mother must have squeezed much tighter, or dug her fingernails into her sister's arm or something, for Aunt Bobby suddenly started to thrash around wildly in her grasp. Mother let go with one hand and hit her in the face. Aunt Bobby took a swing at Mother. In an instant, they were pulling each other's hair, kicking at each other and screeching like a pair of alley cats. It only lasted a few seconds, then the crying began. Mother held her face, wailed about her osteo-myelitis and accused Aunt Bobby of destroying her bridge-work (she hadn't) before heading for her room. Aunt Bobby screamed at Mother's departing back that she had knocked a tooth loose (she hadn't) and ran to *her* room. Aunt Bobby's room, referred to as "the crow's nest," was located above the garage and could only be reached by its own staircase at the far end of the house.

I finished the dishes, went to the family room and turned on the television. I must have stared at the screen for some ten or fifteen minutes before I realized that I had no idea what the show was all about. I had frequently been upset by the way Mother treated Aunt Bobby, but this time I couldn't get my mind off it, perhaps because I had unwittingly made it worse by butting in. I turned the television off and went to check on Michael. He was happily ensconced in his room watching tele-vision and I headed for the crow's nest.

I climbed the stairs, knocked on the door and entered at Aunt Bobby's invitation. I explained to her apologetically that I just plain didn't like the way Mother treated her and was puzzled as to why she let Mother get away with it. Aunt Bobby begged the issue for a few minutes but, at my persistent urg-ing, her emotional dam burst and her story poured forth.

"You see, B.D., ever since we were children I've known that Bette was the important one. Mother geared our whole lives to my sister. Bette came first and I was just a tagalong. I never got new clothes, just my sister's hand-me-downs. I was told that *she* had to have *new* clothes because she was going places in the world. Bette was temperamental even when she was little. If she had a tiny wrinkle in her dress she'd throw an unholy fit about it and, to make matters worse, everyone would rush around and find her another dress. If I got upset about something I was told not to be tiresome. Bette was the only one who counted. No matter how mean or nasty she got, it was fine with Mother. It was difficult for me not to hate my own sister, and a lot of the time I hated her guts. The thing was, though, they were right and I was wrong. Everything I ever tried to do went wrong, while Bette became a great success, just like Mother said she would. I came to idolize my important big sister and to love her. It made me feel a part of her importance. Even though she's pulled some pretty nasty stunts on me, I still do love her. When I got married the first time she didn't seem to mind and basically left me alone.

"A few years after my divorce, when Fay was still a little girl, I married David Berry. You were too young to remember him but he was a wonderful man. He was a reformed alcoholic and very open about it. He was a wonderful man. Well, when we got married Bette was angry because she said she needed me and I was letting her down. To get even, I assume, she sent us a wedding present of a dozen cases of liquor, which were waiting for us in the foyer of our house when we returned from our honeymoon. When I confronted her with it, she pretended that she had forgotten about David's problem. Don't ever underestimate your mother, B.D. She's got a mean streak a mile wide when she's crossed. The trouble is, you see, I can't fend for myself out there. Everything goes wrong when I'm on my own and I get scared. I really do need Bette and she knows it. She doesn't mean most of what she says. Tomorrow she'll apologize and tell me how much she depends on me. It's been this way from the beginning. Bette has pressures that she has to vent sometimes and I'm a convenient target. Don't worry about me, B.D., I'm used to it and get over it quickly. It's sweet of you to be concerned, but underneath it all I know she loves me and that's what counts."

After an exchange of pleasantries, I said good night and

prowled restlessly around the deserted downstairs for a while. I didn't like what Aunt Bobby had told me and felt pretty rotten about the way she seemed to have been treated. The Aunt Bobby I knew and loved was the one who would announce, whenever Mother was out for the evening, "Liberty Hall" in ringing, gleeful tones. That meant that there were no rules and that giggles and laughter were welcome until further notice. All tension would leave the house and, in an instant, we were on vacation. That was my Aunt Bobby . . . a friend and confidante. I was sorry that I had gone to the crow's nest.

My room was beyond Mother's on a circular balcony overlooking the front foyer. As I passed her door on my way to bed she called out, "B.D.! Come in here." When I entered her room she thrust an icebag at me and told me to fill it. When I brought it back she applied it to the side of her face and, sitting with her legs crossed Indian fashion on her bed, she began rocking to and fro and moaning.

"Is there anything else you need?" I asked stiffly.

"Brother!" she gasped. "You don't even care if I'm hurt, do you?"

"I'm sure you'll be just fine in the morning, Mother," I replied brusquely. "If there's nothing else you need, I'm going to my room to read."

"Why don't you sit with me for a while?" she whined. "Or don't you have time for your poor old mother anymore?" Her pathetic routine set my teeth on edge and I blurted, "I had plenty of time for you at dinner but you ended that rather abruptly, didn't you?"

"That damned Bobby!" she exploded. "She gets so nasty at times, I can't stand it."

"Aunt Bobby?" I challenged. "All *she* did was cook a perfectly delightful meal which you proclaimed was inedible and threw on the floor. How can you—"

"Don't, B.D.!" she cried. "I can't stand it! Can't you see that she deliberately ruined that beef just to get me? *Brother!* You always take her side. You think she's so damned sweet, don't you? Well, let me tell *you* something, my dear. Bobby's always been madly jealous of me. When we were little everyone saw her as the sweet, perfect little darling. She made me sick! *Jesus!* They soon found out who had the guts in the family, though. Let me tell you something, Bobby's always tried to drag me down . . . but she's never *won*. Ha! Even her bouts in the loony bin were kept from the press and didn't hurt me. But they sure cost me a pretty penny, I'll tell you that much. She was in the rubber room at Payne Whitney more than once . . . and what I went through visiting her I can't describe. All those horrible crazy people and my sister one of them. Well, I made it through the nightmare and Bobby always came out of it eventually. Of course, she was too stupid to even make a go of her marriages and I inherited Fay too. So, you see, I know how to handle Bobby. She's a tough customer, but she knows she has to behave in my house or I'll kick her out on her ass. *Well*, at least she's great with you kids . . . for that I'll always be grateful." Abruptly her tone changed. "Good night, B.D. Please turn off all the lights before you go to bed. I hurt too much to move."

"Good night, Mother," I said, kissing her on the proffered cheek.

8

What Ever Happened to Baby Jane? was to be shown at the Cannes Film Festival and personal appearance tours of New York and London theaters were scheduled. Mother wanted me onstage with her during the tours and I agreed to do it if she promised to take me to the film festival. She didn't want to travel all the way to France and had no interest at all in the Riviera. No interest in the Riviera? That was like shooting me through the heart. I was outraged.

In the end she gave in and our visit to Cannes was booked, publicized and thus assured. I was really looking forward to this trip and in exchange was more than happy to give it my best at the personal appearances.

Since we were not due to leave until early in May and my sixteenth birthday would be on May 1, there was one personal matter I wanted to take care of before we left. In California you gain certain rights on your sixteenth birthday, one of them being the right to change your name and nullify any adoptions. I was determined to sever all ties to Gary and change my name back to my real one, Barbara Davis Sherry. The hearing was set, coincidentally, for May 1, the judge granted my petition and the deed was done.

We left for New York, stopping in Chicago on the way for a nightclub crawl arranged by Mother's then lawyer, Tom Hammond, in lieu of a sixteenth birthday party. At least there was no Maypole dance.

The first item on Mother's agenda in New York was attending a huge banquet marking the occasion of the fortieth anniversary of *Time* magazine. Everyone who had ever appeared on the cover of either *Time* or *Life* was invited. The invocation was delivered by Cardinal Spellman and among other speakers were Lyndon Johnson, Nelson Rockefeller and Dean Rusk. I don't believe I have ever seen so many famous people all in one place at one time, even at the Kennedy inauguration. I had met quite a few of them before, which bolstered my self-confidence but, nonetheless, I was awe-struck. I recall speaking to Eddie Arcaro, Helen Hayes, Harry Belafonte, Bob Hope, Hedda Hopper, Danny Kaye, John Philip Sousa, Ed Sullivan, Milton Berle, Dave Brubeck, Omar Bradley, Henry Ford II, Barry Goldwater, Vince Lombardi, Casey Stengel, Jackie Robinson, Darryl Zanuck, Herman Wouk, every available Rockefeller and every conceivable Kennedy.

It was an incredible evening and I was thrilled to have been a part of it. One thing, however, will stay with me when all the other memories have faded. I was used to the idea that my mother was a star, that she was internationally famous. I was used to people, strangers from all walks of life, coming over to Mother in restaurants or on street corners to say hello and perhaps shake her hand or get her autograph. But in that place, on that night, people who themselves were legendary came over to my mother, apologized for bothering her and said that they admired her and had always wanted to meet her. It was an extraordinary experience because that night I became aware that my mother was more than a world-renowned actress, more than a star . . . that she was, in fact, a living legend.

There was a *Baby Jane* press party at "21" one night. Mother and I were escorted by the literary agent Jay Garon. Shortly after we arrived, Joan Crawford and her entourage swept into the dining room. Joan was dressed from head to foot in aqua and was seated, with careful foresight, at the opposite end of the room. She gave a haughty wave of the hand toward Mother and called out, "Hello, darling Bette! Bless you." Mother leaped out of her seat, thrust forth her arms as though to embrace the multitude and emoted, *"Jesus!* Look at that broad! The turban matches the blouse which matches the jacket which matches the skirt which matches the shoes which match the pocketbook which matches the gloves. *Shit!"* She threw back her head and gave vent to a wild cackle, slapped her thighs and finished, "Can you believe her? She looks like she just came from a fire sale in Macy's basement."

The personal appearance tour was a real experience. We rode in a huge bus with twenty-five uniformed New York policemen in addition to a couple of detectives. I had no idea that security was so vital and felt it to be a serious case of overkill until we reached the first theater. The crowds were unbelievable and we were mobbed by thousands of people at each stop. The only way to get safely into the theaters was to stand in the center of a circle of New York's finest, all with their arms locked. It was truly incredible and even a little frightening at times. People were reaching through the police cordon and trying to tear at our clothes. I had thought that this sort of hysteria occurred only for Elvis, not Bette Davis. It took the combined strength of all the cops to maintain their circle and get us into the theaters through the surging, screaming masses. We emerged unscathed each time but each time it seemed amazing to have done so. The time spent onstage talking to the audience, singing and presenting the Baby Jane dolls was a breeze by comparison. Mother and I (God help the poor audiences) sang the ballad from the movie as a duet, answered questions and then told everyone to look under their seats for a slip of paper reading "DOLL." The lucky few who found such a slip were the proud winners of a full-size Baby Jane doll. The New York tour lasted two days, was a resounding success and, unharmed by Mother's worshippers, we readied ourselves for England.

The tour of the London theaters went exactly as it had in New York, police, crowds and all, except that at the last theater, Mother, in a rare moment of spontaneity, invited all the policemen to come up on the stage and join us in one final rendition of the ballad. The bobbies loved it and it was a big hit with the audience.

Our arrival at the airport in Nice was greeted by the usual

welcoming committee of fans and also, because of the festival, a large representation of reporters and cameramen. Mother held an impromptu press conference and bowled them over by speaking French. The same thing happened upon our arrival at the Carlton Hotel in Cannes with the same success. The press coverage of Mother was very kind and she was sincerely delighted to be so warmly welcomed. The only thing that upset her was that the papers insisted on referring to me as a "statuesque, green-eyed blond beauty." I thought it very flattering but Mother was incensed over the use of the word "statuesque." "Why the hell can't they just say tall? *Shit!* They always have to exaggerate everything."

"For crying out loud, Mother," I protested, "maybe they would if I were just tall, but I'm tall and busty. Let's face it, compared to most girls my age I'm an Amazon. At least they think I'm beautiful." It was a good thing that Mother came to accept my point of view, since the same description appeared endlessly in papers and magazines for the next couple of weeks.

The beauty and magnificence of the French Riviera is legendary and no attempt on my part to describe it could do it justice. Suffice it to say, therefore, that I was spellbound. The hills, the beaches, the boulevards, the villages, the new and the old. It was all breathtaking. So was the apparent opulence: villas, yachts, vineyards, art collections and the most expensive automobiles the world has to offer. It was all there and so was I, sixteen years old and experiencing it for the first time. Not only that, but upon alighting from the plane at Nice, I seemed suddenly to have graduated from being just my mother's daughter to one of the "Beautiful People."

Our suite on the seventh floor of the Carlton overlooked the outdoor dining terrace and the Mediterranean beyond. I convinced Mother that forcing me to stay in the suite to help unpack would be cruel and unusual punishment when the whole world was out on the beach waiting just for me. Viola Rubber, a stout gray-haired lady of indeterminate age whom we had first encountered in San Francisco and who had come to work for Mother after *The Night of the Iguana,* stood in for me but, upon my return from the beach, I discovered that I had a date for the screening of *Baby Jane* that night, and also for the party afterward, with an executive of the production company, a man named Jeremy Hyman. I moaned and groaned and protested at length that I would much prefer to go unescorted, but Viola was unshakable in her position that it was all arranged and that Seven Arts wouldn't hear of their star's daughter attending the screening without an escort. Mother really surprised me by jumping in on Viola's side, no doubt having decided that things would be better all around if I were stuck with some fat, cigar-smoking producer type rather than roaming around footloose among all those lecherous Frenchmen. The argument lasted for several minutes before I finally resigned myself. It was not the first time that something of the sort had happened and there was always the remote chance that my date would not be an absolute bore, improbable but a remote chance. I primped and dressed and we all had an early dinner in the suite.

Precisely at 7:00 P.M., the arranged time, the doorbell rang. I went to the door, Mother and Viola hard on my heels, and opened it. There stood a tall, handsome young man in a dinner jacket who politely inquired if Miss B. D. Sherry was ready. "My name is Jeremy Hyman and I'm her escort to the screening of *Baby Jane* tonight." While I stood there, speechless for the first time since my introduction to Joan Crawford, he was peering over my shoulder looking for the kid in pigtails he'd been stuck with for the evening. The moment was broken when Mother began jumping up and down behind me in the attempt to get a look at my escort. I got over my surprise, introduced myself, stepped aside to introduce Jeremy to Mother and picked up my stole. He offered his arm and as we strolled down the corridor, I heard Mother say to Viola in one of her stage whispers, "My God, Viola, what have you done? The son of a bitch looks like Leslie Howard! I thought you said he was a producer."

Jeremy had heard Mother just as well as I had and I watched him suppress a smile as we continued down the corridor. Believing that some sort of explanation was due, I said, "That was because we all expected you to be like all the other business escorts I've been stuck with, short, fat, bald, generally smoking cigars and dropping the ashes on my dress. You were a bit of a surprise . . . a pleasant one for me but a bit of a shock for Mother, I'm afraid." While we waited for the elevator, Jeremy confessed that he, too, was pleasantly surprised, that I was so unlike what he had been expecting that he felt a little awkward.

By the time we were comfortably ensconced in the back of our limousine, Jeremy relaxed enough to tell me what had taken place within Seven Arts regarding our date. It seemed that Viola had called Ken Hyman, Jeremy's cousin, who was the executive producer of *Baby Jane* as well as the ranking member of the Seven Arts contingent, stated in no uncertain terms that Miss Davis's daughter had to have an escort and that Jeremy Hyman was acceptable to Miss Davis for the purpose. Ken had given the news to Jeremy and added that it didn't make any difference what was acceptable to whom, Jeremy was the only available bachelor and was the escort whether he liked it or not. Like me, Jeremy had become incensed and admitted that he'd said something like "Davis's daughter? Forget it! Everybody knows Davis is a pain in the ass and the daughter probably is too. Sixteen years old, braces and braids. Why can't she just go with her mother?" Ken had prevailed and Jeremy was stuck with the date but then, to make matters worse, word had filtered through the grapevine about how angry Jeremy was. Everywhere he went for the rest of the day, someone would add fuel to the fire with a snide comment about cradle robbers. His reply to them all had been "The things I do for my company!"

After the screening, the distribution of people and cars was changed before proceeding onward to the party. Mother, Bob Aldrich, Jeremy and I found ourselves in the same limousine. By this time, Jeremy and I had discovered that we rather liked each other and, moreover, that we shared a common passion for horses. We were still discussing horses as the limousine left Cannes and headed inland to the party. Mother, whom I watched out of the corner of my eye, was clearly in distress. The last thing she had intended was that I find a soul mate and, as salt on her wound, Jeremy really did look quite a bit like Leslie Howard. Since Mother had had a thing for Leslie Howard, she must undoubtedly have been assuming that I would immediately develop a thing for Jeremy. For the last few months, Mother had been talking about all the wonderful things she and I were going to do together. The essence of her scenario seemed clear: I would be her traveling companion for the rest of her life. I could almost sense her mind working as she pondered ways to break up my newly found friendship before it got out of control.

The procession of limousines wound inland and zigzagged up a steep hill until we arrived in the cobblestoned square of a quaint little village. We were greeted by a group of villagers and goat carts filled with flowers and were then led along a footpath which ascended almost to the top of the hill before cutting sharply to the left and around to the other side. Completely hidden from view until we arrived on its doorstep was a charming old inn nestled into the side of the hill and surrounded by trees and gardens. Below us and for miles into the distance we could see the twinkling lights of villages in the valleys.

A beautiful buffet dinner was served and, by pure chance, Jeremy and I wound up at a different table from Mother. When a group of guests went upstairs to enjoy the breathtaking view from the balcony, Jeremy suggested that we join them. The view was indeed memorable and, after we had gazed in rapt silence for some time, we realized that everyone else had returned to the party and left us alone. The Fates were at work that night and the thread binding me to Mother's side was to be cut even shorter than I might have guessed. Jeremy and I kissed.

I had read lots of romantic novels and had always considered the descriptions of such moments to be great fun to read but otherwise pure artistic license. On the balcony of that lovely inn I discovered that the writers were not exaggerating. I saw shooting stars, heard bells and, when we finally stepped apart, I felt dizzy. Neither of us was aware of it quite yet but, only hours after having first met, we had fallen in love.

We returned to the party doing our very best to look blasé but I had somehow managed to get lipstick on Jeremy's collar and was terribly embarrassed by the sly looks directed our way. When I told him why we were getting all those leers, he made me feel better by whispering, "Don't worry about it. Nothing could upset me right now." On our return to Cannes, Jeremy told Mother that he would like to take me for a walk along the beach and we were off before she could object. We walked, talked and stopped to embrace for hours. Jeremy dropped me at my suite at four-thirty in the morning, hardly the way either of us had expected the evening to end.

At 8:00 A.M. I was wide awake and ordered breakfast. Mother had heard me come in and expressed amazement that I was up so early. "I suppose you had a marvelous time while I was stuck with all those boring people. *Brother!* Well, at least he was an Englishman," she said, implying that anything would have been better than one of the dreaded French lechers. At that moment the phone rang. It was Jeremy, inviting me to the beach. I accepted, grabbed my beach robe, which I hurriedly threw over my bikini, gulped the last of my coffee and headed for the door.

"Where do you think *you're* going?" Mother demanded.

"To the beach with Jeremy," I replied, opening the door.

"Aren't you going to wait for him here?"

"No, we're meeting in the lobby."

"*Christ!*" Mother yelped as I was closing the door. "The sun isn't even up yet and I don't like you meeting in the lobby. It isn't proper and I do not approve!" I heard the last part of her objection faintly as I was heading for the elevator.

We were the only ones on the beach at that hour but we didn't care. Slowly, as the beach filled up, Jeremy had to suffer the comments of those who the day before had heard him say, "The things I do for my company." The standard greeting was "Hello, Jeremy. Still a good company man I see." We spent the morning together, enjoying every moment of each other's company, but then I had to attend a publicity luncheon with Mother. We arranged to meet later and I hurried off to change.

On the way to the luncheon Mother inquired about my morning on the beach. I said that I had had a pleasant time. "We swam all the way out to the float in the harbor, talked for a while and swam back."

"What did you talk about?" Mother asked, an edge coming into her voice.

"Mostly about horses. He told me about fox hunting in England and the farm country in Kent where he grew up. Things like that."

"How old did you say he is?"

"I didn't, but he's twenty-nine."

"Has he ever been married? Is he engaged?"

"No."

"I don't like this, B.D.," she suddenly snapped. "I see a whole different look in your eye. You're going to get kicked in the teeth just like I always did. You're much too young for a man like that to take seriously. He's either playing you along and you'll be dumped, or he wants you because you're my daughter. Take my word for it . . . I know about these things."

"Oh, Mother," I protested, "I only met him last night. Don't get so intense. We're having fun together, that's all. Oh, by the way, I'm meeting him at the beach after lunch. We're going for a boat ride round the bay . . . and since he's going to the cocktail party on Sam Spiegel's yacht, I told him I'd love to go with him." Even as I was speaking I knew that I had made a big mistake. I should have let things quietly go their course but, in my excitement and enthusiasm, I had blurted out too much and Mother was reading between the lines.

"Oh, *brother!*" she exploded. "You can forget spending the afternoon with him. I didn't come all this way to sit on my ass in a hotel room while you run around on your own. Not on your life I didn't! As for tonight, we'll see."

"I promised to meet Jeremy this afternoon and I will not break my date," I stated belligerently. "Nor will I break my date for this evening. What's wrong with you? Join us at the beach if you like. You're perfectly welcome."

"*Ha!*"

"I'm going, Mother!"

"All right! Go! But we will talk, young lady. I didn't want to go to that goddamned party tonight anyway . . . so go with him!"

"Fine! I shall! But I thought Bob Aldrich was escorting you to the party. When did that change?"

"Just now, that's when! Let's just drop it."

Jeremy and I spent a lovely afternoon. We took off in a speedboat and, after taking in the scenery for miles on either side of Cannes, we went out and circled the U.S.S. *Enterprise,* which was anchored far out in the bay. I had never seen an aircraft carrier up close before and I was amazed. It was a city afloat. After the boat ride we returned to the beach and swam and sunbathed until it was time to dress for the evening.

We met some friends of Jeremy's for cocktails on the terrace first, then took to the sea again in Boston Whalers, which had been provided to transport the guests out to Sam Spiegel's yacht. It was a nice party and I met several interesting people. At one point in the evening Jeremy and I were approached by a navy commander who, after making small talk for several minutes, invited me out to the *Enterprise* to have lunch with the admiral the next day. I was about to accept when Jeremy butted in with some double-talk about our plans for the next day not leaving time for lunch on the *Enterprise*. Since we hadn't even discussed the next day, I thought his attitude a bit preemptive, but I kept my mouth shut for once. Even when the commander, as an afterthought, extended the invitation to include Jeremy, he remained intransigent. The commander said the invitation remained open and moved off to speak to someone else. I turned to Jeremy and asked stiffly, "What was that all about? What right—"

"First," he interrupted me, taking my arm and steering me out of hearing of anyone else, "thank you for keeping quiet back there. Second, I apologize for seeming so presumptuous. Third, very reliable sources have it that the admiral has an eye for the ladies." I was flabbergasted. Too many things I had only read about were happening at once, and to think that Joan Crawford had accused me of not leading a sufficiently sheltered life. "Are you sure?"

"No," he replied, "but ask yourself two things. Why, when it was perfectly obvious that we were together, did he only extend the invitation to me after you had turned him down, or at least I had turned him down in your behalf? More important, why does the commander always ask pretty girls, and only pretty girls, out to the ship for lunch or dinner, never for a date ashore?" I thought about it and decided that I could live without taking any meals aboard the *Enterprise*. We left the party and went ashore to finish the evening dancing at Whiskey-a-Go-go.

To our astonishment a small army of photographers awaited us at the jetty. We knew there was gossip; it was to be expected. This was the Cannes Film Festival and two young people, one of them a star's daughter, had been seen together for a day and a half. It was the number of photographers waiting just for us that was amazing. Apparently we had moved from "an" item to "the" item. They shouted questions in a dozen different languages and took countless pictures of my front and Jeremy's back as he stood on the edge of the jetty, stared steadfastly out to sea and pretended that he didn't understand any language being spoken. The only thing I told anyone was that my date's name was Jeremy. The next day the newspapers reported that I had been in the company of a young German, which was good for a chuckle. They followed us all the way to Whiskey-a-Go-go and a couple of them even pursued us inside. Jeremy drove them crazy by ducking behind me every time one of them got lined up for a shot. He tried to explain that he hated having his picture taken, but this was difficult to understand since, being my mother's daughter, having my picture taken seemed to be a natural part of life. I suggested that if he wanted to avoid being photographed, he'd better drop me like a hot potato and run for his life out the back door. Jeremy didn't run and, by the next day, had decided to come to terms with the problem. He stopped ducking behind me whenever a photographer loomed before us and began to answer questions politely. He still didn't like it, but at least the press got the story straight.

Over Mother's increasingly strident protests that I should mingle, I met Jeremy on the beach the next morning with a promise that I would rejoin her in time for a publicity luncheon in Nice. After a pleasant few hours with Jeremy I returned to our suite to again be grilled by Mother. "All right, B.D. What did you two talk about this time?"

"Oh, I don't know. Not much really. We just sort of chatted about this and that," I replied, doing my best not to get testy. Mother clomped about the room for a few minutes, moving pieces of bric-a-brac needlessly from one place to another, then whirled on me and said, "Well, you won't be able to see much of him from now on. We have a very busy schedule ahead of us. I suggest that next time you bump into him, you say good-bye." This was pure poppycock and we both knew it; however, common sense prevailed and rather than risk Mother getting hysterical and proving her point by leaving Cannes or something (she had walked off many a movie set for far less cause), I tried to look appropriately downcast as I went to my room to change. With my door safely closed, I clenched my fists and almost choked on a silent scream of frustration. I knew that I was lucky to have the freedom I enjoyed, but Mother had given it to me, had urged me to take it. It seemed that I was free to do absolutely anything I wanted, particularly if I were willing to recount the engrossing details to Mother, but "a different look" in my eye was anathema. I would have to be careful.

When we arrived in Nice the photographers were out in full force. For their benefit we stopped at a little sidewalk stand and tried on all kinds of hats. Mother bought one for each of us, mine being a cute natural-straw affair with a narrow, curled brim, a high crown and a pink chiffon scarf tied around it. The luncheon was pleasant enough but, whereas Mother usually stayed at such functions for precisely as long as protocol required and not a moment longer, this time, knowing that I was anxious to get back to Cannes, she pretended to be having the time of her life and dragged it out until she was all but asked to leave.

I had told Jeremy that I would meet him on the beach back in Cannes at 3:00 P.M. and here was Mother playing games and there was nothing I could do about it. I excused myself to go to the ladies' room, found a telephone and rang the Carlton. I had them call his room, page him in the bar, the restaurant, the lobby, the beach and the terrace without success and then left a message at the desk explaining my delay. When I turned away from the telephone, Mother was standing there, puffing on a cigarette, tapping her foot and staring at me squinty-eyed. "You sneaky bitch! *Jesus!* Going behind my back to call that man!"

"I'm sorry," I hissed, anger getting the better of me, "but I had a date to meet him at three and it's damned near that now, thanks to your loving-everything-French routine in the dining room!"

"If he's *worth* a shit, he'll wait for you no matter when you get back."

"I'm damned if I know why he should if I don't show up and don't call. You sure as hell wouldn't let *me* wait for a date who hadn't had the decency to call."

"That's different," stated Mother.

"*No!* It most certainly is not!" I shot back.

"Well," said Mother smugly, "he's just going to have to wait a little longer, isn't he? I want to go back to the hat stand and get a hat for Bobby. Come on. Viola, tell the car to meet us down there. We'll walk."

I don't know whether I turned purple with anger but I must have been very close to it. Fleeting images of deliciously violent acts came to mind, but there was nothing I could do except grit my teeth as I followed along and smiled for the cameras. Mother walked as slowly as she could, pretending to find architectural marvels everywhere and irresistible objects for sale in every shop window. When we finally reached the hat stand Mother said, "God, what a long walk! To hell with Bobby and her damned hat. I need a drink. Let's get back to the Carlton."

By the time we reached the hotel it was quarter to five and Mother was looking very pleased with herself. I changed in seconds and ran all the way, taking six flights of stairs rather than waiting for the elevator. Startling the milling movie moguls and careering off Alfred Hitchcock and Tippi Hedren as I burst through the lobby, causing several sets of screeching brakes as I dashed across the Promenade de la Croisette, I arrived at the foot of the steps leading down to the beach only to have my heart sink. There, a short distance away with his back to me, Jeremy sat talking to a gorgeous girl. I stood for a moment, trying to decide what to do, when Ken Hyman called from the other direction and waved to me to join him. I strolled over to Ken's group, trying to look relaxed and nonchalant, and he invited me to sit down beside him. He whispered, "Sit tight and don't worry about a thing. I'll be right back." He went over to Jeremy, said something to him, and both of them returned.

"Hello," said Jeremy stiffly. Ken tried to help. "Why don't you both take a swim while I order you some drinks?"

"Hello," I said, smiling unsurely at Jeremy. "I'd like that if you would." His return smile looked equally uncertain, but he extended a hand to help me up and on the way to the water I apologized for being so late. Not wanting to admit to my troubles with Mother, I said that the luncheon had dragged on much longer than expected. Jeremy made typically English "No need to apologize, these things happen" noises and then I asked if he had received my message.

"What message?"

"I called you somewhere around two-thirty or three to let you know that I'd be late. They paged you everywhere but when they couldn't find you I left a message at the desk."

"That's odd," he replied, sounding stiff again. "I've been here all day and neither heard a page nor received a message."

"Well, I did call," I insisted plaintively, but there was no noticeable lessening of the tension.

We swam for a while and then went back up the beach for our drinks. We were still having difficulty making conversation. Jeremy's nose was obviously out of joint and I was feeling more than a little insecure. When everyone else packed up and repaired to the hotel to dress for dinner, Jeremy and I followed along slowly. We both wanted to thaw the ice but neither of us knew how. As we were passing the desk the concierge called out, "Oh, Mr. Hyman . . . there's a message for you." Jeremy took the envelope, read the message, and then smiled even as he blushed to the roots of his hair with embarrassment. "Good grief! You really did call at quarter to three," he exclaimed.

"What's the big surprise? I told you I did," I retorted indignantly. He became even more embarrassed and then put an end to all the uncertainty when he said, almost shamefacedly, "I'm really very sorry for doubting you but . . . well . . . I was already upset because you're leaving for Paris in the morning and this was our last chance to be together. Then you didn't show up and didn't call and I figured that I must have misjudged you altogether. That made me feel like a fool and I got angry." He looked absolutely wretched and finished lamely, "I'm sorry. I behaved boorishly."

I was so relieved and so happy that I couldn't think of anything to say. I just stood there and grinned like an idiot. Drawing confidence from my obvious reaction, Jeremy said, "If you'll forgive me for doubting your word I'll pick you up at seven and we'll go to the Colombe d'Or for dinner."

"Terrific!" I replied, not trying to conceal my eagerness. "I'd love to. By the way, what time is it now?"

"Twenty past six. I'm sorry about having to rush you but

it's a long drive to St. Paul de Vence and we must be on time. I have an admission to make," he went on sheepishly. "This morning I presumed a lot and made a reservation for us for nine."

"Don't worry about a thing. We California girls are quick-change artists. I'll be ready."

And so we repaired to our rooms to change, one step closer to our destiny together. We have never forgotten, though, how close to success Mother came. The little straw hat with the pink scarf tied around it, which Jeremy liked enormously at the time, later became symbolic of our time together in Cannes and the first of Mother's many failures at coming between us. I still have the hat, lo these many years later, and even wear it upon occasion.

The drive to St. Paul de Vence was a tour guide's dream: tiny walled-in vineyards, charming villages and exquisite scenery, everything neat and clean whether inhabited by rich or poor, another zigzag lane up another hill to another village at the very top. The Colombe d'Or, which must have been a medieval stronghold in its origins, was now a hotel and restaurant. At first I was struck by its antiquity but, on entering, my mind boggled. On every wall of every room hung the works of artists one expected to see only in museums or in the collections of millionaires. Chagall, Braque, Dufy, Utrillo, Matisse and many others of like stature, as well as lesser-known artists, were everywhere. I was told that the *patron* had hidden all of these artists from the Nazis during the Occupation and had fed and housed them without charge. They, in return, had expressed their gratitude in the only way they could.

We dined on *loup,* a Mediterranean fish of unusual delicacy, and drank a wine from a vineyard we had passed on the way there. After dinner Simone Signoret, who lived at the hotel, told us that we ought to go to the lounge since they were going to screen *Stagecoach.* In response to my querying look, Jeremy explained that Europeans loved westerns and that if John Wayne had got a dollar every time a bootleg print of *Stagecoach* was screened, he could have retired on the royalties. We declined politely, saying that we had to get back to Cannes early, since I was leaving in the morning, and we only had time for a walk in the garden. The French are marvelous. If anything even remotely smacks of romance they become all smiles, knowing looks and suggestive winks. We weathered all of the above, made our good-byes and completed our tour of the hotel on the way out. The gardens were step-terraced and magnificent in themselves but there were dozens, perhaps even hundreds, of nightingales singing in the valley below. The closest I had ever been to a nightingale was Keats's ode and I was overwhelmed by the beauty of their song.

Jeremy and I sat on a stone bench for I know not how long, just listening. Then, as we stood to leave, he held me at arm's length, his eyes boring right through me, and said, "I have never said this before because I've never felt this way before, and I don't want you to answer in any way. I've fallen in love with you. Now, let's get going before something happens to spoil it all."

I was glad that he had told me not to answer him. The drive back to Cannes gave me time to try to make sense of my emotions, but it was all too like a fairy tale. I believed him and was elated but was afraid to say anything committal lest it all turn out to be an illusion. I was afraid that at any second I would wake up and find myself in a hotel in New York. I know we talked on the drive down, but I don't remember a thing. Back at the Carlton we kissed each other good night, but tentatively, as though standing on eggs.

9

Mother had had enough of airplanes for the time being, so she hired a limousine to take us to Paris with an overnight stop on the way. Where we would spend the night was left strictly to chance. We left the Carlton at 7:30 A.M. and Jeremy was waiting in the lobby when we came down. Mother stopped as she went past him and, in a reading she might have learned from Joan Crawford, said, "Good morning, Mr. Hyman. Thank you for taking such good care of my daughter. I hope we meet again someday." As she strode briskly off to the waiting limousine, there was no doubt in anyone's mind that her hopes ran to the precise opposite. Jeremy asked me to call him from wherever we spent the night and, as we exchanged very formal kisses on the cheek, I promised that I would.

Even though the countryside through which we drove abounded in spring colors and should have been totally uplifting to the spirits, I was miserable. Mother became thoroughly disgusted with my moodiness and managed to make things worse by delivering a seemingly endless recitation of all the wonderful things she and I were going to do together, world without end, amen. When we finally stopped for the night at yet another quaint little village, I breathed a mighty sigh.

We got two rooms at an inn, a single for Viola and a double for Mother and me. As soon as the bellboy had deposited the bags and left, I picked up the phone.

"What are you doing?" Mother barked.

"Calling Jeremy."

"I won't have it, B.D."

"I gave him my word, Mother."

"Well, you shouldn't have, should you?" Mother said cockily. "Women don't call men . . . for any reason! If he gives a shit, he'll get in touch with you."

"You're being ridiculous. No one knew where we were spending the night and I'm not playing hide-and-seek, even if you are. Just because you want me—" I was interrupted by a knock on the door, which was probably just as well.

While Mother went to answer the door I slipped through the adjoining door into Viola's room and made my call from there. Fortunately for me, the French phone company was firing on all cylinders for once in its life and I got through to Jeremy almost immediately. He was obviously in a room full of people and Viola was hanging on every word I said, so we exchanged a few niceties, said how much we missed each other and agreed that Jeremy would call me the following night at the Crillon in Paris.

I went back to our room and found Mother with a giant bouquet of American Beauty roses. They had arrived with a hand-written card reading, "To Bette. All my love. Julio." Mother read the card and exploded, *"Christ!* He must have had us followed."

A couple of months earlier, in California, I had met a woman by the name of Mary Rollefson at a party given by a mutual friend. Shortly afterward I was invited to one of Mary's lavish bashes at her estate on top of a Beverly Hill. In Beverly Hills, during one's teens, one never questioned invitations to parties . . . one just went. I did and, despite the difference in our ages, Mary and I hit it off immediately. She confessed that she had an ulterior motive in wanting to get to know me. A very old and dear friend of hers was a man by the name of Julio Lobo. Julio Lobo was a sugar baron, not just any old sugar baron but a world-class super heavyweight. His estates in Cuba had been confiscated by Castro and, although it was a deep emotional loss to him, it was a mere drop out of his economic bucket. His financial empire was worldwide. He had sugar refineries all over the place and was on the boards of directors of sugar monopolies in many countries. Mary said that Julio had long had a great passion for Mother and, since he fervently believed that the Castro regime would be toppled and that he would be able to reclaim his estates, she suspected that Julio wanted to marry Mother in order to be able to return triumphantly to Cuba one day with her as his personal Eva Perón. It had all sounded marvelously intriguing and I had eagerly agreed to go along with whatever plot Mary wanted to hatch.

A few weeks later Julio was in California on business and Mary invited Mother and me to a party in his honor. I knew better than to try to persuade Mother to go somewhere to meet an admirer, so I kept quiet about Julio and pleaded with her to come and meet Mary, extolling her virtues and insisting that Mother would adore her. She was very balky about it but I won out and we went to the party.

There was an enormous ice sculpture on the buffet table when we arrived. It spelled out "WELCOME SUGAR KING" and I quickly steered Mother past it. All the food was Cuban and there was a Cuban combo in peasant costume playing Cuban music. Mother looked at me questioningly and I said that Mary was big on ethnic motifs and that I guessed this must be Cuba night. Mary and her husband, Ivan, came over and introductions were performed. Ivan was an engineer who was generally off in some far-flung outpost building a bridge or something, which was why I hadn't met him before. Mary asked Ivan to take care of Mother for a few minutes so that she could steal me away to introduce me to someone I might find interesting. As we crossed the patio Mary whispered, "Julio's in the bar waiting to meet you."

Ever since Mary had laid out her plan for getting Mother and Julio together, I had been entertaining images of a billionaire Ricardo Montalban type sweeping Mother off her feet and everybody living happily ever after. Mary ushered me into the bar and over to a totally bald man, about five feet tall, seemingly in his sixties and with a piece of his skull missing. I later learned that it was the result of a bullet during the revolution. Julio's manners were Continental and his charm soon overcame my surprise at his physical appearance. He told me how thrilled he was that Mary had met me and how very much he appreciated my inveigling Mother into coming to his party. The conversation continued until Ivan entered the bar with Mother and steered her our way. I introduced Julio to Mother and said, "It seems that Mr. Lobo is the sugar king in whose honor the ice sculpture was carved." While Julio was kissing Mother's hand, she gave me a "What the hell is this all about?" look but, having done my bit, I rushed off to disappear in the crowd by the pool.

For quite a while I managed to avoid confrontation with Mother. Whenever I caught sight of her, Julio had a firm grip on her arm, and whenever she saw me she made frantic signals which I ignored. After about an hour, however, she suddenly appeared at my side without Julio, grabbed my elbow and gritted, "You and I are going to have a chat, young lady . . . right now." She shoved me ahead of her into the ladies' room and locked the door. "What the hell is this all about? That awful little man has been clutching me ever since I arrived."

"What's what all about?" I asked, all wide-eyed and innocent. "I think Julio is charming and you certainly can't hate him for worshipping the ground you walk on."

"I can do anything I damned well please, young lady, and you just remember it," Mother snarled. "You got me into this mess. Now you can damned well get me out of it!"

"You're a big girl, Mother," I said, still all innocence. "If you want to leave, all you have to do is call for our car and leave. It's hardly a big deal. And you don't have to worry about me; I have a date with Danny Milland to go to another party in Malibu."

"I can't just leave," Mother whined. "He's probably waiting for me outside the door . . . and anyway, it would be rude to the Rollefsons."

"Oh, give me a break, will you, Mother, and stop being so dramatic! What do you think he's going to do . . . kidnap you? And as for being rude, when did you start worrying about that?"

"All right, B.D., you just go to your party and have a ball. You obviously don't give a shit about me anyway!" Mother was still carrying on as I unlocked the door and left. I paid my respects to the Rollefsons, found Danny and took off for Malibu.

Mother was in no better humor the next morning. Julio had made things worse by asking Mother to thank me again for bringing her to meet him and, in addition, two bouquets of flowers had been delivered first thing that morning: American Beauty roses for Mother and pink roses for me. Mother had read both cards. Hers read, "To the most important woman in my life. Love, Julio"; mine, "I will always remember your kindness. Fondly, Julio." Mother opened with "All right, B.D. You're not going anywhere until we have this out. What on earth possessed you to get me into this mess? It isn't funny, you know."

"Of course it's not funny. It wasn't meant to be."

Two hours of intense debate later, Mother still refused to see any merit in the original idea. I was still defending the concept and insisting that she would make a fantastic Eva Perón, at the same time finding it difficult not to dissolve into laughter at her complete disarray. The simple fact was, Mother had no idea how to cope with someone who was mannered, charming and at the same time in full control. Beneath Julio's public veneer, one could sense the iron that was the real man and Mother couldn't deal with it. She liked to be able to push people around and then bewail the fact that there were "no real men anymore."

It soon became apparent that Julio was not a man to readily accept defeat. No matter where we were, a bouquet of American Beauty roses arrived every morning, always with a hand-written card. About once a week there was a letter instead of a card, repeating his offer of marriage. There were also random phone calls and gifts. And, as if all that wasn't enough, Julio knew every detail of Mother's daily life: whom she had spoken to on the phone, how many cigarettes she had smoked, what she had read. It really intrigued me but it was driving Mother insane.

During all this, Julio had given Viola precise details of what to do if Mother ever needed help of any kind, wanted any favor whatsoever, or wanted to get in touch with him. Viola had been given a name that was listed in the telephone directories of virtually every major city in the civilized world. All Viola or

Mother, or I for that matter, had to do was look up that name—it was the same one everywhere—dial the number, ask for John Smith, give our name, wait until John Smith came on the line and said, "Hello, Miss Sherry [if I were the caller]. What can I do for you?," tell him what was wanted and it would be done. I kept hoping that Mother might need something badly enough to put this to the test. I didn't have to wait much longer.

So, here we were at a tiny inn in a village located somewhere between Cannes and Paris and Julio had done it again. Since the bouquet was enormous it was hardly likely that the chauffeur had been bribed to secrete it in the limousine. It was even less likely that the village had a florist, let alone a florist with several dozen American Beauty roses ready to hand. For once I found myself having to agree with Mother. Julio must have had us followed. But then we hadn't seen any traffic to speak of all day long. A car following us would have stuck out like a sore thumb. We were completely at a loss. Mother was spitting nails, and my suggestion that she marry the man and put a stop to it that way went over like a lead balloon.

When we arrived at the Crillon Hotel in Paris we found that our reservations were fouled up. The suite Mother had reserved was still occupied by an ambassador who had extended his stay at the last moment. The concierge wrung his hands in Gallic distress while he tried to explain that there were rooms but no suites available until the next day. Mother was clearly on the verge of creating a major scene when Viola suggested that we wait by the reception desk for a moment while she went to call a friend. Mother started to ask a question but Viola scurried off and disappeared around the corner to the pay phones. She returned within five minutes and told us we should go to the bar and have a drink while her friend sorted out the problem. I managed to get a few private words with Viola on the way to the bar. "Who did you call?" I whispered.

"I looked up the number and called John Smith," she whispered back.

"What happened?" I was all agog.

"It was just the way he said. A woman answered and I asked for John Smith. She asked my name, told me to hold on and in about thirty seconds a man came on the line and said, 'Good evening, Miss Rubber. What can I do for you?' So I told him and he said to go to the bar and have a drink."

"What do you think he's going to do?"

"Let's get a drink and wait and see."

Mother was complaining bitterly about "sitting here like refugees" but, between Viola and me and a double Scotch, we kept her more or less under control. When another twenty minutes had passed I heard a great stir in the lobby and excused myself to see what was happening. A very overwrought-looking couple with piles of luggage was checking out with bellboys dashing hither and yon in a frenzy of activity. I went back to our table and reported that something seemed to be happening but I wasn't sure what. Just then a bellboy rushed up and said in English, "The manager's compliments, Miss Davis, but the ambassador has been called home for consultations and the suite you requested will be ready in half an hour. If you will be gracious enough to have dinner in the meantime, courtesy of the hotel, the manager will be eternally in your debt." Viola and I exchanged glances while Mother looked dumbfounded. When we finally confessed what Viola had done, Mother's reaction was *"God!* It's all too much. Order me another double Scotch." She was right . . . it was a bit much. The feeling of power was giddying, but I was fully confident that I could learn to live with it if I had to.

As we were registering I learned that Jeremy had called and left a message for me. He was flying to Paris the next morning and had made a reservation at the Crillon. I was on cloud nine. Mother was silent. I met him at Orly Airport and we spent four glorious days touring Paris. We devoted two full days to the Louvre and even that was barely enough to scratch the surface. We wandered in the Tuileries Gardens, ate lunches under the blooming chestnut trees at little cafés on the Champs Élysées, saw the Arc de Triomphe and visited the Eiffel Tower.

The creaky old elevator that ascends one of the angled legs of the tower put the fear of God into us, though neither of us would admit it. Our original intention had been to go straight to the top, changing elevators at the halfway platform, but on arriving at the platform we suddenly developed a pressing need for something to eat. We went into the restaurant and forced down the most atrocious food imaginable, drank several cups of dreadful coffee and fortified ourselves with an embarrassing number of snifters of cognac. When no further stalling tactics were left we took ourselves reluctantly to the elevator shaft for the final ascent, only to be told that it had just closed for the night. The relief of each of us was so apparent to the other that we dissolved in giggles.

Tom Hammond, Mother's lawyer, arrived in Paris and immediately organized a party at the Lido in Mother's honor. He invited several people, including Olivia De Havilland and her husband, Pierre Galante, and a young Frenchman with some sort of title by the name of Jean-Yves as an escort for me. Mother had carefully neglected to tell Tom about Jeremy. When I told Tom that I was already quite satisfactorily escorted, he was loath to cancel my date, not wanting to be rude, so instead he enlarged the reservation to make room for Jeremy.

Mother was thrilled with Jean-Yves, assuming that the attention of a titled Continental would distract me from Jeremy, or at least irritate him enough to cause him to leave. She failed on both counts. Jean-Yves was very attentive, resembling an octopus when we danced, and I was about to grind my heel into his foot when Jeremy cut in. Mother didn't feel that I was paying enough attention to this "divine man" and kept barking out, "*À droit*, B.D., *à droit!*" She persisted all evening, vainly attempting to get me to spend more time talking to Jean-Yves on my right than to Jeremy on my left. That she was issuing her coded instructions in Jean-Yves's native tongue apparently didn't occur to her. This was greatly amusing to Olivia and her husband, particularly after I quietly explained to them what it was all about. At the end of the evening my French escort asked Mother for my hand in marriage. It seemed that he was a land-poor gentleman looking for an advantageous marriage who thought that he'd found one. Mother promptly gave her consent, beaming radiantly at me as she did so. Needless to say, I declined his kind offer and sent him packing.

"*Shit!*" was Mother's only comment.

Jeremy had to return to London the next morning to go back to work while Mother and I had one more day in Paris before leaving for Rome for a business meeting. Once again we parted, this time at the airport. We again agreed to stay in touch. We talked and kissed for so long that Jeremy missed the shuttle bus to his plane and had to wait two hours for an- other flight. Neither of us would have minded two more hours together except, unfortunately, I had fled the airport in tears before Jeremy discovered that you took a bus first or you didn't fly.

That evening, back at the Crillon, Viola smoothly an- nounced that she had just had a call from Rome to the effect that it would be more convenient to hold the meeting with Mother in London if she would be so kind as to change her itinerary. She added that Mother had nothing to worry about since she had already made all the reservation changes. While explaining this and a few other details, Viola slipped me a sly wink.

Extraordinary lady, Viola. She had ways of arranging things which never ceased to amaze me. It was she who had engi- neered my blind date with Jeremy. Now it seemed that she would go to considerable lengths to keep the romance on track, for I hadn't the least doubt that she had called Rome and told the people there that Miss Davis would prefer to meet in Lon- don. She was obviously pleased with our progress to date and even more obviously convinced that we were the perfect match. Neither Jeremy nor I was ever able to fathom what had prompted her matchmaking scheme in the first place, nor would Viola, until her death eighteen years later, ever say more than it seemed like a good idea at the time.

I was slightly worried about calling Jeremy with the news. It might, after all, have been a shipboard romance and now it could look as though I were chasing after him. On the other hand, he would certainly hear that we were in London, prob- ably within minutes, and if I didn't call him he might assume that I had lost interest. I called him. He sounded positively ec- static that I would be there the next day and, before I realized what I was doing, I told him that I loved him. I felt much bet- ter for finally admitting it but remained on tenterhooks until our plane landed at Heathrow and I found Jeremy waiting for me.

For the next four days, except for minimal amounts of sleep, we were inseparable. Mother realized that she was essentially powerless to do much about it and had, for the time being, given up trying. Jeremy took me out to the country and showed me the beauty of Kent and Surrey. We ate at pubs and I learned to drink English beer. We visited Tonbridge, where Jeremy had gone to school, and attended evening services at the school chapel (Mother never would believe that we had been to church). We picnicked on a village green and watched a cricket match. Jeremy tried to explain the rules to me but I had difficulty coming to grips with a game that could go on for days and then end without a winner. We went to a donkey derby which, I learned, had been held annually for centuries to benefit an orphanage. Children frenziedly urged their donkeys around a small racecourse in a field while hundreds of spectators picnicked on the grass and bet on the races with bookmakers who were laying odds and taking bets just as they do at real racecourses. It was fabulous.

We left London at dawn one morning to go riding. Jeremy had borrowed a beautiful Irish steeplechaser for me from Bridget Walters, the woman who owned the stables where he liveried his horse. I was introduced to Bridget and, chatting with her, I began to learn something about Jeremy's boyhood. He and Bridget had been next-door neighbors for ten years. Until that moment I had been at somewhat of a disadvantage. My life was an open book compared to his and it was fun to hear details of his past from his friends.

It was a gorgeous day and when I agreed to his suggestion that we take a long ride, Jeremy said, "O.K. Let's nip over to Toys Hill and I'll show you where I grew up and introduce you to the Pages." Nip indeed! We rode cross-country, literally over hill and dale, through Chartwell (Sir Winston Churchill's estate) and, at the end of three hours, arrived at Toys Hill. The house in which Jeremy grew up was a picture-book Tudor cottage built at the end of the fifteenth century. We weren't able to go in because Jeremy's mother had moved to Sussex, but he told me that it had a tile roof because a V-2 rocket had landed in the field next to the house during the war and blown the thatched roof clean off the house, doing no other damage. I wondered what would be left of our modern houses if a V-2 rocket landed next to them. When we rode into the barnyard of Scords Farm the Pages—David and Elizabeth and their three children, Anne, Robert and Margaret—ran out to greet us. After a great chorus of hellos, David took the floor. Jeremy had spoken much of the Pages and of David in particular, telling me that I would never meet nicer people but that David had a singularly un-English knack of saying whatever was on his mind and damn the consequences. As a matter of fact, when David became a magistrate a few years later, a teenage delinquent was brought before him and David gave him a spanking right in the courtroom.

"Hyman! You dirty old man!" he bellowed. "What's all this I keep reading in the papers about you gallivanting around with some sixteen-year-old girl?" He paid not the slightest attention to his wife, who was looking at me and kicking him in the shins while he was putting his foot in it as usual. Jeremy grinned mischievously and answered, "David. Lizzie. I'd like you to meet B. D. Sherry, the sixteen-year-old girl." There was a great silence while David turned beet-red and foomfled, followed by much laughter. Then, in his inimitable fashion, he tried to cover up his faux pas. "Well! I must say! It isn't really fair to spring a ruddy Amazon on me and expect me to know she's only sixteen!"

We had lunch at the farm and I was given a tour of all the pets by Margaret and the stables by Robert. I also heard many anecdotes about Jeremy since he had worked for David for a few months while waiting for his call-up notice to do his mandatory two years in the armed forces.

I heard about the time David sent Jeremy off to do some harrowing. When it started to rain Jeremy, instead of packing it in, produced an umbrella from somewhere and continued on, steering the tractor with one hand and holding the umbrella with the other. He would never reveal where he got the umbrella.

Then there was the time when Jeremy was dispatched with the manure spreader for the first time. David carefully told him not to go too fast downhill with the spreader in operation. Jeremy didn't ask why, so David didn't tell him. Naturally, Jeremy paid no heed to David's warning and was rewarded with a ten-pound blob of cow dung hitting him in the back of the head.

I heard many other funny stories but I also learned that Jeremy's casually mentioned "two years in the armed forces" were spent as an officer in the Royal Marines Commandos. It impressed the hell out of me and I couldn't wait to see Mother's reaction to this bit of news.

It was getting late and, much though I regretted it, we had to be on our way. We had the long ride back to the stables and then the drive to London. I had loved England before but I was beginning to cherish every inch of it, not only the countryside and the beautiful old villages and buildings, but the people as well. I had met only city and movie people before and they were not much different from their counterparts anywhere else in the world, give or take a few cultural niceties. Now that I was meeting Jeremy's friends, an entirely new perspective was opening up for me. Bridget had lent me her best horse, an unusually gracious gesture under any circumstances. The Pages had accepted me as one of their own. It was very warming and my reception and immediate acceptance everywhere we went will always be among my fondest memories.

The day before Mother and I were to return to California, the Fates again smiled on Jeremy and me. Mother's meetings had gone well and she would be doing *The Empty Canvas* for Carlo Ponti in the fall to be filmed in London and Rome. We would be back in London in September. This permitted Jeremy and me to continue to be sensible and see how our feelings would withstand the test of time and separation. We were very proud of ourselves for not being impetuous. After all, we had only known each other for ten days.

Mother and I had been back at Honeysuckle Hill for three days when Jeremy called. He said that he had written me a long letter but, after mailing it, found that he couldn't stand the suspense . . . would I marry him? When I unhesitatingly agreed, he asked to speak to Mother. He asked her permission to marry me and, in one of her most memorable reversals of form, Mother replied, "It's about time! B.D.'s miserable without you," and handed the phone back to me. That seemed to settle that but an engagement party would have to wait six weeks until Jeremy was scheduled to be in California. I would also have to wait for my ring since he wanted to put it on my finger himself. That was all right with me but, suddenly, six weeks seemed like an eternity.

10

Mother's change of attitude in granting her consent to my marriage which, at sixteen, I needed unless I wanted to run off to a foreign country, turned out to be a mixed blessing. I carefully refrained from asking why she had given in so easily since it was entirely possible that she was unaware of the age requirement. I didn't have to wait very long, however, before she painted a perfectly clear picture for me.

At first she rushed about enthusiastically, telling one and all of the romance of it all, arranging a massive engagement party, discussing a wedding gown, considering which church to hold the wedding in and generally having a grand time. The atmosphere could easily have led one to believe that it was she who was getting married rather than I. This mood prevailed for about two weeks but then, one morning, my bubble of cheerful anticipation was burst.

I trotted merrily down the stairs as usual, bent on a quick breakfast before going to the beach with friends. "Good morning, everybody," I chirped as I strode briskly into the kitchen. Aunt Bobby was at the stove filling the kitchen with delicious bacon smells. A pitcher of orange juice and the steaming coffeepot were on the counter. Mother was at the breakfast table eating boiled eggs and toast.

"Good morning, B.D.," said Aunt Bobby. "How would you like your eggs?"

"Scrambled, please, with bacon," I answered, pouring myself a glass of juice and taking my place across from Mother. She had not even said good morning but, as I raised my juice, she blurted, "You better be nice to me and love me a lot. This is a great thing I'm doing for you. There aren't many mothers who'd let their sixteen-year-old daughters get married. I'll tell you that much right now!"

She got up from the table and went to the counter to refill her coffee cup. I sneaked a look in Aunt Bobby's direction, hoping for a clue as to what had started this but she continued to busy herself at the stove, neither looking at me nor reacting to Mother's outburst. That in itself told me something. If Aunt Bobby had been surprised she would have done or said something, reacted in some way. My view of her unyielding back told me that this, whatever it was, had started before I came into the room. It didn't help much but at least I knew why Mother's opening line had been such a non sequitur. I waited for her to regain her seat, stayed cool and said with wide-eyed honesty, "I thought you'd changed your mind about Jeremy and were all in favor of the marriage. If that's not the case, you've certainly been putting on a good act for the past few weeks."

"*Ha!* So that's what you think, do you?" she barked, spitting bits of egg all over the table. "Well, let me tell *you* something. That English bastard hasn't even *tried* to woo me over, so why should I change my mind? Why should I? All he sees is his precious little B.D. He doesn't give a damn about *me!*" She had been eating and talking at once. Now she lit a cigarette too.

I bought time by getting up and going for my eggs and bacon. I should have been flustered or furious or something, but I wasn't. I suppose I had known all along that something was going to happen. What threw me off-balance was Mother's blatant admission of jealousy. I wasn't sure whether she was jealous of Jeremy, me or both of us, but jealous she obviously was. She must have had a bad night, worked up a head of steam and then come down determined either to cancel the wedding or make me grovel. Well, I wasn't about to grovel, but the wedding wasn't going to be canceled either. I was willing to try to be reasonable though. "But Mother," I temporized as I sat down and put my napkin back on my lap, "we've only spent two weeks together, less than that actually. When would you and Jeremy have had the chance to get to know each other? When we've all been together he's always been polite and charming toward you. What more would you want?"

"You know perfectly well what I mean, B.D.," she snapped, glaring at me squinty-eyed. "It's an attitude. I can't describe it, so let's just drop it. Just be damned grateful to me if you know what's good for you!"

She was right in one respect. I did know what she meant. Jeremy was in love with me and, except for asking Mother's consent to our marriage, he didn't give a damn about her. She was used to my dates making a big fuss of her and suddenly she was faced with a prospective son-in-law who wasn't even impressed. She couldn't stand it and was going to try to make my life miserable in return. Well, damn it, I wouldn't let her. I glared straight back at her and said stiffly, "Mother, you know how much Jeremy and I love each other. I'd have thought that that in itself would make you happy. Maybe in time it will. So, you're right . . . let's drop it." I stabbed a huge forkful of eggs and shoved them in my mouth as an exclamation mark.

Mother jumped up, knocking her chair over backward, leaned forward with her hands on the table and bellowed in my face, "So, you think that's all there is to it, do you? Well, it's not that simple!" She snarled viciously, "You don't give a damn about me. All you care about is your precious little love affair! Well let me tell you something, young lady . . . if I wanted to I could take him away from you right now!" She took another cigarette from the pewter cup and messed about scratching a kitchen match under the table while I almost gagged on my eggs in fury.

I jumped up too and bellowed right back at her, "Good God, Mother, are you out of your mind? One minute you can't stand Jeremy . . . the next minute you're going to take him away from me! Well, if you want to show your future son-in-law what a weirdo you are, go ahead and try it! But if you think he's one of those sycophants I used to get stuck with who went out with me in order to be able to fawn all over you, you're in for a hell of a shock. Just don't come running back to me with how rude he is when he tells you and your warped mind where to go! So go ahead and try it . . . I dare you!" I was so outraged that I just stood and glared at her while she sank back into the chair, which Aunt Bobby had righted, placed her hands over her face and started to sniffle. "Don't do this to me, B.D. . . . not today. You know that all I want is the best for you. I know all about men . . . they're shits, every one of them. I just don't want you to get kicked in the teeth like I always was." Then, dissolving into wracking sobs, "Have it your way, but you just wait and see . . . he'll dump you. Then you'll realize that the only person who really loves you is me. You wait and see."

I continued to stand, glaring at her pathetic form in silence. It was too late for Mother to object to my adulthood. I'd been a woman since I was twelve when I had, at her instigation, begun dating. The argument was ended, at least for today, and I had no desire to rekindle it. Mother finally got up and went upstairs, sobbing all the way. I knew from experience that she would remain in exile for hours, possibly the rest of the day or even night, then emerge all smiles and good cheer as though nothing had happened.

My days were filled with helping to plan the engagement party, writing to Jeremy, talking to him on the telephone and telling everyone all about him and my excitement at the prospect of living in England. The weeks passed, Jeremy arrived and our feelings, if possible, were stronger than ever. I loved my ring and, like all newly engaged women, always managed to place my left hand so that the ring would be conspicuous. Jeremy was only going to be with us for a few days so, for the sake of convenience, he stayed in our combination pool-guesthouse. He had no idea of the trouble between Mother and me and I had no intention of burdening him with the knowledge if it could be avoided. I stayed fully alert all weekend in order to be able to head off any unfortunate scenes before they developed. As it turned out, I needn't have worried. Mother played the model New England hostess and Jeremy, not knowing that there was anything to worry about in the first place, was the perfect English guest.

The engagement party was held at the Bel-Air Hotel. It went without a hitch and we enjoyed it enormously. Among the guests were Paul Henreid, Joseph Cotten and his wife, Patricia Medina, Rosalind Russell, Whit Bissell, Jules Stein, Elizabeth Montgomery and Rock Hudson. Hedda Hopper, of course, singled Jeremy out for much attention. We were a news item and anything interesting she might glean from him could be used in her column. Jeremy was of the New York and London film worlds and neither knew nor cared that everyone in Hollywood kowtowed to Hedda. He found that he liked her, danced with her several times, kidded her about everything and unwittingly endeared himself to her. From then on, whenever Jeremy flew anywhere or we did anything together, Hedda gave it the first line in her column. Press agents and publicity departments had been known to offer fortunes just to be mentioned at the bottom. Jeremy was a bit embarrassed by this newly found and unsought attention, particularly when the Seven Arts publicity department asked him how he had managed it. There was, however, one fringe benefit. Mother was like everyone else in Hollywood in one respect; she wasn't exactly awed by Hedda or Louella Parsons but she was, at least, forever concerned with what they might say. The fact that Hedda was so taken with Jeremy wasn't enough to convince Mother that he wasn't all bad, but it at least gave her pause to think. From my standpoint, it was both rewarding and lots of fun. Rewarding because it successfully kept Mother quiet for a while, and lots of fun because of the envy it engendered among my Hollywood friends.

Jeremy returned to London, promising to come back for a few days in about a month. Again I wrote a lot of letters and talked to him frequently on the phone. Mother and I went to work on the organization of the wedding. Mother changed the plans daily. At first the wedding was to be held in California because that's where *we* were. Then it would be fairer to have it in New York because that was halfway between where Jeremy was and where we were. Then *that* didn't make any sense because that was where none of us were. So it would be in London because that was where we *would* be. Then Mother couldn't stand the idea of trying to organize a wedding five thousand miles away and it was back in California again.

With that problem out of the way, there was the question of a date to be addressed. It couldn't be before Christmas for all sorts of reasons so, after some discussion, December 28 was selected. When feelers were put out, however, it turned out that there were any number of people whom we wanted at the wedding who wouldn't be able to make it that close to Christmas. January 4, 1964, was settled on.

Now all we had to do was pick a church. All Saints Church in Beverly Hills was the obvious choice, but that gave rise to another question. There was the main church that seated two thousand and the chapel which only seated a hundred fifty. It didn't take long to decide that the chapel was the more desirable alternative. Mother told me to tell Jeremy not to invite more than seventy-five people and to keep it lower than that if he could. It wasn't long before his guest list arrived and there was no problem due to his reluctance to impose upon too many of his friends the burden of flying all that way just for a wedding.

Mother's ill humor had resolved itself into more or less regular, twice-weekly tirades denigrating her son-in-law-to-be. The cause of it was probably a combination of her basic hatred of men, her natural reluctance to see me move away and her distress over the unending delays with respect to *Four for Texas*. She had signed to do this picture along with Frank Sinatra and Dean Martin, with Robert Aldrich directing. For one reason and then another, it didn't seem able to get off the ground, which left Mother with nothing better to do than pick fights with me. She had also signed to do *Dead Ringer* for Warner Bros. the following year and, out of nowhere, the start date for *Dead Ringer* was moved up to early August. Bob Aldrich released Mother from her *Four for Texas* contract and she went to work. I was particularly relieved since it put an end to the twice-weekly tirades.

Dead Ringer (which bore a marked resemblance to a picture Mother had made in 1946 called *A Stolen Life*) was directed by Paul Henreid. The story was about twin sisters, one good and one bad, two murders and an accomplice-lover played by Peter Lawford. Mother was very happy, thanks to Jack Warner making a tremendous fuss over having her under his wing once again. It was a shame that the script wasn't much, even with all the hours Paul and Mother invested in it trying to improve it.

I divided my time between wedding preparations and visiting Mother on the *Dead Ringer* location at Greystone, the magnificent old Hollywood mansion built around 1920 by the Doheny family, which has since been preserved as a Hollywood landmark. Mother had absolutely forbidden me to buy any clothes for my trousseau until she had the time to do it with me, but once the picture was finished she had at it with gusto.

She gave her new role, Mother of the Bride, all it was worth. She bought me enough clothes for several brides, insisting that it was barely enough, and choosing a winter coat almost became the cause of a major argument. I saw any number of wool coats with fur collars and cuffs that I loved, but Mother had it in her head that I must have a fur coat, and a fur coat had to be mink or it didn't count. I protested at length and got nowhere, so off we went to the furrier. As soon as we got there Mother developed a pressing need for a new mink coat herself and quickly chose a black one. I didn't like dark furs on myself, feeling that they looked too old for me, and we had something of a bitter set-to over it. The furrier saved everyone's bacon by disappearing for some time and then producing a scrumptious blond mink with a shawl collar and bell sleeves. I caved in. It was gorgeous and I had to admit that I loved it. Mother was thrilled.

Mother, Viola and I flew to London in September, by which time most of the wedding details had been taken care of. I was bubbling with excitement at the prospect of spending some real time with Jeremy. Although we had known each other for four months and been officially engaged for almost three, we had actually spent only about three weeks in each other's company, broken up into a few days here and a few days there.

Mother went straight into meetings with the Ponti people and learned that there had been a last-minute change in plans. *The Empty Canvas* would be filmed entirely in Rome. She breezed into the hotel suite that evening aglow with pleasure. "I'm *so* sorry, B.D.," she said, oozing malicious satisfaction out of every pore, "but you won't be able to spend the next couple of months with your fiancé after all. We're leaving for Rome immediately and will only be back in London on our way home."

I was devastated. An earthquake had struck and I was being swallowed up in a bottomless pit. I went numb all over and, choking back a sob, I ran to the bathroom to cry in private. At first I was desolated, unable to think of anything but two more long months with Mother which should have been spent with the man I loved. Then anger crept in to replace the hurt. Her posture and tone of smug, self-righteous glee had said it all. She was thrilled, elated, triumphant and she hadn't even the decency to pretend otherwise. I wasn't just angry, I hated the hypocritical, vicious bitch. I hated her guts. Despite everything she had ever done to me or anyone else, I found it hard to believe that she would deliberately be so loathsome.

There was a gentle knock on the door. "B.D.?" It was Viola. "It's all right, dear, I've sorted it out. You and I are staying here for two or three weeks before we go to Rome." I opened the door and threw myself into Viola's arms, crying and laughing at once. "Are you sure? Are you certain? You mean she won't change—"

"Calm down, dear, calm down," Viola said, hugging me and patting my back as she might a little child. "It's all taken care of. Don't worry about a thing." I wiped at my tears and whispered a thank-you. "It's all right, dear," she said with a reassuring smile, "you don't have to whisper. Your mother knows you're very upset. She's in her bedroom changing." I took a deep breath and asked Vi how she had done it. She smiled and replied, "Not now, dear. Use the phone in my room and call Jeremy. Tell him that it's important you have dinner with your mother tonight and that you'll explain in the morning."

Not a word was spoken by Mother regarding the incident or the new arrangements. All she talked about at dinner was how tricky the script was, how much she disliked the supporting members of the cast, the language difficulty she would encounter working with Italian technicians and what all-around hell she was about to go through. When she left for Rome the following morning she sweetly instructed Viola to take seriously her duties as chaperone. "You know that B.D. is the only thing I love and her happiness the only thing I care about. Be sure to take good care of her. I'll miss you both." With a tiny sob of emotion, a brave smile and a regal wave of the hand, she departed.

Jeremy had to go to work every day, so our time together generally began with lunch at one or another of his favorite restaurants. Sometimes he had to go out to a studio and I went with him; at other times, when he had to spend the day in the office, I puttered about London, going places and seeing things which Jeremy and others had recommended to me—Harrods, Fortnum's, art galleries and so forth. It was a wonderful feeling to be on my own in a foreign city without Mother dictating my every move. I found that I enjoyed my time alone almost as much as my time with Jeremy. Evenings were a whirlwind of restaurants, nightclubs, parties, gambling casinos and meeting more and more of Jeremy's marvelous friends and acquaintances. On weekends we drove out to the country. We visited his favorite pubs, I met his friends the Goads, I got to know the Pages better and we did some riding. There always seemed to be more things to do and more people to meet but not enough time for it all.

The weeks flew by so quickly that I was startled when Mother called and announced that Viola and I must leave for Rome within the next day or two. This time, our parting was really tough on both of us. Now that we'd had some time together we had discovered that, in addition to being in love, we liked each other. Had we been of the same sex, we might well have been best friends. It was an exciting new awareness and convinced us more than ever that we were very fortunate to have found one another.

Mother was as happy as a lark when Viola and I arrived in Rome, but her happiness was to be short-lived. After three days of accompanying her to the set, Carlo Ponti and Sophia Loren's grandiose estate, Villa Ponti, I came down with appendicitis. Mother, naturally, wanted me in the hospital nearest to her hotel but, partly because I spoke no Italian and partly because I much preferred the idea of being near Jeremy than being with Mother, I protested strenuously and at length. Mother was fit to be tied and insisted that I was too sick to make it to a London hospital but, somehow, Viola produced a doctor who said that my chances of a normal, healthy recovery from the operation would be greatly improved if I were not in such an agitated emotional state. Mother called me a bitch and accused me of inducing the appendicitis in order to get back to London.

By the time my plane touched down at Heathrow, Mother had spoken to everyone several times each. Jeremy and the doctor were waiting at the airport and the surgeon was standing at attention at the hospital, instruments poised. All went well and in four days I was released, the doctor advising that moderate exercise was highly desirable but there should be no riding for two or three weeks, but that was all right, Jeremy and I were back together and I was safe until the stitches were removed and I underwent a final checkup.

Tim Goad, whom I had met with his wife, Sarah, on one of our weekends in the country, ran a shoot in Surrey in which Jeremy had a gun. They were meeting on Saturday and we decided that pheasant shooting constituted moderate exercise. Jeremy told me that ladies were welcome but neglected to mention that they didn't carry guns. I didn't find out until we got there just what ladies did do.

As if in possession of a crystal ball, Mother phoned on Friday evening to say that I shouldn't go anywhere since she was coming to London and wanted me in attendance upon her arrival.

"When are you getting here?" I asked.

"I don't know for sure . . . maybe tomorrow evening."

"Is that fairly certain?"

"No. It could be Sunday . . . not later than Monday or Tuesday."

"Do you mean to say that you want me to sit here and do nothing for four days just in case you show up?" I protested. "It's not fair! Anyway, the doctor says it's important that I get moderate exercise."

"*Well*, you'll just have to walk round and round the suite, won't you?" Click, dial tone.

I mulled over the probabilities and reached the conclusion that there was no chance of Mother arriving the next day. She would have packed already if she were leaving Rome the next morning and, if she had packed, she wouldn't have been so evasive about her arrival time. Sunday was a possibility, but Monday or Tuesday was more likely. Satisfied with my analysis of the situation, I saw no reason to phone Jeremy and bore him with Mother's latest attempt to mess things up. Shooting it would be. I went to bed early in order to be ready for our dawn departure for Surrey.

It was a beautifully crisp fall morning as we left London on our way to the Goads'. God was in his heaven and all was right with the world. Tim and Jeremy had known each other since childhood and their friendship was delightfully casual. Sarah's father, Uvedale Lambert, was Master of the Old Surrey and Burstow Fox Hounds, the hunt of which Jeremy was a member. They gave us a lovely breakfast and I had the chance to get to know them a little better. I was particularly taken with Sarah who was extremely erudite with a sharp sense of humor.

Three more people arrived, and it was time to move off to the appointed meeting place where the gamekeeper, Cyril Hibbard, and the other guns were to congregate. When Tim was satisfied that everyone who was coming that day had arrived, he rounded up Sarah, me, a couple of other wives, Hibbard and the paid beaters and said, "If you'll string out across there"—pointing to a woodline—"we'll beat that one up first." Then he turned his attention to the guns. "Let's go, gentlemen, it's a fair walk to the other side."

Although I knew vaguely what the term beater meant, I had never been on an English shoot before and was not too sure what was expected of me. I whispered to Sarah, "What do I do now?" She whispered back, "Find a big stick and bash your way through the brush until you get to the other side. Make as much noise as you can all the way but, when you near the far edge, whoop and holler at the top of your lungs. One wouldn't want the fortunate few with guns to mistake you for something edible when you break into the clear." Now I knew why wives were welcome. Beaters had to be paid to beat, wives didn't. This wasn't quite what I had expected when Jeremy suggested we go shooting but, if this was the custom, by golly I'd bash brush with the best of them!

So off we went, the fortunate few to take up their stands at the far side of the wood and the beaters to beat. By listening to the others I learned that the beaters were supposed to maintain a semblance of a straight line and occasionally give vent to cries like "Runner headed left!" if a pheasant ran to the left instead of flying as it was supposed to. When we were halfway through the wood, the first shots were fired and the shooting continued until the beaters broke cover at the far side. Then everybody searched for the birds where they had dropped and we headed for the next wood to do it again. It doesn't sound like much fun for the beaters but I actually enjoyed it.

Things continued thus until we were about two thirds of the way through our third wood, when I heard Sarah let out an unusual cry. "A brace of lovers running right!" I thought she was kidding until I heard someone to my right shout, "There they go, by George, and he's carrying his trousers!" The progress of the lovers through the brush was marked by loud crashing noises, then a few seconds of silence, then Tim's voice in the distance. "Hold your fire! I don't think they're going to rise!" We finished our drive, gathered up the birds as usual and sat down for lunch and a good chuckle over the plight of the ill-fated lovers. It turned out that Tim was the last to have seen them, a couple of fields away and moving well, the boy still carrying his trousers in his panic.

When lunch was over and we were walking to the next wood, Hibbard came up beside me and asked, "Beggin' your pardon, Miss, oi know hit's none o' moi business, but are you gettin' married soon?"

"Not for a couple of months, Hibbard . . . why?"

"Well, Miss, to tell you the trufe, that Mr. Oiman 'asn't been able to 'it the broad soid of a barn since 'e met you, Miss. I was 'oping you'd get married soon so's 'e'd get 'is moind back on business." I wasn't sure why Hibbard was so upset but I promised to see if there was anything I could do about it. When I had the chance to talk to Jeremy later, I mentioned my conversation with Hibbard. He explained that the guns seldom kept more than a brace of birds each and that the rest of the bag became the gamekeeper's perks. I suggested to Jeremy that he get his act together because, judging from the expression on Hibbard's face, he was about to lose hearth and home and it would all be his, Jeremy's, fault.

By midafternoon the Scotch mist which had moved in earlier turned into a steady drizzle. I expected that when we finished the ongoing drive we would pack up for the day and go home. Not so. Nobody seemed to notice that we were soaking wet and we just pushed onward. By the time we had bashed and sloshed our way through another wood, the steady drizzle had become a veritable monsoon. To my great relief, somebody finally noticed. "Raining a bit, isn't it?" This astute observation, rather than begetting thoughts of dry clothes and warm places among the other sportsmen, merely elicited the following comments.

"Yes . . . what a bore."

"Bit of bad luck, what?"

"It might stop."

"It might at that."

"Why don't we drive one more cover and see what it looks like then?"

"All right with me. How about the rest of you?" This was followed by a chorus of assents during which both Tim and Jeremy asked how I was holding up. I said that my stitches felt fine and that if the rest were determined to go on, I was game too. Tim said he didn't think the rain was going to let up and this would most likely be the last drive. I found that heartening and, when it indeed turned out to be the case, I was not in the least disappointed.

Back at the Goads' house, we changed into dry clothes and thoroughly enjoyed the hot tea laced with brandy with which Sarah plied us. She was also kind enough to run our wet togs through the drier. When we were fully fortified we headed back to London, stopping at a pub on the way for something to eat. Jeremy took me straight to my hotel so that I could get an early night, having every intention of doing the same thing himself. He was fortunate, he did get an early night. When I walked into the suite, there was Mother, pacing about the room with both barrels loaded and puffing on her cigarette like a fire-breathing dragon.

"Hi, Mother! When did you get here?" I ventured, trying to sound pleased to see her.

"*Ha!* What do you mean, when did I get here? You knew damned well I was coming today! You were supposed to be here, you bitch!" she snarled, stabbing a freshly lit cigarette into an ashtray.

"You said you *might* be here today," I snapped back, "or

maybe tomorrow, or maybe Monday or Tuesday."

"Bullshit! Don't tell me what I said, my dear!" she shouted, lighting another cigarette and stabbing her finger at me. "I told you to *be* here! Now where the hell were you?"

"I went on a shoot with Jeremy," I answered hotly. "Didn't Vi tell you?"

"She handed me some shit about your going to the country with that selfish bastard!" she shouted even louder. "Anyway, that's got nothing to do with it. You were supposed to be *here*!"

"Mother," I shouted back, "I told you I wasn't going to just sit here for four days and I was trying to tell you my itinerary when you hung up on me! And what's all this about selfish bastards?"

"You know perfectly well what I mean!" she screeched, darting to the ashtray and crushing another unsmoked cigarette, then whirling on me. "That son of a bitch thinks he owns you! Well let me tell *you* something, young lady, he doesn't! And if you don't start obeying me, he never will!"

"I've got news for you, Mother!" I bellowed. "Nobody *owns* me, and that includes you, whether you know it or not!" She backed away, glaring at me squinty-eyed, and moving toward the telephone she hissed, "Well now. We'll just see who's in charge around here. You're a minor and you can't get married without my approval." There was a pause while she lifted the receiver. "Let's see how you like it when I tell your precious Jeremy that the wedding is off and I won't permit him to see you again."

Gritting my teeth and clenching my fists at my sides, I stated in as calm a tone as I could manage, "Mother, you put that receiver down and take back every word you just said or, so help me God, I'll walk out of this hotel and you'll never see me again." There was a short silence before Mother dropped the telephone on the floor, burst into tears, clasped her hands over her face and pleaded piteously as usual, "Don't do this to me, B.D. Not tonight. You know I'm dead. You can't do this to me. *God!*"

"The hell I can't, Mother!" I barked. "Now I'm supposed to feel sorry for you because you're exhausted from sitting on a plane for a couple of hours. I had an operation a few days ago and you couldn't care less how *I* feel. All you care about is who's in charge, who gets to spend how much time with whom and your bullshit orders that never make any sense. I've had enough of your drivel. I'm going to bed. You can let me know in the morning whether you've decided to *approve* of the wedding. Good night!" I started toward my room but had an afterthought. "One more thing. While you're deciding whether or not to bestow your almighty approval, bear in mind that it had better be final. Threaten to cancel the wedding one more time and I'm gone!" With this, I stormed into my room and slammed the door, neither knowing nor caring what Mother would do next.

Mother was as chirpy as could be at breakfast the next morning. She was full of interest in whatever plans Jeremy and I might have and suggested that we three get together soon for dinner since she didn't see nearly enough of her charming son-in-law-to-be. She made no mention of the previous night and, having said my piece in full for once, I was content to leave well enough alone. When I met Jeremy later in the day I gave him a synopsized version of what had happened and suggested that now would be a good time to make our trip to Sussex to meet his mother. From past experience, I knew that Mother would probably stay in a good mood for two or three days. We would be silly not to take advantage of it.

Our drive to the south coast the next day was blissfully uneventful and the chances looked good for a meeting between the two mothers without incident. Jeremy's mother, Dorothy, who had been widowed for a year, had a 450-year-old cottage in East Preston. Mother exclaimed about how quaint and lovely it was and the meeting went without a hitch. Dorothy was distinctly cool toward me but Jeremy had warned me in advance that she was not a naturally warm person and not to expect a big welcome. We had lunch, made idle chitchat and returned to London. From Jeremy's and my standpoints, the day was a complete success. We had all met, convention had been satisfied and nothing had gone wrong.

The next day we learned that Jeremy had to return to the New York office. He was philosophical about it, albeit very disappointed. I was miserable. I was not, after all, going to become part of this world I had come to love so much, and I was more than ever grateful that we had had this time together in England. Mother was jubilant.

As the weekend neared I became more and more excited. Saturday was to be my first day of fox hunting in England. Jeremy had hired a good hunter for me from Bridget and had laid on a van to take our horses to the meet. There was only one problem . . . I had to pass a doctor's examination first. I was convinced that I was perfectly fit to ride and although Jeremy agreed with me, he was adamant about consulting the doctor first. I put off the examination until the last possible moment to improve the odds but it was no use. I was told that light riding was all right but hunting was out of the question for at least another week . . . possible adhesions and all that. I was bitterly disappointed but Jeremy came up with a thought which helped a little.

He phoned the Pages and invited their son, Robert, to come as his guest and use the space vacated by me in the horse van. Eleven-year-old Robert was tickled pink. He had often been hunting but had never vanned to a far-distant meet before. The fun part for me was that Lizzie agreed to take me hilltopping (dashing about the countryside in a car and watching the hunt as best one can, usually from hilltops). It turned out that Lizzie had wanted to watch Robert hunt for ages and now had an excuse.

Saturday arrived and off we all went. I was soon to find out that hilltopping could be an adventure in itself but, when we first arrived at the meet, I ate my heart out: horses, hounds, pink coats, top hats and I was on foot. I had never seen Jeremy in a top hat before and thought him very dashing. The hunt moved off to draw the first cover and Lizzie whizzed off in what seemed to be altogether the wrong direction, but I quickly learned that she knew the ground like the back of her hand. Sure enough, the hounds "found" and shortly I was treated to the spectacle of the fox, hounds, huntsman and whippers-in, closely followed by the Master (Sarah's father) and the field, thundering by below us and jumping everything in their way. Jeremy and Robert were right up there and Lizzie admitted that, although she had great confidence in Robert's horsemanship, her heart was in her mouth at every jump. There were stragglers all over the place, looking for ways around the obstacles, going through gates and riding along the road. Lizzie explained that some people really rode to hounds while others had a more leisurely approach to the whole thing. Since there were few "good" foxes, those that run for miles without going to earth, climbing a tree, hiding in a drainpipe or otherwise spoiling the fun, the leisurely types generally caught up with the "thrusters" sooner or later, provided they knew the country well enough not to get lost altogether.

Once Lizzie got an idea of the hunt's direction we were off again, and again she managed to find us a good vantage point, perhaps too good. The chase had covered several miles at this point, not necessarily a good fox yet but giving it serious thought, and the number of riders still hard after the hounds had thinned noticeably. Jeremy was clearly in view among them, not surprising since he had meticulously sought out a horse which, though ugly, could "jump anything he might come across including the van he came in," but there was Robert right behind him. Good horsemanship was one thing but Robert's horse had been purchased with an eye to soundness and dependability, not speed and spectacular jumping ability. I found myself loudly cheering Robert on but Lizzie, I noticed, had suddenly paled.

"Oh, my heavens," she almost whispered, "did you see that thing the huntsman just jumped? It's awful-looking, and Jeremy's going right after him. I'm afraid Robert's going to try it too. He's going to think that not even trying would be letting Jeremy down. I can't watch, Barbara." (Lizzie is the only person in the world who calls me Barbara.) She turned her back to the unfolding drama and continued weakly, "Tell me when it's over, won't you?" I assured her that I would and looked carefully at the dreaded obstacle which the huntsman, and now Jeremy, had jumped. It was a forbidding-looking thing, I had to admit: a steep muddy bank sloping down to a wide drainage ditch with what looked to be a four- or more foot timber fence beyond the ditch and another steep muddy bank sloping up on the far side. Apparently Lizzie was right for, although the other riders, thrusters though they might be, turned and galloped off to the left looking for an easier route, Robert headed straight for the jump. His horse lost its footing in the mud and went down on the takeoff side. When he got up, Robert still astride, I said, "It's O.K., Lizzie. His horse lost its footing before it could jump. Robert'll go around it now." Lizzie breathed a sigh of relief and turned to look at her son. Robert didn't even glance in the direction of the riders going around, but trotted his horse back a few yards, turned him and went at the jump again. Lizzie stood frozen to the spot, mouth agape, while Robert, eleven years old on his small, steady horse, successfully went where grown men on big expensive hunters had feared to go.

When the day was over and we were back at the farm for tea, I kept Robert company while he rubbed down his horse and fed and watered him. "Why did you take that dreadful great jump when you could have gone around it with the others?" I asked. Jeremy had already told us that in the excitement of a good chase he had completely forgotten about Robert and, apart from that, it would never have occurred to him that Robert would try to stay up with the front runners.

"Well," Robert stammered, face turning bright red, "you must promise not to tell Jeremy, but I was absolutely petrified. It just seemed that I ought to do it. He was kind enough to invite me and I just couldn't let him down." There it was again. Lizzie had said that Robert wouldn't want to let Jeremy down, and now Robert had used the same phrase. I understood what they meant but I wasn't at all sure that I could ever fully comprehend such a strong sense of obligation in this context. Be that as it may, Lizzie hadn't criticized Robert's judgment and I wasn't about to rain on his parade. "Good show!" I said, sounding as British as I possibly could.

The flowers and gifts had continued to arrive from Julio Lobo and Mother was accepting the daily deliveries as a fact of life. When Julio himself suddenly appeared in London and invited Mother, Jeremy and me to dinner, Mother got into a terrible dither and didn't want to go.

"Oh, come on," I urged her, "he's invited all three of us right off the bat. What possible harm can come from having dinner with him? Besides, he's charming and he's interesting and Jeremy and I will go even if you don't." There was a bit more of the same, but I carried the day and Mother accepted.

Over dinner at Claridge's, Julio continued to press his suit and laid out for Mother the most incredibly generous and indulgent provisions of a proposed marriage contract. As dinner progressed I learned that Mother had led Julio to believe that it was I who objected to their marriage, so I quickly emphasized, under a barrage of dirty looks from her, that this was not the case. In fact, I went on, Jeremy's father was dead and we would very much like to have a father in the family. Julio beamed with pleasure, believing that the main obstacle had been swept aside. Mother, however, went off on a tack that despite my approval she could not, after all her unhappy marriages, contemplate another one. By the time dessert was served, Jeremy and I had become completely silly and began a singsong chant of "We want a da-ddee, we want a da-ddee . . ." Mother was so rattled that sputtering and gesticulating was the most she could manage, while Julio took it as a signal to continue his efforts.

A few days later Julio invited us to attend a party marking the fiftieth anniversary of the merger of Tate and Lyle, the British sugar and syrup monopoly of which he was a director. It was white-tie and was held in the ballroom at Claridge's. Julio never left Mother's side and took every opportunity to bestow knowing smiles on his allies, Jeremy and me. The party was probably riveting for the attending sugar and syrup potentates but, for us outsiders, it was nothing more than an endless series of introductions to staid, laconic people whose names we would never recall. Except for one name, that is . . . John Smith . . . London variety of course and dressed in a brown suit and winklepicker shoes and seemingly invisible to the potentates in white tie.

Since there was nothing more amusing to do, Jeremy determined to discover the man's real name. "After all," he said to the brown-suited one, "nobody is actually named John Smith, certainly not dozens of them all over the world working for one man." Jeremy coaxed, cajoled, pleaded and promised never to reveal the truth to a living soul. He finally had his way. John Smith took Jeremy into an empty adjoining room, searched it thoroughly for "bugs" and then, under an oath of silence which I am now breaking, revealed his true identity. He whispered into Jeremy's ear, "James Bond." Jeremy received this trust of confidential information with "No wonder you changed it to

John Smith . . . tough to be inconspicuous with a name like James Bond." "Quite," said James Bond.

Mother had only another day or two of "looping" to do on *The Empty Canvas* (dubbing her own voice whenever the sound quality was poor at the time of shooting, usually on location) and we would be returning to the United States the following week. The upcoming weekend would be my last in England and again Jeremy and I discussed the advisability of my going hunting. We decided against it. If the least little thing were to go wrong, Mother would be able to use it as an excuse to postpone the wedding. The reward of one day's pleasure was far outweighed by the risk involved. The remaining days passed quickly by and I began to contemplate marriage and the future.

11

Jeremy would not be leaving London until mid-December and would not have enough time to get a home organized prior to the wedding. In view of this I was to go to New York, again with Viola as chaperone, to find us a suitable apartment. Before I left London, I made a list of the furniture Jeremy would be shipping and, on the flight to New York, Mother added to it with things she wanted to give us. Mother went on to California and Viola and I moved into a hotel to pore over newspaper rental ads.

I found a satisfactory apartment on the second day of the search, delivered the proposed lease to Jeremy's lawyer and dashed off to Macy's for carpets and curtains. We had agreed on green carpets before I left London but I was suddenly surrounded by oceans of green and my confidence evaporated. Choosing things for Mother had been simple, if I liked it, she would too. But this was different and I found myself unable to make a decision. I wanted to phone Jeremy to discuss shades and tones of green with him but it might take an hour or more to get the call through. In a flash of inspiration I asked the salesman if I could borrow a directory and use his phone to make a local call. He lent me his desk and I looked up the number.

John Smith, New York variety, said that he would be happy to be of service and asked me to hold on. In a few minutes he was back on the line. "Mr. Hyman is delighted that you've found an apartment and says that, of the carpets you mentioned, the Kelly green sounds like the best choice. John still has him on the line, so is there anything else you can think of?"

"That's great," I enthused. "The Kelly was my favorite too. Would you ask him if he likes floral prints in curtains?"

"Hold on," he said, then, less than a minute later, "Mr. Hyman says he loves floral prints and you too."

"Please tell him I love him too," I replied, "and thank you for your help."

"You're perfectly welcome, Miss Sherry, any time. By the way, John says to wish you the very best and tell you that James Bond would also have picked the Kelly green."

We hung up and, with Julio's unknowing help, I finished decorating the apartment on schedule. Sadly, Julio abandoned his pursuit of Mother's hand not long after this. Jeremy and I had truly liked him, but we were never to see him again.

Viola stayed in New York while I flew to California to pack up my trousseau and ship everything east. Mother was perfectly charming and helpful throughout, in fact a little too much so. Had I accepted everything she wanted to contribute to my new household, there wouldn't have been room for Jeremy's things from England. Matters resolved themselves amiably enough though and I was back in New York in time for Jeremy's arrival from London.

I met him at the airport and on the way into the city I told him excitedly of all I had accomplished. I was terribly nervous about what he would think of my decorating skills and probably babbled too much until we got to the apartment. To my great relief, he loved everything. We spent a few days together before I returned to Honeysuckle Hill for a quiet but pleasant Christmas with Mother, Michael and Aunt Bobby.

Jeremy arrived on December 27, bringing my wedding present with him. It was a matinee-length strand of perfectly matched rosé pearls with a diamond clasp if I wanted to wear them as a choker. They were exquisite. Mother cried over them, telling Jeremy how wonderful and sentimental he was. "You're quite a guy," she sniffled. "*Shit!* I'm so damned *proud* to have you for my son-in-law."

Except for our civil ceremony, all we did for the next week was swim, sunbathe and go to parties. We had a civil ceremony because, as he was leaving New York, Jeremy had been told by his accountant that shifting the wedding to the next year would cost him significant additional taxes. When Jeremy told me how much was involved in so seemingly trivial a technicality I felt ill. I insisted that we broach the matter to Mother, feeling sure that I could convince her that a civil ceremony four days early was no big deal. The following events occurred over the next three days:

1. Mother had hysterics and stormed out of the room.
2. I continued to argue my case at every opportunity.
3. Mother shouted and cried and called me a "barter bride."
4. Jeremy suggested that we seek the opinion of the Church since the whole thing was really a question of morality.
5. Mother quickly agreed, believing that the Church would be as shocked as she was.
6. The Church was consulted and, to Mother's utter dismay and ever-lasting confusion, the reverend said, "A marriage should be based on solid foundations and financial considerations unquestionably constitute a part of those foundations. Provided that the marriage is not consummated prior to a proper wedding in a house of the Lord, I see no reason not to hold a civil ceremony and I commend your practicality."
7. Mother's press agent, Rupert Allen, entered the fray and argued that we would have to announce it to the press if we held a civil ceremony on New Year's Eve.
8. Mother asked why and Rupert answered that they were bound to find out anyway and would write whatever they wanted to.
9. Jeremy was dead set against it and asked Rupert what

on earth the press could say that could do any harm even in the unlikely event that they found out.

10. Rupert immediately stated that the press would say I was pregnant.
11. Even Mother could see the absurdity of Rupert's assertion, there only being four days involved, but he continued to argue for a press release.
12. Jeremy finally got angry with Rupert, stated that there would be no more grief if the secret leaked than if it were announced, and accused Rupert of wanting to make the announcement for no other reason than to curry favor with the columnists by giving them a hot scoop.
13. Mother flew into a rage at Jeremy for impugning the motives of her press agent who, she said, ". . . only has my best interests in mind." She promptly authorized Rupert to make the release.
14. The shit hit the fan.

The civil ceremony was held on the evening of December 31. Rupert made the announcement and for two days the telephone never stopped ringing. Mother would never have admitted it in a million years, but I suspected that she wished she'd listened to Jeremy. Reporters were trying to make a big story out of it. Wedding guests who had stopped in Las Vegas on the way to L.A. were wondering if the wedding had been canceled and if they should stay in Las Vegas. People in the east wanted to know whether they should still fly west. People in England wondered if they should fly anywhere. More reporters tried to make a big story out of it. Jeremy was furious and wanted to kill Rupert Allen. I felt much the way he did. Seeing him so angry, Mother quickly brightened and rushed about saying, "I told you so," despite the fact that it was she who had precipitated the crisis by telling Rupert to go ahead with the press release. It only went on for two days, but those two days were murder.

Then January 4 was upon us and all the trials and tribulations that had preceded the wedding faded from memory. The chapel decorations were stunning, pine branches and pink carnations, and everything and everybody looked beautiful. The only problem that arose at the next-to-last moment was that I had sentimentally chosen lilies-of-the-valley for my bridal bouquet since they were the first flowers Jeremy had ever given me. The only place in the world where they were blooming in January was France, a fact Mother kept hidden from me as tradition requires that the groom pay for the bouquet. They were flown in in the nick of time but I never did find out what they cost. My wedding dress, which I had designed myself and which required an amazing number of fittings at I. Magnin, was worth every minute invested in it. The velvet was from Lyons and the rosepoint lace from Venice. I felt like a fairy princess, just the way brides are supposed to feel. The most memorable moment of the marriage ceremony, a complete surprise to Jeremy and me, came when the groom was told, "You may now kiss the bride." As our lips touched a recording of the most beautiful cathedral bells began to peal joyously through the chapel. It was an extraordinary moment that we shall never forget. Whenever there is a royal wedding or jubilee shown on television, one of us always comments, "How about that? They're ringing the bells for them too."

The reception at the Beverly Wilshire was splendid and went on into the wee hours of the morning. Huge quantities of rice were thrown with carefree abandon. Then Jeremy and I went into hiding at the Beverly Hills Hotel, registering as Mr. and Mrs. Ronald Cosgrove in order to elude the press.

Ronald Cosgrove was Mother's idea. Not only had she given us one of the most beautiful and extravagant weddings imaginable but, when we arrived at the Beverly Hills, we found that the suite reserved for the newly married Cosgroves had been planned with equally meticulous care. There was a bar which included champagne in an ice bucket and an enormous tray of canapes. There were flowers everywhere. The bed, however, was the *pièce de résistance.* Mother had made up the bed using a wedding present of black silk sheets, piped and monogrammed in white. Laid out on one side of the bed was a white satin marabou-trimmed peignoir with matching marabou slippers and, on the other side, a pair of white silk pajamas trimmed in black. Upon the pillows she had placed a hammer and a screwdriver with white satin bows tied around them.

All of Mother's forethought was greatly appreciated. Not only did we succeed in eluding the press, but it was a wonderful end to a most memorable occasion in our lives. We went off to honeymoon on a fishing boat in the Florida Keys without a care in the world.

PART II

1

1964

Throughout my life Mother had had my portrait painted by a wide range of artists. There were two by my father, Sherry, and one by Spurgeon Tucker when I was little, and whenever Mother encountered another painter she liked, she commissioned another portrait. This continued until I was fifteen when the last of them was done, a remarkable mirror image of me dressed in emerald-green chiffon. As part of my dowry Mother allowed me to choose one portrait to have for myself. Jeremy had seen most of them and I thought it best to talk it over with him before deciding. He had always liked the one of me in green chiffon but, since he had been collecting British sporting art for years and one of the portraits was a life-size version of me in riding clothes by Willard Cummings, he leaned toward that one. Apart from the riding attire, he liked the painting for itself. It was not a literal likeness for, although done when I was fourteen, the painting depicts a woman who could be anywhere from fourteen to thirty-four. I agreed with his preference and we accepted the Willard Cummings.

Upon our return from Florida I found a letter from Mother awaiting me. It was very fat and contained countless photographs of her activities. Among them was one encaptioned,

"B.D. SHRINE." There was the green-chiffon portrait hanging over the dining-room mantel. There was a light above it and, below it, a bouquet of flowers bracketed by a pair of burning candles. The accompanying letter informed me that Aunt Bobby and the staff had been instructed that the light was never to be turned off and the candles were to be ever-burning and replaced whenever necessary.

Mother went to work on *Where Love Has Gone,* a picture based on the Harold Robbins novel. This was a tale reminiscent of the life story of Lana Turner, whose daughter, Cheryl, killed her mother's lover with whom she also, unbeknownst to her mother, had been having an affair. The movie was set in San Francisco and concerned an upper-crust family of which Mother's character, Mrs. Hayden, was the matriarch. Susan Hayward played the mother and Joey Heatherton the daughter. From the very beginning Mother was loudly vocal in her dissatisfaction with the whole project, about the only things that pleased her being her wardrobe and working close to home. With all the things she was angry about and all the people she was fighting with, the last thing I expected was that she would concern herself with trying to attract my attention.

It began with a phone call in which Mother told me that she was dating a twenty-seven-year-old man and that she thought she had found true love again. In case I hadn't noticed that her new true love was three years younger than my husband, she mentioned it at least half a dozen times. Another phone call, this time from a friend of hers, advised me that the young man was a homosexual and suggested that I do something before Mother made a public spectacle of herself. Mother's next call was to let me know that she was moving into her young man's Malibu beach house. Another of Mother's friends called to make sure that I knew that the house was a totally dilapidated dump used by the young man's transient friends and that many of the friends were dopers.

The flow of news continued for ten days or so. I heard that Mother was prancing about the beach in a bikini, going to hippie parties and generally disporting herself like a stereotypical teenager. I was never sure whether Mother's so-called friends who provided me with the running commentary were really her friends or simply people she had had call me as part of her overall game plan. Whatever the truth of the matter, I maintained a strictly neutral tone with everyone, including Mother, avowing that she was an adult and that where she lived, with whom she lived and what she did were entirely her business and that I had absolutely no intention of interfering in any way.

Next, Mother called to announce that she was going to marry her new love. I had to say my piece. "Frankly, Mother, I find your behavior ridiculous and rather sad," I said formally. "It is, however, your right to lead your life as you see fit and I haven't the slightest intention of letting you get me involved."

"Oh, B.D.!" she wailed. "Can't you see that I need your approval? You're the only thing I love and I wouldn't do anything to upset you."

"In that case," I replied, "you have my approval. I have to admit, though, that I find it odd that I'm the only thing you love when you just got through telling me that you're about to marry the new love of your life."

"*Christ*, you're a cold bitch! You know perfectly well what I meant. I love him and I'm going to marry him no matter what you say!"

"I don't know why you're going on about it. I've already told you it's all right with me. If you want to marry a homosexual, it's entirely up to you. Maybe it'll work out."

"*Brother!*" she shrieked. "You really want to spoil things for me, don't you? Well, maybe he was once, but he isn't now. All he needed was a real woman."

"Mother," I said, moving to end it before I lost my grip on my self-control, "I have now said everything I intend to on this subject. Right this minute, I have to admit, I find myself more concerned with having dinner ready on time. So . . . if you'll excuse me, I'll say good-bye and wish you the best of luck in your new adventure." For once in my life *I* hung up on *her*.

It was only a few days before Mother was on the phone again. It seemed that she and her young man had had a desperate lovers' quarrel and broken up. "Don't worry about me," she sniffled. "I'll get over it. It's not the first time I've been kicked in the teeth and it probably won't be the last. Men are *shits* . . . you'll see."

Where Love Has Gone had begun in animosity and it ended the same way. Sometime after Mother had finished filming and had turned her thoughts to her next project, the picture which was ultimately titled *Hush, Hush, Sweet Charlotte* (after an assortment of aborted titles like *What Ever Happened to Cousin Charlotte?* and, less politely, *The Return of Baby Jane*), the producer and director of *Where Love Has Gone*, Joseph E. Levine and Edward Dmytryk, respectively, wanted to change the end of the picture. For reasons no one could quite understand, they wanted Mrs. Hayden to suddenly and inexplicably go insane. It would have to be sudden and inexplicable since they wanted Mother to shoot only ninety seconds of film. Mother refused to do it. Levine claimed she had a contractual obligation, took her to court and got an injunction preventing her from doing another movie until the matter was resolved. Mother argued in court that Mrs. Hayden had been rational throughout the story and that it would be utterly inconsistent and artistically unacceptable for her to go insane in ninety seconds. The court agreed with Mother and she thumbed her nose at all of them with great satisfaction.

Mother phoned during early April to announce that she was coming to New York to see our apartment. I carefully explained that Jeremy and I tended to be quite busy at times and tried to pin her down as to just when she was coming. She remained as vague as ever. A couple of Mondays later, with no advance warning at all, she phoned to say that she had checked into the Plaza for an indefinite stay. I invited her for dinner the following evening. She said that she didn't want to wait that long and, besides, she had already invited Leonard Sillman to come as her escort that very evening. I told her that we already had plans for that evening and it would have to be Tuesday. "God, you're a cold bitch!" she barked. "I fly all this way to see you and you tell me you're too busy! *Well* . . . have it your way!" Click, dial tone.

I didn't hear from her again until noon on Tuesday when she called to say that something very important had come up and she would have to change our dinner date to Wednesday.

"Wednesday's out," I said. "We have to go to a premiere."

"In that case make it Thursday."

"Thursday's out too. We're having dinner with some business people from France."

"*Well!* I guess I'll just have to change *my* plans, won't I?" she said scathingly. "It seems you and your husband are too important to even be polite anymore!"

"I'm being perfectly polite, Mother," I answered, bristling. "You're the one creating the problems."

"Oh I am, am I?" she shouted. "Well, we'll just see about this busy schedule of yours when I get there this evening." Click, dial tone.

I called her back immediately. "I don't appreciate being hung up on in the middle of conversations. Now . . . are you bringing Leonard or not?"

"Of course he's coming. I already told you he was." Apparently she'd forgotten that she'd started all this by trying to switch nights. "And I didn't hang up on you. I wouldn't do anything that rude."

"O.K., Mother," I said, "I'll see you and Leonard at seven o'clock as planned."

"Six o'clock! I told Leonard six o'clock! Don't try to change that on me too."

"Six o'clock will be fine, Mother. I'll look forward to seeing you then."

Mother had an obsession about being on time, almost a religion in fact. Promptness was right up there with honesty and being a Yankee and she would frequently arrive way early, beaming at her hosts as though she had accomplished some miraculous feat. I called Jeremy at the office to let him know that Mother was coming at six instead of seven. When he got home I warned him about her tendency to arrive early.

"She won't do it to me more than once," he commented, grinning over his shoulder as he went to take a shower.

At five-fifteen Jeremy was getting out of the shower when the doorbell rang.

"I'll get it," I called to him, putting on a robe and starting for the door.

"No, you don't," he said, wrapping a towel around his waist.

"This one's mine." He went to the door, dripping wet with towel around him and opened it wide. There stood Mother and Leonard Sillman.

"Oh, hello!" Jeremy said, exaggerating his English accent. "How nice of you to come three quarters of an hour early." He made a motion ushering them in. "Please help yourselves at the bar. B.D. and I will join you as soon as we're dressed." With great poise he turned and strolled sedately back toward the bathroom, closing the hallway door behind him.

It was the last time *ever* that Mother arrived early at our house.

Huge boxes of clothes began to arrive from Bergdorf Goodman. I kept the first two, not because I needed the clothes but because I knew that refusing them would upset Mother. I made a great point of finding them lovely and thanking her but I also asked her to stop sending them. When the third box arrived, despite my best efforts to head it off, I phoned her without opening it and said, "Mother, I really do appreciate your kind thoughts and the fact that you love me, but I've nowhere to put all this stuff. The closets and drawers are jammed full and I can't wear it all as it is."

"Oh, B.D.," she sniffled. "You know you're my life. Don't do this to me."

"Mother, please understand what I'm saying," I pleaded. "I'm not trying to hurt your feelings. It's that I have absolutely no room in the apartment for more clothes, and that's all there is to it."

"So that's it, is it?" she flared. "Jeremy's jealous! He doesn't like me sending you presents."

"Jeremy has nothing to do with this, damn it!" I snapped. "It's exactly what I said it was . . . no more and no less."

"All right, B.D., have it your way. But sooner or later you'll realize what a bastard he really is! Good-bye!"

Mother, Jeremy and I went to a cocktail party at Joshua Logan's. Among the assembled notables were Elizabeth Taylor and Richard Burton. During the course of the evening, while Jeremy was paying rapt attention to a dissertation by Richard

Burton on the several ways of reading a certain line of Shakespeare, Mother, Elizabeth and I all found ourselves sprucing up in the master suite at the same time.

"Bette," said Elizabeth, "I'm dying to know the truth. How did you and Joan Crawford get along during *Baby Jane?*"

"*God!*" Mother replied. "That monster woman! How do you *think* we got along?"

"Is it true she's as fixated with germs as everyone says?" asked Elizabeth.

"*Jesus!*" Mother replied. "I take it you've never been treated to a tour of her apartment. It's true . . . . all of it. Everything's covered in plastic and the toilet seats have sanitized paper slipcovers. The woman's quite mad!"

When Elizabeth finished laughing she said, "It really must have been interesting with both of you on the same set."

"*Ha!*" Mother retorted. "The crew had it *rough* with Joan. At least with *me* they had a pro, and *brother* did they know it!" A minute or two passed while we powdered and primped, then Elizabeth said, "I've always promised myself that if I ever had the chance, I'd ask you a personal question. May I?"

"Of course," Mother replied. "I'm an honest Yankee dame." Elizabeth looked slightly ill at ease, but then came out with it. "I've heard it said that you and Mary Astor had an affair years ago. It it true?"

"*God!*" shrieked Mother. "Every son of a bitch in the world's been asking me that for twenty years. *Shit!* Everybody *knows* I adore men! I married four of them, for Christ's sake!"

When Mother called one day, I had a cold and it was impossible to disguise the congested sound of my voice.

"You have a cold, haven't you?" she asked, as though expecting me to deny the obvious. I chuckled and said, "I sure have."

"Well, what are you doing about it?" she demanded.

"Taking aspirin, keeping warm and drinking orange juice like a good little girl."

"Don't be flip with me, young lady! Has Jeremy sent for the doctor?"

"Oh, come off it, Mother!" I snapped. "It's only a cold. If

it doesn't go away by the weekend I'll stop by Jeremy's doctor in Westport when we're there, but I seriously doubt I'll have to."

"You're crazy! You can't go out with that cold. You'll get pneumonia. Christ! I'm sending someone over!"

"Oh no you aren't. Just calm down. It's only a head cold, for crying out loud."

"Only a *head* cold? *Ha!* If Jeremy doesn't know how to take care of you, at least *I* do." Click, dial tone.

I dialed the hotel immediately but it was no use, Mother's line stayed busy. I didn't know what to expect next. It could be anyone from a man she'd met in the lobby of the Plaza who claimed to be the world's foremost authority on colds to a team of specialists flown in from Switzerland. I called Jeremy at the office to warn him of what was afoot. I asked him to work late or have a drink with the boys or something, explaining that I'd prefer to have whatever Mother did over and done with before he came home to having him get into high dudgeon and throw people out of the apartment.

"Are you sure it's just a cold?" he asked. "It hasn't got into your chest or anything?"

"I'm exactly the same as when you left this morning. Does that answer your question?"

"Of course it does," he replied, the merest hint of asperity creeping into his voice, "and you have to admit that your mother presumes too much. This is as good a time as any for me to straighten her out, so why not?"

"Because it's easier to let some doctor look at me than to waste a lot of time and energy arguing about it. I agree with you in principle," I said soothingly, "but I'd rather you picked a different issue at another time."

"All right," he agreed reluctantly, "if you insist. But I'd really like to explain a few facts of life to her."

"Another time," I insisted. "Why don't you call me whenever you're ready to come home and I'll bring you up to date then?"

"O.K., but I still don't like it."

My husband's desire to "explain a few facts of life" to Mother had more to do with what had gone before than what was happening now. After the Leonard Sillman dinner, there had been a strange dinner with Mother in her suite at the Plaza. She spent the entire evening hiding in her bedroom, pretending to make and receive "very important calls that just can't wait," and then popping out to say something rude to Jeremy before retiring to the bedroom again. We'd written it off at the time as a reaction to all our business-related engagements and her proving to me that she was busier and more important than my husband. Worse than that by far, though, had been my seventeenth birthday party. Mother had insisted on giving one and had inveigled me into providing a guest list to augment the people she wanted to invite. There were sixty people present in a banquet room at the Plaza. Everyone who had been on my list, I was to learn, had been called by Mother and virtually *ordered* to bring an expensive present. On top of that, she got roaring drunk, insulted some very nice people, swore at the top of her lungs and tried to force grown men to do a Maypole dance. Yes . . . there was a Maypole. Jeremy had become so livid that we left before the party was over.

As I set about making steak-and-kidney pie for dinner, I never doubted that I was doing the right thing. I had always tried to avoid confrontation with Mother, only going toe to toe with her when I completely lost my temper or was overwhelmingly bound up in the principle of the moment. I knew that Mother loved me and that I loved her, and I respected her accomplishments and what she was. Avoiding degrading arguments with her was second nature to me and, just as naturally, I was beginning to do whatever was necessary to keep my husband from having a showdown with her.

I had cubed the steak and was cutting up the kidneys when the doorbell rang. I went to the door and opened it, still wiping my hands on a dish towel. I was confronted by two ladies carrying three heavy-looking leather valises. One was wearing a nurse's uniform, so I felt safe in assuming that the chic-looking one in the gray, two-piece silk suit was a doctor. She introduced herself and said that she was the ear, nose and throat specialist.

"How do you do?" I said, ushering them in. "Please excuse my appearance but I'm in the middle of making steak-and-kidney pie. Would you like a cup of coffee?"

"No, thank you," said the doctor. "I'm rather pressed for time. Would you be kind enough to show me to the patient?"

"I'm the only person here, so I guess I'm the patient."

"I don't understand," said the specialist, clearly irritated. "Are you Mrs. Hyman?"

"Yes, indeed," I replied, confirming her worst suspicions.

"But your mother sounded panic-stricken. She said that you were very ill with a serious throat infection and that your husband refused to do anything about it. That's why I came at once."

"I'm afraid you've been misled," I said. "My mother can't accept that I've grown up, I'm afraid. Now that you're here, though, I guess it would be best if you gave me a quick examination. At least you'll be able to report back to her with a clear conscience."

"That would be best, if you don't mind."

After finding my temperature, pulse, blood pressure, respiration, ears and glands normal, my nose and sinuses congested and my throat mildly irritated by postnasal drip, the specialist announced, "You have a common cold, but we'll take a throat culture and blood sample just to be safe." I looked for signs of humor in her eyes when she pronounced her diagnosis, but there were none. While the nurse was packing up the paraphernalia, the specialist wrote me a prescription for an antihistamine to dry up my runny nose, then took her leave assuring me that my cold would go away in a few days.

I was just putting the steak-and-kidney pie in the oven when the phone rang. It was Jeremy, wanting to know if the coast was clear. "It's safe now," I said. "A thoroughly teed-off ear, nose and throat specialist recently diagnosed the common cold and left in a huff."

"In that case," he said, sounding a little more sarcastic than the situation warranted, "am I safe in assuming that I have permission to come home now?"

"Don't you start too!" I snapped. "One pain in the ass in the family's enough."

"Oh, come on," he chided, "can't you tell when I'm kidding?"

"I'm sorry, but when my mother's lurking in the scenery I

get jumpy. Hurry home and I'll tell you all about the good doctor when you get here."

No sooner had Jeremy mixed us each a drink than the doorbell rang.

"Are we expecting anyone?" he asked.

"Not that I know of," I replied with a sinking feeling. He went to the door and opened it. Mother elbowed him out of the way, swept into the apartment and placed herself in front of me with her jaw thrust forward and her hands on her hips. "What are you doing out of bed?"

"I was never in bed, and anyway, why are you here?"

"Because I knew something like this would happen," she snarled. "Now, you get into bed and stay there!"

"You'd better hold on for just a minute, Mother. I'm a big, grown-up, married lady and the only person around here who can order me to bed is my husband."

"Oh, my *God*!" she howled. "You mean he makes you do *that*, even when you're *sick*?" I was so taken aback that I just stared at her, giving Jeremy the chance to speak for the first time.

"I think that's about enough, thank you, Bette. B.D. is not the sick person here . . . you are. It would be best if you left now."

"He's right, Mother. If you keep this up, someone's going to regret it. Besides, I have to finish preparing dinner. The steak-and-kidney pie will be ready in half an hour."

Mother, who had grown completely popeyed while we spoke, spun on Jeremy and spat, "You English *bastard*! You're going to *kill* her!" She whirled toward me. "And *you*! You're like a lamb going willingly to the slaughter. *God!* I can't stand it!" She grasped her head with both hands and looked more than a little crazed. Jeremy opened the front door and said icily, "Like I said, Bette . . . you'd better leave." She started for the door, then stopped, apparently realizing that she was doing as she was told.

"Good night, Mother," I said forcefully, but it didn't stop her from taking one more shot. "You've cut out my heart!"

Jeremy took her firmly by the arm, steered her the few remaining steps to the door and, ushering her through it, smiled at her and said, "I would that it were true." She was spluttering a garbled imprecation even as he closed the door on her.

Two days later I received a call from Tom Hammond, Mother's lawyer-manager. "B.D.," he began, "you've got to stop upsetting your mother like this. You know you hold the key to her state of mind. How can you be so careless in your responsibility to her? How—"

"Whoa!" I said. "What on *earth* are you talking about?"

"What I'm talking about, as if you didn't know, is the awful way you treated your mother when she sweetly, with nothing but maternal concern, sent a doctor to treat your illness and then stopped by to see how you were."

"Surely you jest!" I cried. "First she presumed to send a doctor to my apartment to diagnose a head cold, which is exactly what I told her it was. Then—"

"She was worried, B.D. You know how your asthma complicates your colds."

"Nuts, Tom! I outgrew that with puberty eight years ago. That was only an excuse, and she didn't stop there, you know. Oh, no! After the fancy specialist and her attending nurse left in a huff because I only had a cold, Mother . . . dear concerned Mother, had the nerve to barge in, not stop by as you suggest, but barge in, hurling all sorts of nasty, rude accusations at Jeremy in *his* apartment with *his* wife and presume to tell me how I'm to conduct myself with a head cold. It was a real thrill, Tom!"

"That may well be. Your mother is neurotic and we all know it . . . all the more reason for you to be sensible and understanding. She needs you . . . you hold her emotional state in the palm of your hand. You can't afford to be cavalier with her. When she feels rejected by you her whole world crumbles and it affects her career as well. You know full well she depends on you."

"Oh, swell! Am I supposed to let her dictate my every move and Jeremy's as well? That's absurd and you know it."

"B.D., all you have to do is be a little accommodating. Let her do what pleases her. How does that hurt you? She's very generous."

"Too generous, Tom, but I can't get that through to her either."

"You mean about the clothes from Bergdorf's? I've tried

not to criticize you for that, but now that you've brought it up—"

"I didn't. I—"

"It doesn't matter, B.D. Please, for the love of your mother, why can't you just accept them? Give them away if you want to, but don't reject them. To your mother's way of seeing things, you're slapping her in the face and refusing her love. It hurt her very much, it really did."

"Look, this is getting us nowhere, Tom. First of all, I *did* accommodate her. I stopped Jeremy from giving her a piece of his mind and convinced him not to make an issue over the doctor. So, he honored my wishes, and it would all have been forgotten if Mother hadn't barged in here loaded for bear later that night. It's too much, asking him to accept that kind of garbage."

"I realize it's difficult, but you have to convince him how vital it is. Also, both of you must remember that she lives in California. She's only here for a few weeks. You can put up with it for a short time, now can't you? Then she'll be gone and you'll be left alone. Tell Jeremy to think of her as just another dipsy-doodle, neurotic star in a Seven Arts picture whom he has to accommodate until the picture's finished. O.K.? He knows how to do *that*, for heaven's sake."

"How am I supposed to have a marriage and let Mother take precedence over my husband? It won't work."

"Please, B.D.! She's in a terrible state and in this mood she could do anything . . . have a nervous breakdown . . . maybe worse. She can't sleep or eat because of what you did. You must call her and convince her you still love her and that everything's all right."

"Tom, you can't lay all this at my doorstep. It isn't fair. I do my very best to avoid confrontations with her. . . . I *hate* them. However, there *is* a line to be drawn."

"Perhaps, but now is not the time to draw it. She can't handle any more rejection. She needs you, don't you see that? This lady is one of the world's greatest and most famous stars and all she needs is your love. She'll calm down once she gets used to your marriage. Right now, it's still an open sore . . . let it heal and then draw your line if you must . . . but if you do, be very, very careful. You have a responsibility."

"O.K., Tom," I sighed. "It still doesn't seem fair, but perhaps you're right. She isn't around that much and I guess I can do my best when she is."

At a dinner party for a dozen or so people, including Olivia De Havilland, Mother's bosom fixation reared its ugly head. She had grasped every opportunity to comment on mine during my adolescence and frequently had much to say about other women's cleavage. It was not uncommon for her to tiptoe in when I was taking a bath and giggle coyly while remarking on how amply endowed I was, or try to fiddle with my neckline if I were wearing a low-cut dress. It gave me the willies.

Olivia's bosoms were always a matter of major concern to Mother. Olivia had a beautiful figure and usually dressed in very flattering, low-cut, square Dior necklines. This style suited her well and it is safe to assume that catching Mother's eye was not what she had in mind when buying her clothes.

During cocktails Mother began to look ostentatiously back and forth between Olivia's décolletage and mine (I was wearing a low-cut pink silk blouse and wishing that I had chosen something else), much as a spectator at a tennis match. When she was satisfied that her odd behavior had attracted everyone's attention, Mother emoted, "Well, my dear Olivia, you've finally met your match. Until now, you've always had the most beautiful bosoms in the room . . . but you've been surpassed!" A lewd expression came over her face. "B.D.'s are better!"

What Ever Happened to Baby Jane? had found its way to the screen mainly because of its low budget. Seven Arts had been unable to resist a vehicle with both Davis *and* Crawford at the price; Bob Aldrich was also scrambling for a backer at that point in time for, having made too many losers in a row, *he,* like his two stars, had been written off as a has-been. The powers that be, famous for their original and innovative thinking, who considered *Baby Jane* a freak success and never allowed for the possibility that the public might simply have enjoyed it for what it was, were quick to ascribe its success to the combination of the two stars. It should have been no surprise to Mother, therefore, when Bob Aldrich packaged her with Joan again in the earlier-mentioned *What Ever Happened to Cousin Charlotte?* Mother it was who detested that title and suggested that the name of the Patti Page lullaby "Hush, Hush, Sweet Charlotte," which had been composed for the picture, be used instead.

Mother played Charlotte, an old southern belle who during her youth had carried on with a married man. When the man fell victim to an ax murder, Charlotte was blamed. She was so traumatized by the death of the man she loved that she actually believed she had done it. Crawford was to have played the scheming cousin who was not only driving Charlotte mad but also blackmailing the dead man's wife, the real culprit. Seven Arts was going to do it but, when Joan became ill and unavailable, they backed out. It was their advertising chief who gave the picture the nickname which so infuriated Mother: *Shut Up Charlotte.* The picture found its way to Twentieth Century-Fox. Olivia De Havilland, to Mother's great joy, replaced Joan and Mother was able to say of Joan, over and over again, "She was petrified of competing with me again. Ha!" Mother had not considered *Hush, Hush, Sweet Charlotte* a horror picture but, after *Baby Jane,* the public did. Mother was furious and ranted that she had ". . . had it with horror movies! If they think they can dig me into a rut, well, *I* have news for *them!*"

Mother came to New York after finishing the picture and invited me to lunch at the Plaza. Conversation was general in nature and perfectly pleasant until she said, "B.D., I want you to have a picture taken in your wedding dress." I was completely at a loss and said, "You what?"

"I want you to go to Bachrach and have a formal wedding picture taken." She said it as though taking formal wedding pictures six or twelve months after the event was an everyday occurrence.

"But you have dozens of them," I protested. "Larry Schiller took the best set of wedding pictures I've ever seen. You have pictures of me coming, going and everywhere in between."

"Yes, but none of them are of you alone. *He's* in all of them!"

"You've got to be kidding! I thought that's what weddings were all about . . . two people getting married."

"*Well! I* only care about *you.* I'm not going to stare at a picture of *him* every day. *Jesus!*"

"Oh, come off it, Mother! You have dozens of pictures of

me all over the place. Look at one of *them*."

"I want a picture of you in your *divine* wedding dress which *you* designed. People flew all over the world gathering the material and I paid Magnin's a fortune for it. *Shit!* I want to *look* at you in it."

"There are all kinds of pictures of me that Larry took; before the wedding, during the wedding, after the wedding, in the church, outside the church, everywhere but on top of the church. One of them *must* be good enough."

"A lot of them *are*, but *he's* in all the full-length ones. I want a full-length one of you alone."

"Then why don't you take the one you like best and cut *him* out of it?" I asked acidly. "I'm fed up with all your crap about my husband! I don't *give* a damn what you think of him . . . just keep it to yourself! You don't even *know* Jeremy. You made up your mind that nobody I married would be good enough and you refuse to be confused with facts. Well I have news for you . . . Jeremy has *his* opinion of *you,* but I don't bore you with it, do I?"

"What do you mean, *his* opinion of *me?* What the hell does *that* bastard have to complain about, I'd like to know?"

"Don't get me started, Mother," I hissed through clenched teeth. "Let's just skip the whole topic. You wouldn't want to hear what he thinks of you any more than he cares what you think of him!"

"Well, isn't that just *ducky!*" she shouted, jumping up and glaring at me with her hands on her hips. "You two obviously don't appreciate what an incredibly considerate mother-in-law I am! I never interfere with you! I'm not like all those parents who try to ruin their children's lives. I *respect* your rights. Obviously you don't give me any credit for letting you do everything *your* way. You don't give a *damn* about *my* feelings!"

Although this was the first time that Mother had held forth on her inverted view of her behavior toward Jeremy and me, it was certainly not the last. As time passed she made minor adjustments in the script, but the essence was always the same. The best part was watching her on television talk shows, extolling her virtues as model mother and mother-in-law. Butter wouldn't have melted in her mouth as, again and again, she told viewing audiences everywhere that she wasn't like other parents, that she made no demands of us, that she respected our rights, that she did everything our way, that she never interfered in our lives, that, in fact, she deserved an award for best performance as a mother-in-law. To Jeremy and me, her performances on these occasions were either hilariously funny or downright infuriating, depending on the temper of our most recent encounter with her.

I sat back and gazed at Mother for a while in a state of mild shock. All she wanted was to interfere in everything, be rude to everyone and my husband in particular, insist on this, demand that and castigate the other and now, by golly, she wanted my applause. The shock wore off quickly as I realized that there was no purpose to be served in pursuing arguments like this. I might never learn to agree to everything Mother wanted without demur, especially in view of her habit of taking simple statements and accepting them as gross insults, but Tom Hammond *did* have a point . . . unfortunately for me. Mother was who she was, behaved the way she behaved and thought as she thought, but she was my mother and she wasn't around to bother us very often.

"Mother," I said at last, trying to accommodate but choosing the wrong words, "have it your way. I'll—"

"Have it my way! Jesus! I never get anything my way! I just can't win with you."

"That's probably the trouble," I said, trying to be reasonable, "you're always trying to win something. So, you've won. When do you want to have the picture taken?"

"The studio's booked with their head photographer for the day after tomorrow at ten-thirty."

"Thank you for taking *my* schedule into consideration," I quipped, realizing as I said it that I wasn't doing very well.

"What's that crack supposed to mean?"

"It's supposed to mean that it would be nice if . . . oh, forget it, it's not worth the bother."

"*Oh?* So I'm not worth bothering with? Is that what you're telling me?" Despite my resolve to be accommodating and the fact that I kept picking the wrong words, I began to fume all over again. It was impossible. "No, it isn't . . . and if you listened to what I was saying instead of imagining insults all the time, you'd know it!"

"Oh! So now I imagine things, do I? Do you think I'm stupid?"

"See? There you go again. I say you're imagining things and you ask me if I think you're stupid! It's *hopeless!*"

"Oh, God, B.D.! Don't do this to me . . . not when I've come all this way just to see you"—tears, hands over face—"You're the only thing I love."

"Come off it, Mother," I said. "If you love me so much, why do you go to such lengths to antagonize me all the time?"

"*Me* antagonize *you?*" she sobbed. "All I wanted was a picture of my only daughter in her wedding dress and you try to *get* me."

I held my peace for a few seconds and then, in an attempt to salvage something of value from all this, I said as calmly and reasonably as I could, "Mother, nobody's trying to get anybody. All I'm talking about is the way you persist in referring to my husband as 'he' or 'him,' never by his name. You don't think that's going to antagonize me?"

"*Ha!*" she burst, back on the attack the moment I lowered my guard. "He hates me! You said so yourself. Do you really expect me to be charming about someone who hates me? It's too much, B.D., too much!"

"I most certainly did *not* say that Jeremy hates you. I said that he has his opinion of you, just as you have yours of him. Is that so unreasonable?"

"Shit! You know he hates me and you don't care. I bet you let him say anything he wants to about me!"

"That's enough, Mother," I said, trying to end it. "You've convinced me that you hate Jeremy . . . and that's why you think he hates you. I'm not going to argue about it anymore. Let's get back to the photograph. I don't think I have anything to do the day after tomorrow but if I do, I'll change it. I'll call the storage company and have the dress delivered to Bachrach, so you better tell them to expect it."

"No," she snapped. "They'll mess it up. I want it here to check it."

"That's fine with me but how are you going to carry ten feet of wedding dress and all that lace across town without messing it up yourself? The storage company will deliver it in a van on a hanger and I'll have them steam it first."

"All right, B.D.," she snapped. "Have it your way. I just hope we don't get messed up."

At the appointed time Mother, the dress and I were at the studio. I had done my hair as I had worn it for the wedding and applied makeup suitable for a photographic session. Mother helped me dress, doing up the dozens of buttons at the wrists and down the back, and we were ready. In the studio everything had been prepared in advance and the photographer began to pose me immediately. When he stepped back and looked through his lens for the first time, he said, "You do a great base makeup, Mrs. Hyman. Your complexion looks just like matte silk. You must have modeled at some time."

"Thank you," I said, "I—"

"What do you mean, base makeup?" Mother snapped. "My daughter has a perfect complexion. She never wears makeup. She's only seventeen, for Christ's sake!" The poor photographer grew very flustered and, stammering, was searching for a diplomatic response when I came to his rescue.

"As I was saying before my mother interrupted, I did do a bit of modeling a few years ago and that's when I learned about base makeup."

"Oh!" said Mother. "But you don't usually wear it. That's all I meant." The photographer caught my eye and I gave him a slight shake of the head. He took my cue and went on with his work.

As he was studying the best angle for my head, he said, "I love the way you've done your hair. It's very clever the way the veil is attached. It creates the effect of a crown of lilies-of-the-valley."

"Of course it does!" blurted Mother. "That was the whole idea! *God!*"

"What my mother means," I said, glaring at her while trying to cover up her rudeness to the poor man, "is that that was the effect we were trying for when the veil was designed, and it's nice of you to notice." Mother muttered something under her breath but, under my angry stare, she clomped off to a corner of the studio and let the matter drop.

Regrettably, the photographer was a nice fellow who apparently enjoyed complimenting people. He did it again. "Your nails look lovely with that luminescent platinum polish." He was staring through his lens again. "They have just the right effect with the white velvet. Twist your torso slightly toward me . . . there . . . that's it . . . perfect!"

"She always wears that kind of polish! *Christ!* What's so special about it?"

"No, Mother." I quickly jumped in, hoping the photographer had learned enough to keep quiet. "I use whatever nail polish I think suits the clothes I'm wearing. You're the only person I know who wears the same lipstick and nail polish all the time. It's sort of your trademark."

"*God!*" she exploded. "I can't say anything right today. Maybe I should leave!" Nobody answered but she stayed anyway.

At the precise moment that the photographer seemed satisfied with my pose, having made countless trips back and forth arranging the folds of the dress and checking through his lens, Mother darted across the room and pushed the veil, which had been meticulously arranged, farther back over my shoulder. The photographer peered through the lens again, then stood there looking nonplussed.

"Did it look better the way *you* had it?" I asked. He hesitated for a moment, peering through his lens again, before saying, "Well . . . I thought so. May I change it a little?"

"Put it back the way you had it, please," I instructed. "You're the expert. That's why we're here." Mother remained silent while the photographer arranged the veil exactly as it had been before her interference, then chirped, "There! That's better! That's what *I* was trying to do."

Again the photographer seemed satisfied and about to start shooting when Mother made another dash across the room, this time to fiddle with the folds of the dress.

"*Dammit,* Mother!" I burst out. "Why don't you sit down and leave things alone? We're going to be here all day if you don't! The man knows what he's doing . . . he does it all day long, for heaven's sake!"

"I'm paying a *fortune* for this! I want it to look the way *I* want it. That's my *privilege.*"

"How much you're paying for it is *your* business, Mother! *You're* the one who wanted this picture taken, so don't expect me to do this again if you mess it up. I'd suggest that since you're paying so all-fired much for his expertise, you let the man get on with what he's an expert at."

"Brother!" She returned to her corner and glowered.

The photographer rearranged the folds of the dress to his satisfaction and took his pictures. A few weeks later a large framed photograph arrived in the mail from California to be followed, shortly, by a phone call. "Do you have the photograph?" Mother asked. I said that I did and thanked her.

"Isn't it brilliant? I chose the frame." I said that it was and that I loved the frame.

"No wonder he's the head photographer! He's brilliant! It feels as if you're standing right here in the room with me!" I had no idea whether he had been the "head photographer." He might have been, but I doubted it. I made agreeing noises anyway.

"It's just wonderful! That you would offer to do this for me! I'll thank you all my life!"

For a week or so after Mother's departure I brooded over my situation. While it was true that she was only in the east every so often, it was equally true that when she was she thought she owned me. My husband considered marriage a partnership in which each of the partners had absolute obligations to the other. He was strong and he was demanding and he detested my mother, not only for her behavior toward him but for the way she treated everyone, including me. I had related Tom Hammond's "you have a responsibility" speech to Jeremy and he had agreed to bear with me for a while. He had made it quite clear, though, that he was significantly less than persuaded by Tom's arguments. The last dinner we had had with Mother before she left was horrendous. She had been insufferably rude and unpleasant and I had felt a strong urge to slap her at one point. Jeremy had grown quieter and quieter as the evening wore painfully on and I had actually seen his jaw muscles working at times. He hadn't spoken a word about her since and, to my repeated apologies, he had only grunted.

I couldn't blame my husband if he held me responsible; I *was* responsible. I hadn't tried to defend her . . . how could I? Her behavior was indefensible. The fact remained, however, that because of me my husband was being subjected to treatment that no one should have to tolerate and both of us knew it. When Jeremy and I were together, we seemed as close as ever but, when he was away at the office, I began to feel that he was a bit moodier than I remembered him. Was there a coldness, an aloofness, at times that hadn't been there before? Or was I imagining things? He had been a bachelor until he was thirty. Was he wondering what he had done to himself, wondering whether I was worth all this?

I found myself curled up on the sofa when I thought about it too much, crying. I *couldn't* lose him! If I were forced to make a choice, I would choose Jeremy and damn my responsibilities, but I dreaded having to make such a choice. I wanted desperately to talk to someone and pour it all out, but I had no one close enough to talk to. I couldn't simply ignore the problem . . . it wasn't going to go away. I would have to face up to Jeremy, try to get him to understand my emotional turmoil and accommodate me as I was being forced to accommodate Mother. Perhaps it *was* nothing more than an overactive case of a new mother-in-law adjusting to her only daughter being married. I wished I could believe it.

I pulled myself together and cooked an elaborate meal. I prided myself on my cooking, but this time I really went the limit: *escargots*, white asparagus vinaigrette, standing rib of beef with Yorkshire pudding and green beans, crepes Suzette. Jeremy was most complimentary. Over coffee I apologized in advance and broached the topic.

"There's been something preying on my mind since my mother left and I'm afraid that if we don't talk about it I'm going to lose you." My voice broke slightly and I struggled for control. Tears only served to irritate Jeremy and that was the last thing I wanted.

"Sweetie, why on earth would you think such a thing?" he asked, a look of shocked surprise on his face.

"Because of my mother. I know how angry she made you and I don't blame you at all, but I have a problem. I—"

"Hold it a second. I've been waiting for you to decide to talk about it and I'm glad that the time has come to clear the air. Now that it has, why don't we make it simple and save a lot of time and trouble. Your mother is an obnoxious pain in the ass! What else is there to say?" The fury which must have been pent up in him for the past weeks was clear in his eyes.

"Yes, yes, darling," I quickly agreed. "I know she is . . . and worse than that. She's all that you could think of to say about her. The trouble is, I'm stuck with her. I can't shut her out of my life and that's my problem. I don't expect you to accept her. I certainly don't expect you to like her, God knows. The thing is . . . could you bring yourself to accept her existence in *my* life if I managed to keep her away from *you* most of the time?" He looked very, very dubious but the anger had faded. "You mean you believe all that bunk Tom told you?"

"Unfortunately, yes. I didn't want to . . . I tried not to. But it's all too true and I know it. She *is* different and I *do* have a responsibility to her. I don't expect you to understand. The question is, can you love and support me in *spite* of my mother? Not condemn me for her? I love you so much . . . I wouldn't do anything to spoil what we have. I'll do anything you say, but I'm pleading for your understanding . . . not of the emotions involved, just the fact that they exist. I'm asking you to leave my wretched mother to me. I'll deal with her when she's around and I'll keep her away from you except on unavoidable occasions."

"Sweetie," he said, sitting down next to me and taking my hand, "I love you very much and nothing will ever come between us, not even your mother. If I'm certain of nothing else, I am of that. That's not even under discussion. What is under discussion is your mother and what to do about her. You ask me to understand that certain emotions exist which you can't escape, but how on earth can you tolerate what she does to you? How can you put up with it? She's the rudest, most importunate person I've ever encountered, or ever hope to. That woman doesn't love *you* or anyone else and you're kidding yourself if you think she does. The only emotions she truly understands are hate and jealousy. She—"

I interrupted him before he got wound up. "I can't defend her, darling. I wouldn't think of trying to. There is no defense . . . but you're wrong about one thing. She *does* love me and she depends on me to love her. Granted, hers is a warped, jealous love but, in its own way, it *is* love. It's all she's capable of and it's intense."

"Look, if you're that convinced, I'll do my best. I'll never understand love on those terms, but I guess I'll have to take your word for it . . . just so long as you understand that it won't be any easier for me to watch *you* suffer than to keep my mouth shut when she's rude to *me*."

"Thank you." I breathed a sigh. "If you can just do that much, I'll be so relieved, you have no idea. I *know* how angry you've been. Whenever she visits New York I'll have lunches and go shopping with her. If I spend enough time with her during the days it should eliminate the evenings which involve you . . . at least most of the time it should. It'll work. I *know* it will!" There must have been desperation in my tone, for Jeremy suddenly became very tender. "I'm really sorry that you've been worried about me . . . us. Your mother infuriates me, but I'd no idea that my feelings were so transparent. I never intended to take it out on you, let alone make you feel guilty."

"There were a few times when I had the feeling that you'd had enough of marriage. I was sinking in despair." He squeezed my hand hard. "You must never do that to yourself again . . . or let me do it to you. Just come right out with it if it ever happens again. As to this, if you feel so strongly about your mother's dependence on you, then so be it. I can live with it if you can. I don't agree with you, but it's your right to feel as you do. She can't come between us . . . nothing can. Believe it!"

"Thank you," I said, and did cry. Jeremy didn't mind. He dabbed at my tears and called me a silly goose. I loved him more at that moment than ever before.

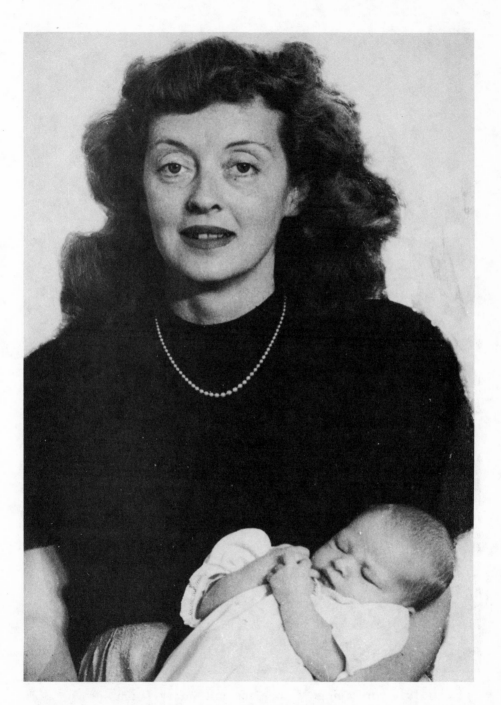

Mother and me, May 1947. I am about one week old.

1948 christening. Mother, me and Sherry. (I am one year old.)

Mother, Sherry, my dog, Schatzie, and me on the front
step of the farm at Butternut when I was eighteen
months old; taken by Grandmother Ruthie

My second birthday party

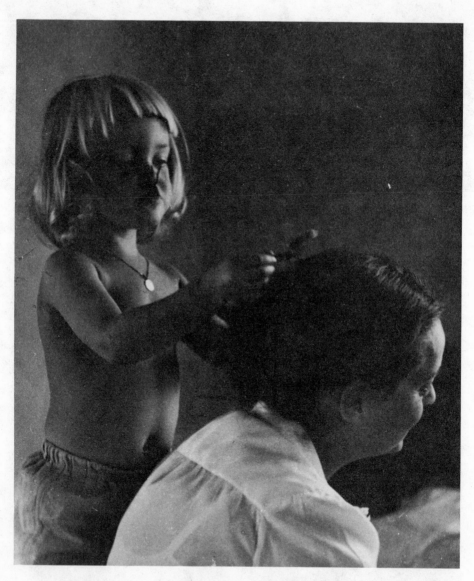

Mother and me at Butternut when I was four; taken by
Grandmother Ruthie

Michael, me and Margot

Witch-Way, Cape Elizabeth, Maine

The hat contest on the *Independence*

At the Grier School in Pennsylvania during a horse show. Mother, as usual, is wearing my ribbons.

Me modeling equestrian attire with my horse in Central Park, New York City, at age twelve

Arriving in Cannes for the film festival (in front of the
Carlton Hotel) *Photograph by Pierre Manciet*

At the Lido in Paris, 1963. *Clockwise from left:* Tom
Hammond, Pierre Galante (O. De H's husband), Olivia
De Havilland, Rupert Allen, Jean-Eve Millet, me,
Jeremy and mother.

2

1965–1966

Despite Mother's efforts to break out of the macabre mold, she received nothing but scripts for low-budget horror movies submitted by nowhere production companies. The only acceptable script, still macabre, came from Seven Arts and was called *The Nanny;* at least it had a plot and would be a decent movie. Early in 1965 she left for England to begin filming, but a snag developed immediately. Mother developed the "worst case of flu known to man" and after a couple of weeks was still in seclusion in her hotel, saying that there was as yet no improvement in her condition. Word came through to Jeremy from London that they were sure Mother was faking it but didn't know why. "Is there anything you might do to help, old boy?" Jeremy asked me if I knew anything about it. I didn't but suggested that he ask the English director whether she was fighting with anybody and, if so, what about. It turned out that her nanny character was being wardrobed in the lightweight dresses worn by modern nannies. Mother had clamored for a traditional, old-fashioned nanny's wool uniform with white collar and had developed the flu when told that this type of uniform was hard to find and out of style for the picture anyway. I told my husband to advise the director that finding Mother an old-

161

fashioned nanny's uniform would also cure her flu. It did.

Mother was back in California in plenty of time for my brother Michael's graduation from Black Foxe Military Academy in Los Angeles before he went on to the Loomis School in Connecticut. Michael wrote me a very sweet letter asking if I could possibly come to the ceremony.

Jeremy and I discussed the matter and, as I had fully expected, he flatly refused to voluntarily go anywhere near my mother. Our agreement had worked quite well and he had seen little of her over the past year. He wanted to keep it that way. He did, however, urge me to go alone for Michael's sake. He rarely saw Michael anymore, but had grown quite fond of him during his California visits prior to our wedding.

Thus it was that I went alone for a three-day weekend in California. Michael was thrilled that I had come all that way just for him and I was happy to be with him. The graduation ceremony was held out of doors on a gorgeous, sunny day. I was very proud of my brother, looking so smart in his uniform. Gary was there, naturally, and I was pleased for Michael that both his parents were present. They barely exchanged a word, but that was probably for the best.

That night Mother arranged a dinner party at the Bel-Air Hotel for Michael and his friends from the graduating class. I acted as hostess and was flattered to learn that Michael's friends thought I was not only "neat" but very pretty too, a couple of the more precocious ones being disappointed to hear that I was married. After dinner I drove them all back to Honeysuckle Hill for card games and Monopoly. When the last of the parents had come and gone, I told Michael what a pleasant evening it had been and how pleased I was that he had invited me. Mother had long since gone to bed and we sat up for half the night comparing notes on parental carryings-on over the past year or so.

Mother had been known, on rare occasions, to permit a few days to go by in harmonious accord and I had been hoping that this, my first visit to her home in eighteen months, would be such an occasion, especially with Jeremy a continent away. I suppose I should have known better than to get my hopes up but I was still a perennial optimist. I hadn't realized yet that for Mother to behave in a civilized fashion for long had be-

come miraculous rather than rare. At breakfast on day three—
I was leaving on a late-afternoon flight—Mother began. "Isn't
it a shame," she said with a sneering smile, "that Jeremy won't
let you stay away longer than three days. I guess he can't bear
to do without you fussing over him." I held my temper in check
and said, "Mother, the last two days have been very pleasant.
Why don't we keep it that way and enjoy our last few hours
together?" She quickly lit a fresh cigarette and busied herself
with smoking and eating at the same time.

After taking enough time to consider her line of attack, she
affected a puzzled expression. "I really don't understand why
you're always so accusing, B.D. I charmingly ask why you can't
stay a little longer and you bite my head off. Did I touch a
nerve or something? It's him, isn't it?" She had been unable to
maintain the puzzled expression and the original sneer was back.
I was determined to give it one more try. "Look, I've been here
two days without us having an argument. Why are you so determined to start one? *Why?*"

"I'm not trying to *start* anything! *Brother!* He's making your
life miserable! That's why you won't talk about it . . . I can
tell!"

"That's it!" I spat. "You've ruined it again. You're so damned
jealous of my relationship with Jeremy that you've become a
nasty, bitter old woman. You beg me to spend time with you
and then you do your best to make me wish I hadn't. You're
nuts! Do you know that?"

"Oh, God, B.D.! Don't do this to me . . . not when you're
leaving so soon . . . it isn't fair. Jesus!" Off she went into her
racking-sobs routine. I sat perfectly still, not uttering another
word in the hope that a long-drawn-out scene might be avoided
if I could only keep cool.

"God, you're a cold bitch!" she essayed. "You didn't used
to be like this."

"That's certainly possible, Mother," I replied, carefully
measuring both words and tone of voice.

"You'll never admit it"—she blew her nose—"but it's all *his*
fault, you know. *He's* done this to you."

"That's possible too. We've been married for eighteen
months."

"Eighteen months. *Brother!*" I waited a moment and, when

Mother lit another cigarette, I tried a change of subject. "Wasn't it a lovely day at Black Foxe? I was so proud of Michael . . . he looked so handsome in his uniform."

"Yes! And that *bastard* wouldn't come! He let you fly all this way alone. Jesus!" She reminded me of an engine with preignition. If I left her alone, I thought, she might just splutter to a stop. I said nothing and stared off into space as though rapt in my recollections of the graduation. It was no use. She suddenly came at me with a broadside which shattered my good intentions. "I didn't want to tell you this, B.D., but your husband has been sleeping around right from the start. I have it from a *very* reliable source." I managed not to shout at her despite the fact that she'd brought me right back to a boil.

"Mother," I said levelly, staring her straight in the eye, "either your reliable source is an abject liar or you're deliberately being despicable. It's pathetic that you would say such a thing and I'd suggest that you keep filth like that to yourself. I won't buy it."

"How can you be so blind?" she shouted, jumping to her feet and striding halfway across the room, then whirling around and striding back again. "He's got you completely snowed! *He's* on a gravy train while *you're* slaving your guts out for him! And you can't see it! *Jesus!* You're killing me with this! You're just too damned stubborn to admit you're wrong! I lie awake at night in sweats . . . I'm so frightened for you! When are you going to wake up?"

What, I asked myself, had I done to deserve this? There didn't seem to be any way to stop her once she got started. I stood up too and we faced each other across the table. "If you don't stop carrying on, Mother, so help me I'm going to leave. I've listened to enough of your garbage!"

"Don't threaten me, young lady!" she barked. "I'm your mother and I know more about you than you'll admit. You owe it to yourself to rethink your marriage. You need freedom . . . *shit* . . . he thinks you're his slave. *I* can see what's going on inside you. You think you can fool me but you can't. Men are *shits*! You know it already but you won't admit it. You're too damned stubborn to admit I told you so. I only hope you wake up before it's too late. That's all I have to say on the subject . . . so let's just drop it." I took a deep breath, choked off what

I really wanted to say and spun on my heel to walk, stiff-backed, out to the pool.

Would this ever stop, I wondered, or would I have to spend the rest of my life letting my mother work off her frustrations on me? I was convinced that that was what she was doing. I lay down in the sun and tried to block it from my mind. Only a few hours more and I would be on my way back to love and sanity. Being with my mother for a few days made sanity look like a gift as precious as love.

I must have dozed off because I was startled by Mother calling out from the house, "*Surprise!* Look who's come for lunch!" I looked up and there stood Bill Simpson (I have changed the name to protect a perfectly innocent man). Bill and I had dated off and on for a couple of years before I met Jeremy, and he had professed to being in love with me and wanting me to marry him. He was a struggling young actor who was in worshipful awe of Mother and I had always regarded him, rightly or wrongly, as among those who dated me in order to get near her. He was a nice-enough guy, but I couldn't imagine why he would suddenly appear like this.

"Hello, Bill," I said, not even trying to conceal my puzzlement. "How are you and what brings you here?" Mother disappeared into the house as soon as I spoke and Bill came over to my chaise, hand outstretched.

"Hi, B.D. It's nice to see you. I'm fine and your mother invited me for lunch." I waved at a chaise. "Sit down. Don't think I'm not pleased to see you but I'm curious about something. When did Mother call you about this luncheon?"

"Sometime last week . . . Wednesday, I think. Why?"

"Did she say anything about why she was inviting you?"

"Sure . . . she said that you were coming home and wanted to see me."

"Forgive my asking so many questions but I'll explain in a minute. Is that all she said or did she enlarge on the coming home and wanting to see you bit?"

"No . . . I don't think so." He mused for a moment. "To the best of my recollection, she just said that it would be nice if I came for lunch with you and her for old times' sake."

"Thanks," I said. "That's all I wanted to know. I apologize if I sounded like the Spanish Inquisition, but Mother and I have had a pretty good go-round and I was curious about what she might have said to you. She seems to be having a hell of a tough time accepting that my marriage is going smoothly and keeps trying to think of ways to mess it up."

"Oh, I see-e-e-e-e," he said. "You thought that maybe I thought—"

"Precisely," I interrupted.

I knew perfectly well why Mother had invited Bill, but now I was satisfied that he was an innocent pawn in her game. Struggling young actors do tend to eagerly accept any kind of invitation from a big name. My only concern now was what she might do next. Bill had always been pleasant company and a gentleman, so it seemed best to sit back, socialize and watch Mother make a fool of herself.

She started bustling in and out of the house, setting up a lunch table on the patio, while Bill and I chatted. Having him to talk to was actually a welcome relief from Mother's persistent badgering. Her announcement that we should come to the table, followed by her coy apology for not being able to join us, simply extended my respite. "You two get to know each other again," she said with an incredibly obvious suggestive leer. "I'd like to join you but I can't. I'll see you both later." Off she went, closing the doors to the patio behind her.

"Wait till I tell Jeremy about this one," I said. "He'll die laughing."

"You mean you're going to tell him you had a tête-à-tête with an old boyfriend?" He sounded shocked.

"Sure I am. Why are you so surprised?"

"Well, it seems awfully risky to me. Are you sure he'll understand?"

"Completely sure. He loves hearing about Mother's little schemes."

"He must trust you a lot," Bill said, almost wistfully.

"He does . . . and I trust him."

"That's wonderful. I hope my marriage works out that well. I got engaged recently, you know?"

"No, I didn't. Congratulations. I hope you're as lucky as I am."

We relaxed and enjoyed our lunch together. I talked about Jeremy and Bill talked about his fiancée who, it turned out, was a girl I had once known slightly. We rehashed old times and he brought me up to date on old friends. When the food and conversation ran out and Bill was taking his leave, Mother popped out of the house. "You don't have to leave so soon if you don't want to, Bill," she gushed. "Why don't you stay for a while . . . take a swim? I know B.D. would like you to."

"Thank you, Bette, that's very nice of you," he replied, giving me the suggestion of a wink, "but perhaps some other time. I have an appointment and I mustn't be late." He shook hands with Mother and me, made appropriate departure noises and left.

Mother ensconced herself in the chaise next to mine and it didn't surprise me in the least when she said, "He's still crazy about you, you know? I could tell . . . it's written all over him."

"I doubt that very much," I replied. "Did you know he's engaged?"

"That doesn't make any difference. He's always been in love with you, probably always will be." She paused and then added, conspiratorially, "If you want to have a quick affair with him I'll keep my mouth shut."

"I don't think so, thank you, Mother," I said, as though turning down a second cup of coffee, meanwhile flopping back and closing my eyes.

"You ought to think about it. An affair now and then is good for a marriage. It adds spice, stops it from getting boring . . . I ought to know." And thus spake a four-time loser. I didn't answer, just lay there hoping Mother would think I had fallen asleep. I heard her chaise creak and thought I had succeeded but, when I risked a careful peek under one eyelid, I saw that she had only gone to the lunch table for a cigarette.

I heard her rubber sandals flip-flopping as she prowled around the patio, then coming in my direction. "I don't understand you, B.D.! I can't believe you're letting this happen to you. You used to be so sharp." She had reached my side by this time and I was aware of her shadow across my face. "Are you listening to me?" she snapped angrily.

"To tell you the truth," I answered, "I'm doing my best to ignore you."

"Is that so? Well let me tell you something, young lady! You better listen to me while there's still time. You may pooh-pooh it, but that English bastard is cheating on you and I can prove it! So why don't you just face facts and stop being so damned blind?"

I sat up and turned to face her. "Mother, that's the second time you've accused my husband of cheating. Now you say you have proof. Well . . . let's have it. I'm giving you one chance to convince me that you're not lying, playing games in the hope I'll leave Jeremy!"

"B.D., you've got to believe—"

"I don't have to believe anything!" I shouted. "Proof is what we're discussing. So where is it? Names, dates, places . . . that's proof!"

"Oh, don't be so rough on me, B.D.," she whined, clasping and unclasping her hands in front of her. "It's not that simple."

"You realize, don't you, Mother, that the only thing you've proven to me is that you're a malicious liar," I said coldly, standing up and walking toward the house. As I reached the doors she shouted at my retreating back, "How dare you turn your back on me? I'm only trying to help you see what's good for you and you treat me like a criminal! Cross-questioning me . . . I can't take it!" When I turned to face her, she put her hands over her face and started to sob. "Oh, God, B.D., why do you always do this to me? You're so heartless."

"One of these days, Mother, you ought to take a long, hard look at yourself. I neither know nor care whether you believe your own bullshit . . . that's your problem . . . the mystery is how you can claim to love me so much and, in the same breath, spout outrageous lies designed to ruin my marriage and my life. You're pathetic!"

"You just won't understand, will you?" she wailed. "I'm only trying to save you from all the heartbreak that I've been through. I'm your mother . . . I care about you . . . I don't want you to get hurt."

"Oh, I understand, Mother, only too well . . . far better than you seem to realize. I'll say one more thing and then I'm going to pack. You'd better come to terms with the fact that my marriage is successful and stop your persistent smear campaign, or you'll force me to choose between you and my husband. I wouldn't do that if I were you."

I went into the house, told the chauffeur to be ready in forty-five minutes, then went upstairs to pack. When I came down, carrying my suitcase, Mother was waiting at the foot of the stairs. "You look gorgeous! It's been wonderful having you here. I just wish it could have been longer. I guess I'll just have to have the guts to face it." She reached forward and clasped my arms above the elbows. "Please thank Jeremy for letting you come to Michael's graduation. It meant a lot to him." The chauffeur took my suitcase and we exchanged kisses on the cheek. As the car pulled out of the driveway, Mother was smiling and waving.

In October of 1965 Jeremy and I moved to Weston, Connecticut. Earlier in the year we had concluded that we were stuck in the east and had bought a house. It was of an interesting design, which our real estate agent described as a "Georgian Colonial back-to-front split." The house had one story in front and three in the rear where it wandered down a hillside. There were five levels in all, the front being a three-level living room with a fourteen-foot ceiling, a dining room and a kitchen. At the back of the living room was an iron-railed balcony with three bedrooms and bathrooms opening onto it. The second floor, going downhill, had another living room opening onto a screened porch, two more bedrooms and a bathroom. The ground floor, downhill again, consisted of a billiard room and a laundry room. We named it Wildwoods and put in a swimming pool the following summer. I was bursting with excitement when we moved in. Not only were we getting out of the city, which we both detested, but I had my own house for the first time in my life.

I had been concerned that Mother would invite herself to stay with us whenever she came east and the only cloud in my otherwise cloudless sky was my dread of the scene which would follow my refusal to be her motel. As it turned out, Mother using my house as a motel would not be the problem. Within a couple of weeks of our taking up residence at Wildwoods, Mother developed a pressing need to live in Connecticut. Her reasons were not compelling. "*Everybody* knows that the movie business has moved to New York. Anyway, I'm fed up with California. . . . I've always wanted to live in Connecticut." *I* knew why she was moving and no amount of public utterance would persuade me otherwise. She actually managed to convince one of her biographers that she had moved to Connecticut first and I followed her there.

Mother sold Honeysuckle Hill, shipped her furniture to storage and moved into the guesthouse of a lifelong friend, Robin Brown, in Westport. She stayed there through the winter until, in the early spring, her real estate agent found a satisfactory house located on the Westport-Weston line, just two miles from our house. She named her new house Twin Bridges, moved her furniture in and started calling me to discuss all the fun we were going to have together. High on her list of "fun" things to do was staying overnight at each other's houses.

It was time for Jeremy and me to discuss coexistence with Mother again. There really wasn't much to discuss. Our agreed-upon plan of reducing Jeremy's exposure to her to absolute minimum had worked well enough and we would have to keep on with it. The only difference would be that now I would have to see her two or three times a week *all* the time instead of only when she was visiting the east. I began to make it a point to drop by Twin Bridges at least twice a week for lunch, coffee or a drink. It didn't solve *all* our problems but it did reduce major unpleasantnesses to a tolerable infrequency.

Nineteen sixty-six was a slow year for Mother. No movies came her way but she did do a week as cohost on *The Mike Douglas Show,* an episode of *Gunsmoke* and she made an appearance on *The Milton Berle Show.* In October she phoned and said that she wanted to have us over for dinner on Jeremy's birthday in November. I reminded her that my husband didn't like birthday parties in his honor.

"Couldn't you let me do it this once?" she pleaded. "Jeremy and I have had a lot of trouble getting along and I want to *do* something for him . . . so he'll *like* me." She sounded so sincere about wanting to bridge the gap between Jeremy and herself that I began to feel bad about denying her the opportunity. "Do you mean just us?" I asked warily. She was too quick with her reply. "Yes, anything you say." It was to be one of many, many occasions when I should have been more suspicious. I said, "O.K., then, if it's just Jeremy and me at your house."

"Great!" she replied, bursting with enthusiasm. "Now! Who do you want to invite?"

"No, no, no!" I panicked. "I said just us . . . you agreed."

"Well, I did. But wouldn't it be nicer to have just a few of your friends?"

"No, Mother, positively not. You keep forgetting that basically you don't like most of our friends. An argument is bound to start over something and I don't want that to happen."

"Well, I have to admit Jeremy's friends aren't exactly my cup of tea," she snorted sarcastically.

"They aren't just Jeremy's friends . . . they're my friends too, and that's exactly what I'm talking about. You're getting snide about it already and we aren't even out of the discussion stage yet."

"I am *not* getting snide! But have it your way . . . maybe you're right. We'll do it with just us if that's what you want."

"I'm glad you feel that way," I said, trying to make it sound as though she'd won a point. "It's a much better idea and, anyway, if it's just us, maybe you and Jeremy can come to understand each other a little better."

"Understand each other? *Ha!* I understand *him* perfectly well. He just won't give *me* a break. Everything's got to be his way. He doesn't give a damn about me!"

"If that's the way you feel about it," I said in exasperation, "why do you insist on having us for dinner on Jeremy's birthday? It sounds to me as if you've already made up your mind that the evening's going to be a disaster. Perhaps we'd better scrub the whole idea."

"Oh, don't start that, B.D.!" she protested, half whining, half challenging. "All I want is my son-in-law to know that I'm a good dame and you won't give me the chance. Now come off it!"

"Why don't you come off it? One minute you want to do something for my husband in order to improve relations and then, the second I agree, you start name calling again. You've got me totally confused. I don't think *you* know what you want. You've got the idea in your head that if you give Jeremy a birthday dinner he'll think you're a good dame, to use your words. That's fine in theory, but if you're going to be rude to him when he gets there, what the hell is the point of it all?"

"All right, B.D., all right. All I wanted was to have you both over for dinner and you try to *get* me. Just let me know if you're coming in time for me to prepare. It's a lot of work, you know, cooking for him."

It was no use saying we weren't coming, Mother wouldn't accept that and I would have to go through it all again. I did have difficulty restraining myself from mentioning that I cooked for my husband every night and didn't find it that much work; however, I took the opportunity to remind her of the understanding. "I've already said that we're coming, Mother, but you've got to promise that it's just the three of us. Do I have your word?"

"All right, B.D., have it your way. *Jesus!* Orders from the Hymans as usual." Click, dial tone.

Jeremy accepted the plans for his birthday with resignation, saying, as he had from time to time before, that what Mother did or said in private had become to him as water off a duck's back; he simply tuned her out. A few days before his birthday, though, Mother rang. "I've invited someone else, but don't worry, you'll approve."

"Listen, Mother!" I bellowed. "We agreed that it would be just us! You promised . . . orders from the Hymans . . . remember?"

"Oh come off it, B.D. You sound exactly like a lawyer. They're people you like. You'll be thrilled."

"Who are they?"

"Oh, all right, but I wanted it to be a surprise. I've invited Mike and Shirley. I haven't seen them since the wedding and they're thrilled."

Mike was the younger brother of Ken Hyman, the executive producer of *What Ever Happened to Baby Jane?* When Jeremy first came to the United States and went to work for his uncle, Mike's father, he and Mike forged a very close friendship. Mike, unlike his brothers and Jeremy, had not gone to work for his father, the head of Seven Arts, which was probably a good thing since his wife, Shirley, was very straitlaced and got the vapors if anyone swore in her presence. There had been friction between Shirley and me from the word go and, as is unfortunately so inevitable in these situations, Jeremy and Mike were to see less and less of each other. Mother was fully aware of all this since she had asked me, not long before, why she never heard me mention Mike and Shirley.

I knew that a disaster was unfolding right before my eyes, but I didn't know how to stop it. To do the obvious—say, stick it in your ear, Mother, and hang up—would bring hysterics, phone calls from lawyers and all the rest. On top of everything else, I could never believe that my own mother actually meant me any harm.

"O.K., Mother," I said lamely, "you've already done it, so there's no point in discussing it further."

"Right!" she gloated. "Stop worrying so much. Everything will be just fine."

Mike and Shirley were getting out of their car as we pulled into the driveway at Twin Bridges. After the usual hugs of greeting we knocked on the door. Mother seemed to be in a pretty good mood, greeting our cousins effusively, giving me a big hug and telling Jeremy how nice it was to see him without a trace of insincerity in her voice. She dispatched Jeremy to the bar to mix drinks for us, but not for her as she already had one in her hand. She was about to take Mike and Shirley on a guided tour when Jeremy said, "Before you disappear, Bette, could I trouble you for a couple of Anacin?"

"Does being in my house give you a headache so quickly?" she retorted. "B.D., why don't you show Mike and Shirley around while I find something for your husband's headache? I wouldn't want him to suffer on my account." So much for her good mood, I thought.

"That's very considerate of you, Mother-in-law," Jeremy said, ignoring her jibe. "I appreciate your concern."

Before anything else was said, I shooed Mike and Shirley off to show them the downstairs. It was a nice old house. The front door, by which we'd entered, opened into a foyer and the main staircase was opposite the door, the living room to the left and the dining room to the right. The dining room was furnished with Mother's famous round table, complete with a lazy Susan, surrounded by potty chairs. The living room was lined with bookcases, with a bar in the corner near the fireplace. Beyond the living room a cute little den opened onto a screened porch overlooking the river. The house wasn't spectacular in age or design, but it was cozy and comfortable. As we returned to the foyer to go upstairs I heard Jeremy's voice from the dining room. "This isn't Anacin, Bette. What is it?" Mother answered, "It's a special headache prescription I've used for years. Take it . . . you'll feel better in minutes."

The upstairs design was not unusual with three spare bedrooms and a bathroom, but the master suite was striking: a big bedroom with a sitting room and enormous bathroom. The tour over, we returned to the living room to get our drinks from Jeremy. Mike and Shirley politely enthused over the house and Mother replied, "Thank you. I like it too." She turned to address us all. "Now . . . I was going to cook a birthday dinner for Jeremy, but I was afraid that nothing would suit him. So . . . we're going to a charming little restaurant which just opened. We'll have another drink and get going." She went to the bar and poured herself another. I looked at Jeremy for a cue. All he did was make a face and shrug his shoulders, so I kept my peace and turned to chat with the others as though nothing were wrong.

We finished our drinks, Mother downing yet another one while we were still on our first, and filed out to get in my station wagon. Jeremy drove and Mother was in the front passenger seat. The restaurant was only a ten-minute drive but, before we got there, I noticed Jeremy's head drooping and snapping up again. I leaned forward and asked, "Are you all right, darling?"

"I don't know," he replied. "All of a sudden I can't keep my eyes open. It's weird."

"Do you want me to drive?" I asked, not alarmed but definitely puzzled.

"No, it's O.K. We've only a couple of minutes to go. I certainly feel strange, though." Mother started cackling and rocking back and forth on the front seat.

"What the hell's so funny?" I barked at her. "What did you give Jeremy, anyway?" She went on cackling. "I knew he didn't really have a headache . . . he's just so *nervous* about everything." Chuckle, chuckle. "I gave him a Miltown . . . to calm him down."

"What's a Miltown?" Jeremy asked.

"It's a bloody tranquilizer!" I bellowed. "What in God's good name is wrong with you, Mother?"

"Oh, don't fly off the handle, B.D." She turned to Jeremy. "Your headache's gone, isn't it?"

"No, it isn't," he replied as we pulled into the restaurant parking lot, "and now I feel strange as well. Thank you very much."

"That wasn't very nice of you, Bette," Shirley ventured. "You really shouldn't give other people your prescription medicines, you know. It can be dangerous."

"She's absolutely right, Mother," I fumed. "You've no right—"

"Oh, shut up, all of you!" Mother shouted. "Let's just drop it, shall we? Jeremy will be just fine. Why don't you all stop worrying about him so much?" She got out of the car and started walking toward the entrance. Realizing that she was alone, she turned, spread her feet and placed her hands on her hips. "Are you coming or not?" she shouted. I was worried about Jeremy; he had never taken a tranquilizer before, and not only were Mother's probably strong but he had had a drink too.

"Do you feel sick . . . would you rather go home?" I asked him. "I don't feel sick," he replied, "just sort of light-headed and sleepy. Perhaps food will help . . . let's go and eat."

When we were seated, after much ado about Mother gracing the establishment with her presence, the waiter asked for our drink orders. Mother ordered a double Scotch but the rest of us declined.

"Would you bring us menus, please?" I asked. "We're all starving and would like to order."

"Certainly, madam," the waiter replied as Mother derisively chimed in, "Yes, by all means. I'm in charge, but whatever makes my daughter happy." While the waiter was gone, none of us spoke a word. We sat, fiddling with our napkins, sipping water and looking anywhere except at Mother or each other. The atmosphere at the table was thick enough to cut with a knife and we were all extremely ill at ease. Except for Jeremy, that is. He seemed to be asleep with his eyes open.

The waiter returned, served Mother's drink and handed out

the menus. By the time we each had one, Mother had gulped down her drink and was demanding another double. She snatched up her menu, peered at it and, on the waiter's return with her drink, announced, "We'll all have Chateaubriand." She clapped the menu closed and held it over her shoulder. The waiter took it and asked, "Would anyone like an appetizer, madam?"

"No!" snapped Mother. "Just bring the Chateaubriand."

"The Chateaubriand is for two, madam. You are five . . . shall I bring two or three?"

"What?" barked Mother. "Oh. I see. I don't eat much. Just bring a double one."

"Very well, madam. How would you like it cooked?"

"Rare."

"Wait a minute," I finally piped up. "I don't know about anyone else, but Jeremy and I like ours medium."

"So do we," said Mike bravely.

"What?" Mother barked again. "Oh. Make it medium then . . . but on the rare side." I caught the waiter's eye and mouthed "medium" at him, but Mother caught me in the act. "*What* did you say?"

"I was about to say that perhaps somebody might like an appetizer, even if you wouldn't," I said, covering up. The waiter was still hovering. "I'll have clams on the half shell, please. So will my husband. How about you guys?" Mike and Shirley ordered shrimp cocktails.

"Two clams on the half shell and two shrimp cocktails," intoned the waiter. "Is there anything else?"

"I'll have another drink," said Mother.

Again we sat and fidgeted, saying nothing. First, Mother's drink arrived and quite quickly thereafter, thank heavens, our appetizers. I nudged Jeremy into wakefulness. When he noticed the clams in front of him he mumbled, "Oh, great . . . clams," then just stared at them. The rest of us started to eat while Jeremy stared blankly at his plate and Mother stared blearily at Jeremy. A few moments passed, then Mother shouted at him, "Wake up and eat your clams, for Christ's sake! You ordered them . . . eat them!" He blinked his eyes, looked at her across the table, looked down at his plate and, sounding much more lively than before, said, "Oh, great . . . clams . . .

I love 'em." To my immense relief, he started to eat.

We ate as slowly as possible, trying to prolong the availability of something to do. Mother was getting drunker by the minute and none of us dared speak for fear of giving her another reason to shout at us. Every time she opened her mouth at this point it was to bellow something at somebody. Each time she did, the whole restaurant fell silent as everyone stared at us. It was like being in an E. F. Hutton commercial.

An eternity passed and the waiter returned to remove the appetizer plates. I asked how long it would be before the steak was ready and he said that he was about to serve it.

"Well, for Christ's sake bring it!" shouted Mother. "These people are starving!"

"Right away, madam," he replied, heading for the kitchen at a virtual gallop. Within seconds a waitress appeared to place an entree plate before each of us. Hard on her heels was the waiter, wheeling a serving cart on which was a large serving dish with a small black object in the middle of it.

"What's that?" shrieked Mother, pointing at the small black object.

"Chateaubriand for four, madam."

"For *four*?" Mother roared, standing up, placing her hands on her hips and glaring myopically at the waiter. "*Shit!* That's not enough for *two*!" All heads turned in our direction and a deadly hush fell over the room.

"I'm terribly sorry, madam." The waiter had blanched visibly. "But this is Chateaubriand for four."

"Sit down, Mother," I hissed urgently. "It's not that important. Just tell him to bring another one if you like."

"What do you mean, it's not important?" she shrieked. "It's a fucking gyp! I'm paying a fortune for this dinner and I won't be cheated!" She stomped off in the direction of the kitchen shouting, "Where's the owner? I want to see the fucking owner! I won't be treated like this! I won't stand for it!" She disappeared through the door into the kitchen and, for the next few minutes, I couldn't make out what anyone was saying. The only certainty was that Mother had found someone to shout at.

Whispered conversations started up at other tables and I looked around at our little group. Jeremy's eyes were slightly more focused and he was staring at me with a quizzical expression. Shirley was sitting with her hands clasped in her lap and her lower lip quivering while Mike stared worriedly at her. Our waiter, in the meantime, had staunchly applied himself to carving the small black object into five slices of steak and was now serving them along with our vegetables. There being little else to do, we started to eat. By the time Mother returned from the kitchen, a look of triumph on her face, we had all, Jeremy included, finished our meager portions.

"Well," Mother crowed, "they won't pull *that* again! *I* told *them* a thing or two! *Fucking thieves . . . Jesus!"* She sat down.

"Mother, *please*," I begged. "Calm down and eat your steak. It isn't worth all this . . . really it isn't."

"You know, Sweetie?" said Jeremy, uttering his first full sentence since entering the restaurant and picking exactly the wrong time to do so. "Your mother's absolutely right . . . it's a ripoff."

"Ha!" cried Mother. "Even that son of a bitch agrees with me!" She jumped up and headed for the kitchen again, lurching unsteadily. "Where's that fucking waiter with the other steak? They said they'd give me someone else's! Where the fuck is it?"

"Oh, my God," squeaked Shirley. "I think I'm going to be sick."

"Oh, swell," I muttered, "that's all we need."

"Oh, shit!" said Jeremy, finally fully aware of what was going on. "I set her off again, didn't I?" Mother came weaving out of the kitchen again, waiter in tow. He was carrying another serving dish with another small black object on it. I was amazed; had I been the owner, chef or whoever Mother had been shouting at in the kitchen, I would have delivered the whole damned tenderloin to the table just to shut her up.

"You enjoy your dinner!" boomed Mother. "I'm leaving! I can't stand this place any longer!" She stormed unsteadily across the restaurant, bumping into tables and chairs all the way. We sat mesmerized at the havoc she wrought, spilled drinks and slopped soup mostly, until she disappeared into the foyer.

"I think we'd better get going," I said, "unless anyone wants more steak." No one did and we hurried after Mother, red of face but trying our best to look dignified.

Safely in our own home, Jeremy and I drank a great deal

of coffee and talked far into the night, trying to figure out what had caused my mother to behave so outrageously. Certainly she had been drunk, but drunk by design. She had started drinking before we ever got to Twin Bridges. Why? What was it that drove her to scenes like this? We couldn't find an answer. All we did was promise ourselves that, no matter what, we would never be seen in public with her again.

3

1967–1970

Mother hadn't made a movie since *The Nanny* in 1965. Again it was Seven Arts which came to her rescue and again it was a low-budget picture to be made in England. Mother went to London in July of 1967 to make *The Anniversary* and this time she made them fire the director and replace him with her old friend Roy Baker. The movie was yet another tale about a family of weirdos and the press again categorized it as a horror story. Again Mother was furious, arguing that it was only a slightly ghoulish tragedy, but a horror picture it remained in the public perception. After reading the reviews, Mother said, "From now on, if a third cousin who is never even seen on screen has committed a murder, or is even thinking about committing one, I'll throw the script in the furnace." I cheered her up, if only slightly, by pointing out that Joan Crawford had been reduced to doing minibudget monster movies like *Trog.*

In September of 1968 I became pregnant. Jeremy and I were ecstatic at the prospect of finally becoming parents and when I shared the news with Mother, she was thrilled. "It had better be a girl," she said threateningly. With a grandchild in the offing her thoughts turned to family and she decided that a big Thanksgiving was called for. She invited the entire Jerry Merrill family for the holiday weekend and, with Michael home from school, Jeremy and me, she was satisfied. It took several dozen phone calls to decide who would sleep where and, as each different permutation of beds, rooms and people was put forward by Mother as the ultimate solution, the only possible way to do it, I agreed with her. The thought of spending some time with the Merrills was very exciting and I looked forward to the reunion with great pleasure. I had hardly seen them since their sojourn at Witch-Way in 1957 when they took care of Michael and me, and Jeremy hadn't even met them yet.

The sleeping arrangements were finally resolved. Jerry and Marguerite, their daughter, Susan, and my brother would occupy the spare rooms at Twin Bridges. Their two sons, Chris and Mark, would stay at my house. Mother also announced that, in order to divide up the "work" of the weekend, I would have to provide dinner for everyone on the night following Thanksgiving.

When the Merrills arrived at Twin Bridges, late in the afternoon of Thanksgiving Day, it was crisp and frosty with a few snowflakes skittering around in the gray sky, just the way New England Thanksgivings are supposed to be. Mother, Michael, Jeremy and I met them in the driveway and there was much hugging, kissing and handshaking. Bags were hauled out of the trunk of their car and we clamored our way into the house. The air was ripe with the delectable smells of turkey, sage stuffing, pumpkin pie and mincemeat. Mark sniffed appreciatively. "It sure smells like Thanksgiving."

"Did you bake the pies, B.D.?" Marguerite asked.

"Yes, I did. You'll be able to see how your protégée turned out."

"There's more to dinner than pies!" Mother blurted. She looked around her. "Michael! Put the suitcases in the appropriate guest rooms. Chris, Mark, leave yours in the hall. You're staying at B.D.'s."

"Fine," said Chris who, as the elder, had the habit of speaking for Mark as well.

"Of course it's fine!" Mother barked. "I planned it that way. It works. Why wouldn't it be fine?"

"It is fine," said Chris. "I just said so."

"Right. *Brother!* At least that's settled." She addressed Marguerite. "Don't you think it's great that B.D.'s going to have a baby?"

"Yes," Marguerite replied, smiling in my direction. "I'm very happy for her."

"What about me?" Mother burst. "I'm happy for *me*. I told her that I expect a granddaughter."

The suitcases were taken upstairs and the visitors retired to unpack, wash up and change. Half an hour later we were all assembled in the living room. Mother made it quite clear that she would accept no help in the kitchen. "Vik and I can make it!" she stated emphatically when offers were made. (Vik Greenfield had replaced Viola Rubber and was Mother's man Friday and secretary. He was in his mid-thirties, was slight of build, and occupied an apartment above the garage.) Until Mother announced dinner, we spent time catching up on the past several years, or getting to know each other.

We took our places as indicated by the place cards and admired the array of traditional dishes spread out on the lazy Susan: butternut squash, creamed onions, mashed potatoes, peas and Harvard beets. Vik entered to sounds of appreciation as he bore aloft an enormous turkey, which he placed on the sideboard. Mother followed on Vik's heels and took up the carving implements.

I leaned across to Jeremy, placed my hand on his arm and whispered urgently, "Go and carve . . . quickly." He looked at me with a puzzled expression. "Why?"

"Don't you remember Vik's chicken?"

"Oh, good grief!" he exclaimed, leaping out of his seat. "I'm on my way."

Several months earlier, Mother had invited Jeremy and me to join her and Vik for dinner. Vik enjoyed cooking when he got the chance and had discovered a recipe for roast chicken with chestnut stuffing. Mother raved about it and wanted to share it with me, allowing Vik the privilege of preparing the entire dinner. We enjoyed the first course of avocados filled with creamed shrimp and then Vik brought in his masterpiece, a delectable capon, roasted to a golden brown, stuffed with chestnuts and resting on a bed of parsley and watercress.

182

It looked like a photograph from a gourmet magazine and we told him as much.

"*Sit!*" Mother instructed Vik. "You've done all the work, so I'll carve." I didn't think anything of it and was puzzled by the way Vik stiffened as he took his seat and Mother took up the carving knife. She planted her feet slightly apart, picked up the fork and, biting her lower lip in concentration, poised the fork above the picturesque fowl before plunging it through its breast and clear through to the wooden carving board beneath. Then, leaning on the fork and swaying back and forth slightly, she stared at the bird in indecision.

"Mother?" I called out, realizing why Vik had looked stricken and wanting to help. "Why don't you let Jeremy carve? He's very good at it."

"*What?*" she squawked, looking up and glaring at me. "What do you mean? I'm doing just fine. Brother!" She took a couple of stabs at the pinned bird without success, the knife sliding around on the oven-crisped skin. "Shit!" she blurted. "This damned bird is too slippery. Jesus! No one could carve this thing." As we watched in fascination, Mother first lost her grip on the carving knife, which fell to the floor, then she placed her right hand over the chicken and wrenched the fork from its breast, flinging the freed weapon across the table and narrowly missing Vik. Then, with determined ferocity, she began to rend Vik's masterpiece asunder with her bare hands. Frequently licking her fingers, she tore pieces of chicken from the carcass, put them on plates and handed them to us. We were never to find out what the chestnut stuffing was like.

As Jeremy dashed to the sideboard I called out, "Jeremy will carve, Mother!"

"I can carve . . . I love to carve," she argued, holding tight to the knife and fork.

"Come on, Mother-in-law," my husband coaxed. "It's traditional for men to do the carving."

"He's right," I added. "Let him do the honors and you can sit down and join us."

"Sit down? Ha! Go ahead and carve if it makes you happy, Jeremy," she conceded, handing him the knife and fork, "but I cannot sit down. I'll pass the plates. Vik?" she called, looking over her shoulder.

"Right here," he answered from behind her other shoulder.

"Oh, *there* you are. Pour the wine . . . I'll pass the plates."

Jeremy carved, Vik poured, Mother passed plates and everyone helped themselves to side dishes. The main course was finished, Mother and Vik cleared the table and I was allowed to serve my own pies. Everything was delicious and the compliments were sufficiently numerous and superlative to satisfy even Mother's requirements. My hopes for a trouble-free evening had risen steadily, but they were soon to be dashed.

With dinner over, Marguerite, Susan and I went to the kitchen to help Mother and Vik with the washing up while the men and boys adjourned to the living room. Mother became incensed that we were presuming to lend a hand. "Vik and I can *make* it! Go and sit with your families."

"Bette," Marguerite protested, "at least let us clear the table and get it all into the kitchen."

"I do *not* want everybody cluttering up the kitchen," Mother retorted in her most ungracious fashion. "Christ! Please just let *me* do it. You and B.D. do this sort of slave labor all the time so, today, in *my* house, you will not. Period!"

Marguerite made one more attempt. "Susan doesn't do it very often. Why not let *her* help?" Mother became positively irate. "Just leave me alone! Please . . . I beg of you!" We gave up and joined the men in the living room.

A quarter of an hour passed and Mother appeared in the doorway, cloth in hand and wearing an apron. She leaned heavily against the jamb, looking frazzled and exhausted, and glared angrily at us. "Considering that I slaved my guts out preparing that enormous dinner for you people, which was my pleasure, you'd think that at least one of you could help me clean up this unbelievable mess. *Brother,* I'll be at it all night!"

She returned to the kitchen. I motioned for everyone to stay where they were, tiptoed to the kitchen door and peeked in. Vik was rinsing dishes and putting them in the dishwasher and was about to tackle the roasting pans. Mother was moving things from one place to another and muttering under her breath. I popped through the doorway and said cheerily, "What can I do to help?"

"Get out!" shrieked Mother. "I didn't mean you. You do

this for your English tyrant husband day in and day out, for Christ's sake! I meant one of the others who've just sat on their asses all day." She strode back to the living room and bellowed, "B.D. is *not* to slave in my kitchen. She runs nonstop for that English bastard she's married to." Jeremy, as usual, pretended to be deaf and went on reading a magazine. Mother continued, "She's also pregnant, in case you've forgotten. Jesus!" She stormed back to the kitchen.

Marguerite was next to get up, saying over her shoulder as she followed Mother, "Let me do it, I understand her." Understand her she might, but Marguerite also returned covered with abuse for her efforts. Then Michael was heard from. "I think I'm 'the others who've just sat on their asses all day.' I'd better go and find out." He went to the kitchen and was greeted with "Well! It's about time you got off your ass."

The younger living-room crowd grew restless, so I fished around for playing cards. There weren't any to be found but I did come up with some dice. Jeremy volunteered to teach Chris and Mark how to shoot craps if it was O.K. with their father. Jerry said that it was and that he would like to join in. I fetched them some matchsticks for counters and they settled down on the floor near the doorway so they could use the baseboard as a backstop. The game was in full swing when the kitchen detail came to join us.

"Well! We finally finished that awful mess," Mother said as she stepped around the crapshooters. "Christ! I hope you all enjoyed sitting around while I did it all." Forced laugh. "I'm kidding. You know it was my great pleasure to serve you all. *Brother!* I'm dead." She collapsed dramatically into the nearest empty armchair and stared about her. The silence engendered by her entrance continued. She suddenly became aware of the group on the floor, apparently not having noticed them when she stepped around them. "What the hell are you doing down there?"

"They're shooting craps," I said. "It was my idea." I hoped that it being my idea might render it acceptable.

"Put it away," she ordered. "We're *not* playing games tonight."

"Why on earth not?" I asked. Stupid question.

"Because I'm *dead,* for your information, that's why not. I'm going to bed." She dragged herself out of her chair and began to ostentatiously empty ashtrays, open curtains for the morning and turn out lights, leaving her guests wondering why they had to go to bed at eight-thirty in the evening.

The rest of the Merrills' visit went fairly smoothly. My dinner the next night was peaceful, mostly because I had reminded everyone to thank Mother, not me. It didn't matter that I was the hostess . . . it was Mother's idea, therefore she must get the thanks. Mother also claimed the credit for teaching me everything I knew about cooking, but an exchange of knowing smiles between Marguerite and me satisfied us on that score.

Mother's career doldrums continued. She desperately wanted to get a "class" picture but, with her determination to live in the east, she was out of the mainstream and nothing but low-budget oddities came her way. Scripts for horror films weighed down her mailbox and I could hardly blame her for refusing even to read them. The trouble was that she had only two alternatives, rejoin the mainstream and thereby raise a higher profile, or make junk movies, and she wasn't willing to do either. Out of economic necessity she agreed, early in 1969, to do *Connecting Rooms,* the script for which she had read two years earlier. She made the movie in England with Sir Michael Redgrave and found some appeal in it because it was about some nice, if misfit, people who lived in a boardinghouse. She enjoyed working with Sir Michael and was comfortable with the movie because it was old-fashioned. Unfortunately, the critics and everyone else thought it a dud.

She was back in Connecticut with time to spare, as she had sworn she would be, for the birth of my child. On June 19 I stopped at Twin Bridges on my way home from a visit to my obstetrician. Sitting in the deep, overstuffed scoop chair in the corner of her dining room, sipping coffee and looking like a beached whale, I gave her the news. "No need to get excited yet, it could be another two weeks." "O.K., B.D.," she said, "but you better call me before you go to the hospital. I want to be there for the birth of my granddaughter."

"It just might be a grandson, you know," I said for the millionth time.

"Oh, come off it, B.D., it's a girl. You know I'm always right about these things."

"Be that as it may, I'm not going to call and wake you up if the baby decides to put in an appearance in the middle of the night."

"Wake me up, damn you! I won't miss this birth, come hell or high water."

"O.K., O.K.," I agreed, just to calm her down. I couldn't tell her that we didn't want her there, but neither did I want to make a promise which I had no intention of keeping. "But if we have to leave in a big hurry and there's no time to call, I promise that we'll let you know the minute the baby's born."

"You bitch! You call me!" She jumped up to get a cigarette but was so agitated that, in trying to strike a kitchen match on the underside of the dining table, she broke the heads off two before succeeding. With her cigarette lit, she calmed down. "Anyway, Jeremy may need me. Have you thought about that? Have you?"

Mother missed my look of disbelief and proceeded to conjure up a mind-boggling scenario. "I can picture Jeremy nervously pacing back and forth, utterly useless as men always are when you need them the most. You're lucky that I'll be there to take care of things, see to your comfort." Getting a faraway look in her eye, she went on, "I'll make sure that your room is properly prepared for you. I'll see to it that the nurses are on their toes . . . they're not going to be blasé around *my* daughter! No, sir, I'll see to *that*! After the baby's born and I've made sure that you're comfortably settled in for the night, I'll round up Jeremy. *Brother!* He'll be a *wreck*. We'll go to a local bar and go on a toot. What a celebration that will be! *Jesus!*" When she came to the end of this fantasy she gazed, spellbound, into space. I was at a loss for words.

Failing dismally in my search for an appropriate response, I said simply, "Surely you jest?" Mother was undeterred. "It'll be great. You'll see." I had to try to get her back to reality. "Mother, I don't want you interfering with the hospital staff and making a big to-do on my account. Aside from that, Jeremy is not the nervous type. He'll stay with me as long as they'll let him and then, most likely, sit in the fathers' waiting room and read a book until they call him."

"What?" shrieked Mother. "*Shit!* I'll take care of that. I've never heard of such a thing . . . he won't read while I'm there!" She finished with a great horse laugh, clearly enjoying the prospect of being able to straighten my husband out.

I struggled out of my chair, said that I had to get going, kissed Mother on the cheek and hurried home. I couldn't wait to tell Jeremy about the terrific plans Mother had in store for him. If it hadn't been obvious before, it certainly was now: My mother was not going to be anywhere near that hospital while I was delivering, not unless I wanted an earthquake of a disaster on my hands. Jeremy was very good at turning a deaf ear to Mother's insults. He had me convinced that at least half the time he truly didn't even hear what she was saying. There was, however, a limit to everyone's forbearance. Mother rushing about the hospital in a frenzy, ordering doctors and nurses around and telling Jeremy how expectant fathers are supposed to behave would be overstepping his limit by a considerable margin.

As I stepped through the door into the foyer of our house, my water broke . . . the baby was hours away, not weeks. I knew three things . . . I needed to get the doctor on the phone, put some towels on the floor and not call my mother. Jeremy came up from the den and helped me to bed, talked to the doctor and then asked whether I wanted him to call Mother while we waited for the labor pains to start.

"*No!*" I bellowed, then went on to tell him of Mother's hospital fantasy. He paled visibly as I talked and no more was said about it.

It was several hours before the pains started but, before the end of our twenty-minute drive to the hospital, they were two minutes apart. Since I had walked into the hospital under my own steam, the nurse on duty was very obvious in her skepticism. "I doubt it, dear," she said condescendingly, placing her hand on my stomach, "but we'll soon see." It seemed to be my day for making people pale . . . the nurse turned white. "The pains are ninety seconds apart! Why are you standing up? You should be in a wheelchair!" Jeremy had been irked by the nurse's attitude and now he had his chance. "If you'd taken my wife's word for it in the first place, she'd be in one by now, wouldn't she?" A wheelchair quickly materialized. Jeremy stayed and talked to me until I was taken into the delivery room. He did, indeed, sit calmly in the fathers' waiting room reading a book until the doctor called to tell him that he had a son and that mother and baby were in the pink.

While he was waiting for the baby and me to be brought out for his inspection, Jeremy called Mother. "Hello, Bette . . . it's a boy and they're both fine . . . Beed was only in the delivery room forty-eight minutes . . . we're naming him Jeremy Ashley." He told me that he spoke in telegramese in order to deliver the salient points before being interrupted.

"What do you mean? *Christ!* B.D.'s had her baby? You bastard! Why didn't you call me? You planned it this way, didn't you? I can't believe that you'd do this to me. God!" Jeremy was much too interested in his new son to recount the entire conversation, but apparently it went on in like vein for quite some time. When Mother came to visit me the next day, she was querulous at first but soon calmed down. She had vented most of her spleen on Jeremy.

Summer and fall passed blissfully by for Jeremy and me. Ashley was a healthy and cheerful baby who never ceased to delight us. Our closest friends in the area, Dick and Josie Hamm, were childless and were happy to be Ashley's godparents. Josie was Swiss and multilingual; she and Ashley had their own personal form of communication involving words like "schnookie" and "schnaukie-pautzie." I have no idea what they meant but Ashley gurgled and smiled whenever Josie used them. Mother hated it. To her it constituted baby talk, one of the foremost things of which she didn't approve. Her many snide comments, designed to compel Josie to "speak English," were completely wasted.

Josie invited Mother, as well as Jeremy and me, to her annual Christmas bash. We deliberately arrived early at the Hamms' in order to give Josie time to play with Ashley before the madding throng poured in. Mother was already there. While I set up a Port-a-Crib in the guest room, Josie took Ashley into the living room and began to speak their "language" and play pat-a-cake with him. Mother collared me on my way back to the living room. "Why do you permit that?"

"Permit what?"

"All that gooing and gaaing and baby talk. Jesus! I never let people talk to *you* that way."

"For heaven's sake don't get so testy, Mother. In the first place, Josie's not gooing and gaaing . . . she's talking to him in Schweizerdeutsch or whatever it's called and, apart from that, Ashley adores her . . . that's all that matters." Mother muttered something else but I ignored it and went to join Josie.

Other people began to arrive and Josie was having a grand time showing off her schnookie to each of them. Every so often, Mother stalked over to Josie and reminded her that Ashley belonged to me, not her, which caused Josie to laugh and explain that "Bette is schnaukie's grandmother."

"It's nice of you to remember," Mother would retort. None of this bothered Josie a bit. She went right on having a good time, utterly oblivious of Mother's growing discontent. Ashley finally began to fuss and I told Josie that it was time for his dinner and bed. I had barely taken him in my arms when Mother loomed at my elbow. "It's disgraceful to disrupt this beautiful party any longer with all this baby nonsense. I suggest, B.D., that you put this tired child to bed." Josie and I exchanged glances as I told Mother that I was just about to do that very thing.

As we were making our way through the crowd, Mother barged ahead of Josie and, when we arrived at the guest room, she barred the way. "I do not approve of a crowd to put a child to bed." I almost pointed out that Ashley had to have dinner first, but reckoned that she wouldn't approve of a crowd for that either. I let her continue, uninterrupted. "It is far too confusing for them. I *never* permitted it when *I* brought up *my* children. Bedtime is a serious affair and the sooner they learn it, the better."

"Yes, Bette," said Josie, departing obediently, but with eyes cast upward in despair. Fortunately, Ashley wasn't very hungry and, little tummy full, he fell asleep in minutes.

As I was returning to the party, Josie popped out of the kitchen and took me aside. "Wow! Your mother is really jealous. I'm sorry if I made things difficult for you."

"Don't give it a thought," I replied. "I know that grandparents are possessive of their grandchildren, but Mother is ridiculous."

"Well, I'll leave schnookie alone when she's around, then."

"Oh no you won't! You're Ashley's godmother and he adores you. Mother will just have to get used to it. It's not that she'd play with him if you didn't . . . she never plays with him. She simply wants to own him or, to use her words, be in charge of him. I'll be damned if I'll let Ashley be deprived of his fun with you because of my mother's hangups."

"I'm glad you feel that way," Josie said. "I've got to admit that I find her attitude overbearing."

"You insisted on inviting her," I reminded. "You can't say I didn't warn you."

"Oh, what the hell?" she said. "She is Bette Davis . . . she just sees things differently."

A little while later I became aware of a major ruckus down the hall. I made my way back and there was Josie, holding Ashley in her arms, his little face wet with tears. Mother was there also, shrieking hysterically, "Don't touch that baby! That's B.D.'s baby and she's in charge! If she'd wanted him picked up and coddled, she'd have done it herself. Put him down, this minute!"

"What happened?" I asked, pushing past Mother but not moving to take Ashley away from Josie.

"Josie has upset the baby," Mother declared, "and she has no business touching him in the first place." She stood back, a look of malicious triumph coming over her face, as though she had caught Josie in the act of a kidnapping and I was the cops.

"What happened, Josie?" I asked again, ignoring Mother's outburst.

"Little schnaukie was crying when I went past the door and I came in to see what the matter was . . . that's all." As the debate went on, Josie had gently rocked Ashley in her arms and now, with his grandmother no longer shrieking in his ear, he was almost asleep again. "Thanks, Josie," I said quietly. "I'm glad you heard him. Excuse me." Mother was still lurking nearby, glaring furiously at Josie. I took her arm and steered her out of the room, gently closing the door behind us. "For heaven's sake, what's wrong with you, Mother? What's so terrible about Josie comforting a crying baby? It's not as if he's at home in his own room, you know . . . there's a difference."

"I thought you wanted him to go to sleep. How is he supposed to do that if everybody keeps rushing in and spoiling him? That's what I'd like to know!"

"If he was sufficiently upset to wake up, he wouldn't have gone back to sleep anyway, so what's the difference? And besides, it isn't everybody, it's Josie . . . and she can pick him up any time she wants to."

"Fine, B.D., fine," Mother snarled. "*I* never permitted such confusion when I was bringing *you* up, but do it your way."

"Thank you," I said, "I shall."

It was a splendid buffet but Mother ate little. She seldom did, sitting or standing. As the party was beginning to get into full swing, music blaring, dance floor packed and with a bedlam of voices, Mother put on her coat, found Josie and thanked her stiffly for a lovely party. "Why are you leaving so early?" Josie asked. "The party's just starting."

"I do not approve of people overstaying their welcome and I most certainly do not drink after dinner. I don't know why all these people lack the manners to know the proper time to leave, but I do know. So, good night." And, indeed, she left, giving me the cold shoulder on her way out.

The next day, Josie phoned. "I know you told me that if I invited your mother it was my problem, so you don't have to say it again, but what was that all about?"

"What was what all about?" I asked.

"All that shit about not drinking after dinner and people not knowing when to leave a party."

"Oh that! That's nothing to worry about. Look, if you're going to socialize with my mother, you'd better start taking 'How to Cope with Bette Davis lessons.' The first thing you have to learn is that none of her rude habits are rude. It's double-think. Everyone else is rude . . . she's being polite. A lot of it relates to her drinking. She—"

"Oh, come on, B.D., I've seen her get plastered several times and I understand that part of it, but she wasn't last night."

"You didn't let me finish," I said. "On the matter of drinking, her position is well known. She's even held forth on it to the media . . . at least about drinking after dinner and drinking white wine, she has." Josie guffawed. "Drinking *what*?"

"White wine. But let me explain the whole thing. You never drink when you're working because that's unprofessional.

Mother is a professional, therefore she doesn't drink when she's working, or so she would have us believe. You never drink after dinner. You can get shit-faced at breakfast and drink all day, which Mother does, but it doesn't count unless you drink after dinner. People who drink after dinner are 'real drunks.' Mother doesn't drink after dinner, therefore she can deny until hell freezes over that she's a drunk."

"What happens if you don't have dinner at all?"

"Aha! Now you've got the idea. If dinner isn't served, you can go on drinking, provided that is that you aren't drinking white wine. The worst of all are people who drink white wine. They're alcoholics. That's why she'll never accept white wine except with a meal. The people who drink it are alcoholics pretending they're not drinking. They're not to be trusted because, in addition to being alcoholics, they're dishonest. It's all very simple when you understand the ground rules according to my mother."

We talked for a while longer and got a few laughs along the way.

"Thank you for explaining it all," said Josie.

"You're welcome," I replied, meaning it. At least she hadn't told me that I was "too hard on" my mother, or that I didn't "understand" her.

Mother had announced on our first anniversary that she would send us one dozen white roses on each anniversary for each year of our marriage. The second, third, fourth and fifth anniversaries had rolled by and every year a bigger and bigger box of roses had arrived. Now we were having our sixth and Mother called. "Since you're determined to stay married forever, damn you, I'm not going to send you a dozen roses for each year anymore. It's too goddamned expensive. *Jesus* . . . I'll go broke! I'll send you one rose for each year from now on."

"Whatever you like, Mother," I said. "I always did think that you'd got a little carried away."

"Yes . . . well . . . the fact is . . . and I never even hinted at this before . . . the fact is, I never thought you and Jeremy would last this long. *Jesus!*"

"You've hardly kept *that* a secret. You've told half the world that you can hardly wait for me to see the error of my ways and come running back to you. I'm sure that it will be a great relief to us all when you come to terms with the fact that I've never been happier."

"Never been happier? Ha! You can't fool me, young lady. If I'd known how long you were going to keep up this pretense, I'd never have consented to your marriage in the first place. Just don't expect so many roses, that's all." Click, dial tone.

Not long after Ashley's birth Mother had flown to the West Coast to guest-star in an episode of Robert Wagner's television series *It Takes a Thief*. R.J. had a soft spot for the older Hollywood greats and held them in high esteem. Mother instantly became enamored of him when he gave her the red-carpet treatment all the way, including an elegant dressing room and a limousine. She and R.J. developed a lasting friendship and he became a family friend. Usually when someone was a fan of Mother's it was so thick that I couldn't bear to be around, but this was not so with R.J. He obviously needed nothing from her and genuinely liked her. When she was in his company she was in splendid fettle, which made it very relaxing for the rest of us. She was also impressed by him as a sex symbol. Quite often, when he was in the east, he drove out to see her and Jeremy and I dined with them several times, sometimes at Twin Bridges and sometimes at Wildwoods. We never worried about such evenings because R.J.'s presence assured us of tranquillity. He and Mother also did a "No Generation Gap" Jim Beam advertisement together. Their photo ran full-page in all the major magazines and Mother was delighted with it.

R.J. happened to be in the east with Tina Sinatra the following spring when Mother decided to give me another birthday party, my twenty-third. Because he was one of the principal guests Mother wanted to invite, Jeremy and I decided to risk being seen with her one more time. The party, a dinner in a private dining room at one of the better local restaurants, was thoroughly enjoyable with Mother on her best behavior throughout.

When Jeremy and I got home after the party, we discussed the mellowing effect R.J. had upon Mother. Thinking back on similar situations, we discovered that there was a constant pattern. Whenever we had been anywhere with Mother, in public *or* in private, and other people had been present who were of sufficient stature to impress her, she had behaved properly. In addition to that, we realized that there were certain people in whose presence she remained abstemious, her lawyer-manager, Harold Schiff (he had replaced Tom Hammond some years earlier), and the Merrill family among them. We were delighted with our discoveries and filed the new data for future use.

We already knew that we could handpick small groups of people to weather Mother's worst when the occasion demanded. We had tested this premise when Mother had insisted upon giving me a twenty-first birthday party. In Maine she had always been good at writing clues for treasure hunts and she wanted to run such a hunt on this occasion. The clues were great, the ten carefully chosen couples could have held their own against Torquemada, and when Mother finished the day well into her cups and was rude to everyone, it begot nothing but cheers and laughter. Jeremy had been so heartened by the sight of a roomful of people as unawed by Mother as he was that, choosing his moment carefully, he proposed his first toast to her since the wedding. The guests fell about with laughter for several minutes while Mother kept shouting at them to shut up, that it was the nicest thing her son-in-law had ever said to her. As far as I know, she never did realize what Jeremy meant with his toast: "To Bette . . . a real *mother!*"

4

1970–1972

After Ashley's birth we entered a comparatively peaceful period in our relations with Mother that was to continue for two and a half years. She remained temperamental, of course, and continued to see things only from her own point of view, but the constant tension virtually disappeared. There was also a gradual lessening of her resentment of Jeremy and her desire to break up our marriage. I wasn't sure whether it was due to my now having things like a maid and a lawn service or to the existence of her little grandson, and I didn't much care. As long as she was finally coming to accept the fact of my marriage and not trying to make trouble and embarrass me at every opportunity, the reason was unimportant.

Jeremy was the ultimate in proud fathers. He took his baby son with him wherever he went. He was forever bundling up a delighted Ashley, putting him in his car seat and hauling him around on errands. Mother's attitude had changed so dramatically that Jeremy, Ashley in tow, fell into the habit of stopping off at Twin Bridges from time to time, to have coffee with Mother on his way home. It was truly amazing. Jeremy told me that she was always pleasant and polite, sometimes even ef-

196

fusive, and that they had begun to get along very well. He believed that it was because of Ashley that the change had come about.

It was almost too good to be true and I asked myself if it could really be happening. My husband's willingness to let bygones be bygones didn't surprise me, but Mother's new attitude was such a complete about-face that I sometimes had trouble accepting it. No longer did she try to ensnare us in her schemes. No longer did I hear about "that English bastard." Instead I heard "How darling Jeremy is with that baby" and similarly pleasant comments. Jeremy continued his spontaneous visits with Ashley, I increased the frequency of my visits, we began to drop by for cocktails now and then and, in due course, began to accept invitations to dinner without hesitation. It was all quite marvelous and because Mother had finally made it possible for my husband to like her, I felt that my loyalty to her through the bad years had been redeemed.

Mother frequently failed to grasp the gist of things and it was invariably the result of her not listening. Everything she saw or heard, she only saw or heard subjectively. She loved to read, but if I had read the same book as she, and we had occasion to discuss it, I wound up wondering whether we had, indeed, read the same thing. The fact was that we hadn't. We had read the same *book* but not the same *thing*. Discussion of a book was rendered impossible because Mother only read with an eye to the role she would play if the piece were made into a movie. If there was no such role, she called the book "utterly boring" and put it aside. If the character she found for herself were only a small part of the plot, she ballooned it into the focal point of the story and, in her recollection of the book at a later date, slanted everything to suit her assumed role.

At dinner one night, Mother's failure to grasp the gist of a conversation reached new heights and Michael was the victim. He was home from college for the weekend and told us about the drug problem on campus. It had become so alarming that the college had set up a roadblock for the purpose of searching cars as they entered the campus. "The trunk of my MG was opened the other day. They told me it was a search for marijuana." Mother, who was coming out of the kitchen as he spoke, snapped, "What do you mean you had marijuana in your trunk?"

"No, Mother," Michael was quick to explain. "You missed the beginning of the conversation. I didn't have anything in my trunk. I said that cars entering the campus were being routinely searched. They're mostly looking for pot. You know I don't smoke, for heaven's sakes, and certainly not pot."

"What do pots have to do with marijuana? Do you mean to tell me you hide it in pots?"

"*Pot . . .* not pots. *Pot* is another word for marijuana. Forget it . . . I didn't have any . . . otherwise I'd have been arrested."

"*Arrested?*" she howled. "Oh my *God*, Michael! What the hell are you thinking of? How can you become a lawyer if you have an arrest record?" She threw her hands over her head in a desperate gesture, then rushed to the bar for a stiff drink.

"Mother, listen to me, O.K.?" asked Michael. "I was not arrested. I don't smoke joints and never intend to." I don't know why he switched to joints, having already explained pot, but he did . . . and quickly regretted it. "So calm down. We were merely having an innocent conversation about the drug problem on college campuses. There's absolutely nothing to worry about."

"Nothing to worry about? Ha! If you aren't stupid enough to keep it in your car, then why do you smoke it in joints? I don't understand you, Michael, I really don't."

"Mother," I said, unable to keep silent any longer, "Michael doesn't smoke anything. He just said that." Jeremy was on the verge of falling off his chair with laughter and was holding his hand firmly over his mouth.

"Come off it!" Mother bellowed. "Michael is the one who mentioned joints. Don't you think I know what I hear? Jesus!"

"Mother, will you please just listen?" pleaded Michael. "I didn't say I smoked in joints. I said I didn't smoke joints. I don't smoke anything. They're all the same thing: pot, joints, grass, marijuana. I'm sorry I—"

"*Marijuana!* Now you're talking about marijuana again. I can't believe this. How can you do this to me?" She ran her hands through her hair in another desperate gesture. Jeremy stepped into the breach. "Look, Bette, Michael wasn't caught with any drugs and wasn't arrested. He assures us that he doesn't use them and I believe him. Since the topic is so upsetting, why don't we drop it at this point with the hope and expectation that Michael will continue to fight the good fight?"

"That's a good idea," Mother conceded, "but before we drop it, there is just one thing. *Michael*"—she stared intensely at my brother for a few seconds—"I beg of you, on my knees, to promise me that you will have nothing further to do with marijuana. Christ! It will ruin you!"

"Mother," Michael began, "I told you that . . . oh, never mind. Yes, Mother, I promise."

"Thank God!" Mother sighed, collapsing into a chair in exhaustion.

Late in 1970 Mother went to California to do a film for American International Pictures. She asked Jeremy whether he knew anything about the company and was not comforted to learn, too late, that AIP had been founded on, and almost exclusively made, low-budget exploitation movies. "Thanks a heap, creep!" was her response to Jeremy's unwelcome input. The picture was called *Bunny O'Hare* and she starred with Ernest Borgnine. Dressed as hippies, the two of them had to race around New Mexico on a motorcycle robbing banks. Mother was in constant fear for her life. She also hated the concept of "all location" filming, which she vowed never to do again. The picture was another dud and Mother sued AIP for mangling, in the cutting room, what she thought would be a film of at least *some* redeeming value.

Upon her return from the coast, Mother had Margot at Twin Bridges for one of her irregular visits and she invited me for lunch. Margot had been at the same school in New York State for many years and regarded it as home. Now nineteen, her mental development had stopped at the age of six but, thanks to the school, she had become very easy to deal with and was always smiling and cheerful when she arrived for her visits. All Margot really wanted was to please people and one only had to be minimally kind to her in order to make her happy. Every so often Mother insisted that Margot spend a week or two with her, but I never understood why. She was grossly inept, even cruel, in her treatment of Margot and my heart frequently bled for the poor child. During each visit Margot would spend a few days with me and I never had any trouble with her. The only truly annoying habit she had was to go on an occasional talking jag and, when she did this, one only had to tell her to stop and simultaneously assure her that one wasn't angry.

When I arrived for lunch, Margot was waiting at the door. With Ashley perched on my left hip, I said hello to Mother and gave Margot a hug with my free right arm.

"Hello, B.D.," Margot said. "Ashley's so cute. Isn't he cute, Mother?"

"I know he's cute, Margot. Jesus! You don't have to tell me he's cute."

"Thank you, Margot," I said. "I think he's cute too. You look very pretty today. That's a lovely dress and I like the hair ribbon that matches it."

"Mother gave me this dress. It's new. Isn't it pretty?"

"Yes, it's very pretty. It—"

"Margot!" Mother barked. "Who the hell else would give you a dress? *Brother!* Go and sit."

"Let's go to the living room," I suggested, starting in that direction. When I was halfway across the dining room, Mother snapped at Margot again, "Don't stand there like a moron, Margot! Go with B.D., for Christ's sake!" I felt the familiar pang. Mother went to the kitchen and I put Ashley on the floor. Margot and I sat down and watched him toddle around for a minute or so before Margot, first glancing in the direction of the kitchen, leaned close to me and asked, with a troubled little frown. "Am I a moron, B.D.?"

"Of course not," I replied. "You're a very sweet, nice girl. Mother doesn't mean to say such things. They're just expressions she uses without thinking, so don't worry about it. O.K.?"

"I *am* a nice girl?" She giggled and squirmed in her way.

"A *very* nice girl," I confirmed. More smiles and giggles.

Mother entered the room and Margot stopped smiling. "What are you giggling about?" I answered, "Nothing much, Mother. Margot's happy to see me, that's all."

"Isn't Ashley funny, the way he stumbles around?" said Margot. Mother glared at her and said scathingly, "I think

Ashley gets around *brilliantly* for his age." Margot stretched out her hand toward Ashley but, before he reached it, he tripped and fell. He chuckled as he got up, but Mother yelled, "If you'll just leave him alone, Margot, he'll be fine."

"Mother," I protested, "it wasn't Margot's fault that Ashley fell down. Please leave it to me to worry about my baby." Margot looked crushed and uncertain. I squeezed her hand. "It's O.K., Margot, you didn't do anything wrong. Ashley isn't that steady on his feet yet." Margot began to brighten, but Mother yelled again. "I'm *thrilled* that you're so wonderful at coping with Margot! Maybe you should have her stay with you if you're so understanding. You try having her twenty-four hours a day!" Margot started to cry and Mother stormed out of the room. I said something soothing to Margot and told her to keep an eye on Ashley, to call me if he got into any kind of trouble.

I caught up with Mother in the kitchen. "You're hurting Margot's feelings. Can't you see that?"

"Shit, B.D.! Don't tell *me* how to deal with Margot. She'd sleep all day if I let her. I have to drag her out of bed, then watch her take hours to get dressed and forever to eat breakfast. Brother! She's so slow it drives me crazy. You think it's so easy . . . try it sometime!"

"I do, every time she stays with me . . . or have you forgotten? It's not her fault that she only has one speed. *I* let her sleep till noon and give her two meals instead of three. That gives me the morning to myself and no hassle."

"Oh, *you* have all the answers, don't you? Just lay off, will you?"

As I went back to the living room, Mother called to Margot, "Would you like Coke with lunch?"

"Yes, please," Margot said. "Would Ashley like a Coke too?"

"Don't be an idiot!" Mother shouted. "Ashley's a baby and babies don't drink Coke. Christ! Stop being so stupid, Margot!"

"It was nice of you to think of Ashley, Margot," I said with a smile. She perked right up.

Lunch was ready and we took our seats, Ashley in his high chair. I should mention that Margot had a strictly limited curiosity about anything except Indians. Indians had captured her imagination and were her favorite topic of conversation. The school had found every available first-grade-level storybook touching upon the subject.

"Do you think there are Indians in those woods?" asked Margot, gazing out of the dining-room window.

"Shit!" shrieked Mother, almost apoplectic at the mention of Margot's favorite and oft-discussed topic. "I'm sick of hearing about Indians. There hasn't been a *fucking* Indian in Connecticut since the beginning of time!" Margot, who would cry at the slightest personal cirticism, was intrepid when it came to Indians. "There *were* Indians here before the white man came."

"Well, there aren't any now . . . so shut up about it!" Margot looked perplexed, and it was obvious to me, if not to Mother, that until she got a satisfactory answer regarding the whereabouts of a tribe of Connecticut Indians, real or imaginary, she would continue to pursue the subject. "Where did they all go? Are they the ones in the state park where I went with my school last week?"

"What?" Mother squawked. "What are you talking about? What state park?"

"The one I went to with my school. They have a whole Indian village there and the squaws ground corn while we watched. *I* could grind corn. *I* could be a squaw." I thought Mother's eyes would bug right out of her head.

If she didn't want to discuss Indians with Margot, all she had to do was give her something resembling an intelligent answer to one question and then announce a change of subject but, for reasons I could never fathom, Mother wouldn't do that. "Are you crazy? Jesus! How can *you* be a *squaw?*"

"I'll be Chief Red Cloud's squaw when he comes to get me. He likes me a lot." Mother was clearly nearing the end of her tether. She jumped out of her chair, planted her fists on the table and screeched at Margot, "Who the *fuck* is Chief Red Cloud?"

"I met him at the Indian village and he said he liked me. I bet he'll come to get me. Maybe he's out in the woods right now."

"I hope he does come to get you," Mother blurted, heading for the kitchen. "I can't take any more of this." Margot looked at me and, with considerable excitement in her voice, asked, "Do *you* think Chief Red Cloud could be in the woods, B.D.? Do you?"

"No, dear," I soothed, "he's not out *there*. He's still at the state park and he already has a wife. Anyway, you know you're too young to get married."

"Some Indians have more than one wife. Do you think he'll wait for me?"

"No, Margot. Red Cloud's tribe only allows one wife. Now . . . that's enough about Indians. It's getting Mother upset."

"Why?" asked Margot.

"I guess Mother doesn't like Indians."

"That's a shame. I'm sure they'd like her."

"That may well be, Margot, but we aren't going to talk about it anymore, O.K.?"

"O.K."

When Mother returned to the table, Ashley was beginning to fuss. I checked whether he needed changing, thanked Mother for lunch and took my leave. On my way out the door, I heard Margot say, "Why don't you like Indians, Mother?" I ran for the hills.

Mother again had an opportunity to work with Robert Wagner when, in the spring of 1971, she did *Madam Sin* with him. Co-produced by R.J. and Sir Lew Grade, the movie was made in England and locations were shot in Scotland's imposing and barren coastal landscape. They had hoped to sell the film as a series, but it wound up as a television movie on ABC.

When she returned from England, Mother asked if Ashley, now about two years old, could spend the day at her house once a week. She wanted to get to know him and have him feel close to her. Things had been going so well that I couldn't bring myself to deny her the opportunity to spend time with her grandson; however, I had to find a way of ensuring his safety. Not only was there Mother's drinking to worry about, but also the existence of the river near her house. Ashley, like any two-year-old, could cover a lot of ground very quickly and I couldn't trust Mother to keep a constant eye on him.

I found the chance to have a private word with Vik. He fully understood my concern and willingly agreed to be Ashley's watchdog. The visits began and worked out better than expected. I got a day off, Mother was happy and Vik got to play with Ashley instead of running perpetual errands. I might have foreseen that it was the *idea* of having her grandson around that appealed to Mother, rather than the chance to actually play with him and get to know him. In any event, Ashley enjoyed his weekly visits until they ended later in the year when Mother went to California. This time it was to do another series pilot with Doug McClure called *The Judge and Jake Wyler*. She expressed nothing but contempt for McClure and thought the whole show stank. It too failed to be picked up as a series.

Mother spent a few weeks at La Costa, a health spa, then went to Italy to make *Lo Scopone Scientifico (The Scientific Card-player)*. This turned out to be disastrous from the start. Mother had never before encountered a bi- or multilingual production with stars from two or more countries, in which each ethnic group films in its own language. Mother and Joseph Cotten were the only English-speaking actors, all the others being Italian, and Mother refused to understand why they wouldn't make *everyone* speak English in her scenes. It did no good to explain to her that audiences in Italy didn't want to hear their stars dubbed from English to Italian. As far as Mother was concerned, that was *their* problem . . . let them shoot the whole thing twice if they wanted to, but everybody in a scene with her should speak English. Even the director suddenly forgot how to speak English and communicated with her through an interpreter. That she stayed and did the picture will always mystify me. She did, however, get revenge of sorts. The picture was a dismal failure, even though the Italian critics gave Mother good reviews, and was never shown outside Italy.

In 1972, Jeremy and I decided to have an open house on Christmas Eve. It was my favorite night of the year and I could never get to sleep easily. It seemed like a good idea to have a party, invite hordes of people, particularly ones with children, and enjoy ourselves until the children were tired enough to go to bed voluntarily. It was one of our better ideas and we still do it.

I laid on a huge buffet, gallons of eggnog and enough soda pop to inflate every child in Connecticut. Over two hundred people came and went during the course of the evening and it was a most gratifying success. Except for one dismal incident, that is.

Mother cornered one of the guests, a close friend by the name of Leslie Kelley. Leslie was an extremely successful career woman; although still in her twenties, she was a computer-program designer. She and her husband, Bill, a chemical engineer, were unable to have children. Leslie was charming, intelligent, attractive and successful but, for some obscure reason, shy and insecure. Mother's instinct for attacking only people who were vulnerable was as good as ever. I didn't hear everything she dumped on Leslie because I was in another room when she began, but certain lines remain clearly in my mind. "You're not a real woman unless you have children." "Why don't you think of your husband instead of your precious little career?" "I don't understand why B.D. invited you . . . this party is for families." By the time I reached Leslie's side, she was in tears. People had fallen silent everywhere and were staring at my mother, and the children on the living-room levels of the house were standing wide-eyed and still.

I took Mother firmly by the elbow and marched her, despite her loud and abusive protests, to the kitchen. With inspired creativity I suggested that if she really wanted to fix Leslie, she should leave immediately in a cab. By doing so, I said, she would make Leslie feel guilty for causing my mother to leave and ruining my party. Mother bought it, left in a huff and the party was saved. I later found out that Leslie's great offense had been to say to Mother how nice it was that she and Bill had a chance to spoil Ashley since they had no children of their own.

Jeremy and I wasted much breath conjecturing as to what had sent Mother round the bend after two or more years of peace. We had always known that being the center of attention was life and death to her, but why had the rude, despicable Bette Davis appeared again all of a sudden? We concluded that being in a room full of children and their parents, all engrossed in fun and Christmas and none of them caring two hoots about famous movie stars, was too much for Mother to bear. Whatever the reason, we were certain the honeymoon had ended, and Mother's subsequent reversion to her old ways would confirm our fears.

5

1973

I began to believe there was more to Mother's Christmas Eve scene than I had supposed at the time. In January she was preparing to leave for California to do some more work about which she was less than excited. She looked thoroughly disgusted and down in the mouth as she told me about the pilot script for a half-hour comedy television series called *Hello Mother, Goodbye.* She hated the whole idea but had to take a stab at it because she needed the money.

Mother bewailed the fact that "doing things for money" was all she seemed to have been involved in for the last nine years. The last thing she had taken any pride in was *Hush, Hush, Sweet Charlotte,* and even that had been pasted by the critics. She felt old and tired and fed up and bored with working. It seemed to her that she worked almost constantly and had little to show for it financially and nothing whatever artistically. Also eating at her was the main thing I was never able to understand— that despite her Yankee work ethic, she resented working for "the dough." She worked hard at projecting an image of working only for the sake of art, never for the money involved. I pointed out again and again that all people worked for money, that there was no disgrace in it and that she should take the highest-paying job available if there was nothing around that inspired her artistically; and to hell with all the worry. Mother maintained that it was less disgraceful to take a *cheap* project out of need than to "soak everyone and be a cheat" with an expensive one. She couldn't get ahead financially because, despite this philosophy, she loved to spend money and did so like a drunken sailor. Earning money and spending money were unrelated in Mother's eyes.

It was in a very discouraged state, therefore, that she left Twin Bridges for California to film *Hello Mother, Goodbye*. This series was not picked up either. While she was out there she did a Dean Martin "Celebrity Roast" and, at the last minute, a guest-star appearance in an NBC movie, *Scream, Pretty Peggy*. It was another thriller and Mother shot her son at the end of it.

My brother, Michael, who had become engaged at Christmas to his longtime girl friend, Chou-Chou Raum, was getting married in the spring. Although Michael had only been home from college for the occasional weekend and for part of vacations, times when Mother was annoyed more often than not by everything he did, she began to affect a state of loneliness and abandonment. In every interview she stated that the only meaning in her life was her work: "In the final analysis, work is all there is. Family doesn't last . . . they all go off. Human relationships . . . ha! . . . they're a joke. All there is is work, and I'm damned lucky to have it." Privately she sought to project an image of devoted mother whose son lived at home and who was bored and fed up with work, but had to do it to provide. She expressed a desire to ". . . buy a shack on the coast of Maine and become an old character beachcomber," but, when I suggested she go ahead and do it if it would make her happy, she told me not to be absurd: "I have my work to do."

Whenever Mother was at her most disillusioned with the film industry, she returned whence she had come, to the stage. This was why, several months earlier, she had agreed to do a personal-appearance tour. In February, on her return from the West Coast, she opened at Town Hall in New York City with a show called *An Informal Evening with Bette Davis*. It consisted of many film clips, selected from her more than eighty movies, and a question-and-answer session with the audience. It was a morale-and-ego boost for Mother at a time when she sorely needed it. The house was jam-packed and she was met with giant ovations each night.

They loved *her* and *she* loved *them*. After New York she took the show to Saratoga, New York, and Princeton, New Jersey, where the receptions were equally tremendous. In March she opened *An Informal Evening with Bette Davis* in Denver, Colorado, and took it to twenty-eight cities, ending in Hartford, Connecticut, in April. She was tired but sufficiently uplifted to fly to Chicago to accept the Sarah Siddons Award and be back for Michael's wedding on May 19.

Michael had completed college and was moving to Boston to attend Boston University Law School. Marriage is not easy for a student, particularly a law student, but Michael and Chou-Chou were determined to forge ahead despite the difficulties that faced them. Chou intended to work full time and they were very happy. Mother had stridently voiced her disapproval but attended their wedding, side by side with Gary.

Mother's outlook was so improved by her reception everywhere during the tour that I dared hope that Christmas Eve might prove to have been an isolated incident. It was not. When Ashley turned four in June, Mother began her new campaign by warning me that I had only one year left and that I had better enjoy it: "Boys turn on you when they're five . . . I know about these things." She followed this by again becoming obsessed with my "dull rut of a marriage." Having gone through her entire routine all over again—affairs on the side add spice, Jeremy had been cheating from day one, etc.—she did at least give me something by which to remember her thoughts on marriage. Toward the end of the usual argument, when I reiterated that I had been happily married for nine years and intended to go right on doing what had brought me my happiness, she said, "Christ! What the hell do you know about marriage anyway? You've been married to the same dull bastard for nine years. You're just like all those other people who claim to be such experts on the subject after twenty years with the same dull man. Brother! They make me sick! *I've* been married four times . . . *I* know what I'm talking about . . . *God,* do I know!"

* * *

There was nothing at all on Mother's career horizon. She was beginning to slide into a depression when Harold Schiff came from New York to tell her that she had to sell Twin Bridges. Her expenses were extremely high and she needed the money. He advised her to find a small rental. She was indignant and recited all the work she had done over the past few years, culminating with the weeks on tour with her show. He said that although she had earned quite a bit from the tour, she hadn't really netted that much after expenses, that the show had been more an exposure than a big money-maker. Mother had to accept her manager's assessment of the situation. Citing Michael's moving away as her reason, she sold Twin Bridges and moved into a charming little house, also on the river and even closer to me in Weston. She named it My Bailiwick and settled all her furniture in.

Mother liked her new home, but the circumstances which had forced her move added greatly to her poor state of mind. She had loved Twin Bridges and hated to give it up. That, coupled with the fact that there weren't even any offers of work, led to an increasingly serious drinking problem. Her drinking had been pretty heavy for many years, but now it became really serious. She not only drank in the morning, she was actually drunk by 10:00 A.M. and stayed that way until bedtime. This, added to the problem of no longer having a separate apartment to withdraw to, became an unbearable strain for Vik. After a couple of stormy months at Bailiwick, he was forced to take his leave of Mother. I was sorry to see him go but I couldn't blame him in the least.

With Vik's departure the last restraint on Mother's drinking was removed. I continued to stop by to see her, but it was increasingly difficult to ignore her state of intoxication and the deterioration of her house. She had stopped keeping things tidy, but resented my trying to pick up for her. She said that now she was alone, there was no reason to worry about it. "Who cares anyway?" she asked one day.

"I care," I replied, "and so do a lot of other people. I know you're feeling down, but you've got to pull yourself together and go back to work. That's what you really need."

"What the hell do you know, B.D.?" she asked resentfully. "You deserted me years ago. Just get away from me! I don't *have* to do a goddamned thing!"

"For your *own* sake you *must*. You can't be happy living like this . . . it's a pigsty. Look around you."

She peered about her blearily and started to whimper like a frightened child. "Happy? Happy? I've never been happy. All my life I've had to fight the world. Everyone has always tried to get me. Well, I had the last laugh . . . I fixed them. They're still trying but I won't let them."

"Mother, nobody is trying to *get* you. If you'll just stop drinking, you'll see things in a better light."

"Oh, is that so? I suppose you think I'm drunk?" She suddenly screwed her face into a frighteningly vicious mask and shrieked, "Get out, you bitch! Get out of here!"

But I was determined to at least *try* to penetrate the alcoholic fog. "I won't get out until you listen to me. Even if you never work again as long as you live, do you want the whole world to say that Bette Davis disappeared into a whiskey bottle? You *have* to stop this drinking. I'll keep on coming to see you, more often if you like, but you've got to promise me that you'll try to pull yourself together." While I was speaking she pushed herself out of her chair, fixed a sickly smile on her face and assumed a shakily defiant posture. When I was finished, she hissed, "You just go back to your cozy little life, why don't you? Go back to the husband and son you say you love so much and leave me alone. You don't approve of me, so get out of here." Then in a scream, "I don't care! Get out!"

Mother's phone rang and, since I was next to it, I answered it. It was her agent and I said as much as I held the phone out to her. She lurched forward and snatched it away from me. "Yes? What is it, Robby?" She listened for a minute, then shouted, "You can tell him to go fuck himself! I won't make that piece of shit! I don't care what he's offering!" She slammed the receiver down.

"What was that?" I asked.

"Some piece of crap that Robby thinks I should do. Well, I won't . . . they'd better get *that* through their heads. I throw all their scripts in the garbage." She cackled wildly at the thought, but I was startled. All this time I had been under the impression that no work had been offered her, yet here she was hanging up on Robby and bragging about throwing unread scripts in the garbage. "Mother," I said sternly, "you really must stop this. You have to work and you know it. You can't just insult everyone who's trying to help you."

"Shut up! I'll work when I get some good scripts and not before!"

"How do you know whether they're good or not when you don't even read them?"

"I just know. I've done pretty well so far without your advice. Stop giving it to me now . . . get out of here!" She stared at me, then screamed, "Get out of here!" She stumbled over to the bar, laughing and talking to herself. I left.

Mother's drinking got worse. There didn't seem to be any time of the day or night when she wasn't staggeringly, slurringly drunk. Understanding her speech was extremely difficult, but since she repeated herself many times over, one could eventually figure out what she was saying.

She called me every day and begged me to come see her, forgetting completely that I had been there the day before. Each time I went I hoped to get through to her, but each time it was the same. Within minutes of my arrival she began to curse me and heap abuse upon me. All of her life, she had had someone on hand to berate. In the early years she fought with Ruthie; then, in succession, Aunt Bobby, Viola and Vik were her whipping boys. Now, there was no one for her to scream at and abuse except me when I visited. I have no doubt that she treated her husbands similarly. I know this was so with Gary.

I ran errands for her a couple of times each week, mostly to buy food. She refused to call the market to have food delivered, although, of course, the liquor supply was constantly replenished. Somebody was delivering that, but she didn't seem to care if there was no food in the house. My stomach had been causing me more and more distress throughout all this and one day Jeremy dragged me to the doctor. Before we left the house, I phoned Mother to tell her that I wouldn't be over until afternoon.

"If you don't come right this minute, when I need you," she said, "you can go to hell!" I said that I would see her later.

The doctor diagnosed colitis, gave me a prescription and

told me to avoid stress. On the way home, Jeremy and I discussed my dilemma. He agreed that I couldn't abandon my mother at a time like this, but urged that I stop trying to be her psychiatrist. "You aren't qualified and, so far, all you've done is make yourself sick. I don't think anything you say will make a bit of difference. Your physical presence and assurances that you love her are all you can offer. She really ought to have professional help."

"I know, but the thought of trying to convince Harold of that is worse than being shouted at by Mother."

"You're probably right, but you mustn't fight with her anymore. Just be there and mumble inanities. If you keep fighting with her about the drinking, you're going to wind up in the hospital yourself."

I went on visiting Mother and did my best to heed my husband's advice. It wasn't easy to do nothing but assure her that I loved her and "mumble inanities." The colitis grew a little worse but I didn't have any violent attacks. Mother's condition remained the same.

One day, Harold called. He said that Mother seemed to be having a drinking problem and asked whether I knew what was causing it. I told him that she had had a drinking problem for several years. It was just that now, being alone, she didn't have anyone from whom to hide it and it had become much worse. He said, as I had known he would, that I was imagining this, that she had never drunk to excess before, that this was something new and that I should do something about it. He said that Robby had told him that Mother was hanging up on people, refusing to read scripts and insulting producers when they tried to talk to her. Nor was she answering her mail.

I informed him that I was all too well aware of all of it, having been to see her practically every day. I told him all that had transpired to date and added that I didn't think I would be able to pull this particular piece of fat out of the fire. I didn't mention the suspicion that had been growing in me for some time, that what was behind all this was Mother's desire to get me so upset that I leave my family and become her next companion. That was, after all, the life she had intended for me until I let her down by getting, and staying, married. I did tell Harold that Mother should have professional help. He said that she would never accept it and, anyway, if word got out about it, it could be disastrous for her career.

At the end of the conversation it was still my problem. A new secretary-companion, even if one were found, would never accept the job with Mother in this condition and outside help was categorically ruled out. I was the one Mother loved, he told me again, and I had to help her, I owed it to her. I agreed to keep on trying.

Within minutes of Harold's call I was beset with such stomach pain and cramps that I had to lie down. Jeremy was out and wouldn't be home until evening. I dialed my doctor's number but he was at a medical convention. I lay there, hoping that the pain would let up. I had taken the maximum dosage of my medicine and then some, but it wasn't helping. At least Ashley wouldn't be home from school for a few hours.

It finally became too much for me, so I phoned Josie to see if she had any ideas. She said that she had and would be right over. She arrived in fifteen minutes, helped me to her car and twenty minutes later we were in the emergency room of the hospital. I wasn't in the mood to appreciate it at the time but, in retrospect, the scene in the emergency room was very funny.

It took the first five minutes to convince the duty doctor that I had any right to be there. He felt that I should have waited for the family physician to get back from his convention. When he finally deigned to consider my plight, it was just like that old joke: "Have you ever had anything like this before?" "Yes, I have." "Well, you have it again." He gave me a new prescription for a sedative, told me to take two pills every four hours until the major attack wore off, then one every four hours until I was well again. He told me to stay in bed as much as possible for a few days and to avoid stress.

Josie took me home, put me to bed and stayed with Ashley until Jeremy got home. He made dinner for himself and Ashley and some soup for me to have with my next two pills. I slept until late the next morning. When I awoke I felt much better. I still had a stomachache, but nothing like the one I had had the day before. The previous evening I had briefly apprised Jeremy of Harold's call, which seemed to have brought on the attack. Now I filled him in on all the details, including my suspicion as to what lay behind Mother's behavior.

We discussed it as calmly and quietly as possible. We agreed that, provided I was fully recovered by the following day, I should give it one more try. Jeremy volunteered to come with me, but I convinced him that his presence would negate whatever slim chance I might have of success. The next day I was feeling better and went to Bailiwick.

I knocked on the kitchen door for a long time before Mother peered through the glass and slurred, "Who's there?"

"It's me, B.D. . . . open the door."

"I don't need any errands today. I'm just fine."

"Mother! Open the door!" I heard the key turn in the lock and pushed the door open. Mother staggered away from me into the living room and literally fell into a chair. I followed her and looked around. It was an unbelievable mess. "Good God! How could you do this, Mother? I'm going to clean up, whether you like it or not."

"Suit yourself," she replied, continuing to gaze blankly at the television set.

The doctor had told me to avoid hard work for as long as possible, but the physical effort of cleaning up Mother's house was preferable to the emotional drain of trying to reason with her, so I set to work. I picked up the clothes which were strewn everywhere, emptied and washed dozens of ashtrays, which were overflowing onto tables in every room, collected and washed the three-day accumulation of dirty dishes that had been left all over the house, threw out spoiled food, wiped the tables and cleaned the floors. Then I went upstairs. The bedroom looked like a neglected slum and smelled worse: stale cigarette smoke mixed with whiskey fumes and the odor of rancid food. Plates of half-eaten meals, empty glasses, liquor bottles, dirty, rumpled clothing and magazines were everywhere. The bed was an indescribable mess with cigarette burns and overflowing ashtrays, dropped bits of food and spilled whiskey all around it. I cleaned all that up too, cleaned the bathroom with its clogged toilet bowl, changed her bed linens, put the soiled linens, towels and clothes into the laundry, then vacuumed the entire house.

It had taken several hours, but I was finished and I still felt fine. Whenever I had passed by her earlier, Mother was still sitting, unmoving, before the television set. Now I went to beard her. She looked up at me accusingly and said, "I can't find my drink."

"I know. I threw it out when I washed up . . . you don't need it. I'm of a mind to empty all the liquor in the house down the drain. Have you looked in a mirror lately? You're a drunk, Mother, nothing but a broken-down drunk." While I waited for her response, I tried to look her in the eye, but she wouldn't meet my gaze.

"Think what you like," she muttered. "It's really none of your business, is it?"

"It damned well is my business, Mother! Someone has to get through to you . . . you're sick. Don't you understand that? You can't go on drinking yourself into oblivion every day . . . you've got to stop!"

"If that's the way you feel," she replied with the same eerie calm she'd been displaying since my arrival, "I guess I no longer have a daughter. You've said what you came to say, so why don't you leave now? I know you don't like me . . . fine . . . just get out of here. And you needn't bother to throw out the Scotch, I'll just get more."

"Mother!" I shouted. "I will not watch you drink yourself to death! Think of your professional pride, if nothing else. You're a great actress . . . your fans don't want to read that Bette Davis is now a sad old drunk, rotting away in Connecticut." I thought that by shouting I might be able to shock her into a reaction: tears, anger, anything.

"So you think I'm a sad old drunk," she said as calmly as before, but maneuvering herself with great difficulty to her feet. "How very interesting. Good-bye. You don't need to come and see me anymore, since I disgust you so." She shoved me toward the front door and, though far bigger and stronger, I didn't resist.

"Mother, face it," I pleaded as we reached the door, "it's not a question of what I think . . . it's a fact. You've become a pathetic drunk. Pull yourself together before it's too late."

"I like it this way, B.D." She pulled open the front door and leaned heavily against the wall. "I have no daughter. That's the way you want it and it's fine with me. I won't stand here and be insulted." I was wondering whether to tell her what I really believed when she screamed, "Get out!" Her white cat strolled into the doorway and she managed to bend over to pick it up. "That's my Belle," she cooed, leaving the door open and lurching away from me down the hall. "You love me, don't you?"

I made certain the door was locked and closed it as I left. During the short drive home my vision blurred with tears, but I didn't know for whom I was crying. I hadn't experienced anything like this before and I hadn't the least notion of what to do next. I wasn't even sure that I still wanted to do anything. I regained my composure by the time I reached home and described it all to Jeremy. "I don't know where to go from here," I finished. "She told me that if I thought she was a drunk, she no longer had a daughter. You wouldn't have believed the state of the house. A pig wouldn't live in it. I cleaned it up because I couldn't stand not to and because it was easier than trying to talk to her. She's so far gone she thinks the cat I gave her is the only thing that loves her."

Jeremy shook his head and looked thoughtful. "Did you tell her you love her . . . that you wouldn't even be there if you didn't?"

"I honestly don't remember whether I did or not, but it wouldn't make any difference if I said it a million times . . . she's not listening to anything I say . . . she's just wallowing in self-pity." He was silent again for a few moments. Then he said, "I'm afraid you're right . . . about why she's doing it, I mean . . . but I wouldn't mention it to anyone else if I were you. Nobody but you and Bobby know her well enough to believe it. I understand your not wanting to tell Harold about your colitis, it sounds histrionic, but you *must* tell him you can't handle this. If you're right, and this is all for the purpose of getting you back, she'll give up after a while. *But,* and it's a big but, if you're wrong, she may drink herself to death without professional help. I happen to think you're right, but I also think you should get Harold to bring in the experts. Her career can survive almost anything. I'll talk to him if you'd like me to." It was nice of Jeremy to offer to call Harold, but even if he did, Harold would insist on talking to me. I would call him myself.

I told Harold about my visit. I also told him that I didn't think there was anything more I could do, that her attitude was wholly different than it had ever been before. He said that I owed it to her to keep trying until I succeeded. He reminded me of all the gifts Mother had given me over the years and asked if I didn't think I owed her something in return. I pointed out that the gift-giving had begun back in Gary's days and that it was Mother's way of apologizing for her bad behavior, just as were the floral arrangements she sent to hosts whose parties she had ruined. I suggested that he had it backward and that it was dirty pool to throw it in my face, reminding him that he, himself, had occasionally asked me to accept a gift I neither wanted nor needed just to make Mother feel better. Harold refrained from comment, but reiterated Mother's desperate need for my help. I finally gave up the struggle and agreed to try again.

When I arrived at Mother's house the next day, I could hear her inside but couldn't get her to open the door. I walked around the house shouting for her to let me in, but it was no use. I went home and called her on the phone but, when she heard my voice, she hung up. I was about to call Harold and appeal to him again for help when it dawned on me that if Mother was well enough to answer the phone, and had her wits sufficiently about her to immediately recognize my voice, her condition must, if anything, have improved.

I went to Bailiwick again the following day and Mother let me in. I cleaned up as I had before and again began my litany about her drunkenness and self-destruction. For a little while she shouted back at me and I thought we were making progress. Then, as suddenly as if I had flipped a switch, she became very quiet again. "Go home and leave me alone," she whispered.

"I don't want to leave you alone. I love you," I said, remembering Jeremy's question, "and I want to help you."

"Don't bother. I won't be around to trouble you from now on."

"What do you mean? You seem much better today. Just cut down on the drinking and everything will be O.K. . . . you'll see."

"All right, B.D.," she sighed. "Go on home. I'm tired now. I'll think about what you've said . . . now go away and let me rest." When I got home, I wasn't sure what to make of it. I thought I'd made some progress but I couldn't be certain.

That night the phone rang. Her voice was hoarse. "B.D.? Do you really love me?"

"Of course I do. I love you very much."

"I love you too, more than anything, but there's nothing left for me now. Tomorrow I'll be gone."

"What do you—"

"Just remember me with love," she interrupted, then hung up. I dialed her number several times but there was a perpetual busy signal. I told Jeremy what had happened and what I suspected and said that I would be back in half an hour.

When I arrived at Bailiwick, the curtains were drawn and there was no sound from within. After all these years, I found it hard to believe, but there was no escaping the obvious: She had done it again. I sat down on the front steps as long-suppressed memories from my childhood flooded in on me.

The first time Mother staged a mock suicide, I was eight years old and Michael three. She required an extraordinary quantity of verbal declarations of love and devotion from us and, because she constantly demanded them, it hardly ever occurred to us to render them voluntarily. The first "suicide" came about when Mother decided that she had suffered intolerably callous treatment at Michael's and my hands.

"Neither of you care a damn about me!" she bellowed. "Well, we'll just see how you feel about it after I'm gone." She had made this speech so often that even Michael was immune to it. I was hard pressed to play out the role demanded of me, but I managed to hide my true feelings and read my lines like a good girl: "Mommy, we care about you *now* . . . *both* of us do, and we don't have to wait until you're gone to know it. Anyway, that's years away, so why talk about it now?"

"Oh, you think so, do you?" she snarled. "You cold bitch! You've torn my heart out . . . do you know that? Jesus! I just can't stand any more of this."

Michael burst into tears and tried to say that he loved her, but Mother shoved him away and said that if he couldn't be a man, then go snivel in his room where she wouldn't have to listen to him. She then broke into hysterical sobbing. I left her howling in the hallway and led Michael by the hand to his room. I told him not to worry and to stay out of sight until the storm blew over. I gave him a big hug and left him playing with his toys. As I was to learn later, Mother invariably staged her "suicides" when the servants were off and there were no other adults in the house. So it was now.

When I left Michael's room, Mother was still in the hallway. "I suppose you told him that everything would be all right," she sneered. "You'll ruin him with all this coddling. It makes me sick! But it doesn't matter now. . . . I won't be here tomorrow." She stood in front of me, squinting her eyes and swaying slightly from side to side as she clutched some small object to her bosom.

"Stop it, Mommy, *please*," I begged. "Michael's only little and he gets upset easily. He'll grow out of it."

"It's touching that you're so worried about your brother. It would be nice if you cared as much about me, which you obviously don't." She stared penetratingly at me, then flung the small object at my feet.

"What's that?" I asked.

"Why don't you pick it up and see for yourself?" She turned and started down the hall toward her bedroom.

I found the object where it had bounced into a corner and looked at it closely. It was an empty bottle of Nembutal, her sleeping pills. As I straightened up, Mother was standing in her doorway, watching me. "As you can see," she shouted down the hall, "I have swallowed them all. I won't be around to trouble you by tomorrow. There's nothing you can do about it now . . . it's too late." She slammed the door and locked it. I stood, frozen in shock for a moment, then ran down the hall clutching the empty prescription bottle. "Mommy, Mommy, please open the door!" I screamed, pounding on the door with all my might. "I *do* love you . . . of course I love you . . . you know that! Let me in . . . don't die . . . oh, please don't die! I love you, I love you! Mommy . . . Mommy!" There wasn't a sound from the other side of the door.

Michael had heard the commotion and came running down the hall. Although he was too young to understand what was happening, he was crying again. I took him downstairs and sat him in front of the television set, then went back to pounding on Mother's locked door. After a while I went back to fetch Michael and put him to bed. I tried pounding on the door some more, then, exhausted at last, slid down onto the floor and cried myself to sleep, my back against the door.

I was rudely awakened the next morning when Mother opened her door. I fell back and banged my head on the uncarpeted floorboards. She looked down at me with a triumphant expression on her face. "I hope that taught you a good lesson. I deserve better from you. I love you more than anything and I expect you to love me in return." As I sat there on the floor and watched Mother walk sedately down the hall, I realized what she had done to me and vowed never to fall for it again. I had believed her . . . she was very convincing. Why shouldn't she be convincing? It was her business. Never again, I promised my eight-year-old self, never again . . . no matter how convincing she might be.

Mother committed "suicide" several times a year after that. Michael believed her once or twice, despite my assurances. He cried outside her door once, which must have thrilled her to bits, but then he too got used to it and stopped paying attention.

It had been a dozen years since she had last tried it on me, but I wasn't going to break my vow. I hadn't then . . . I wouldn't now. The only thing she had forgotten was the empty pill bottle . . . she had always left one outside her bedroom door. I dare say there was one on the kitchen steps now, but I couldn't be bothered to go and see. I couldn't be bothered with any of it anymore. The pain was starting again, so I wearily got up and drove home to take my pills and put my husband's mind at ease. I didn't mind the occasional call for assistance to prevent Mother walking off a picture or something, but the past few weeks had been too much. I was *not* my mother's keeper! I'd paid my dues . . . many times over . . . and now I was stuck with colitis for the rest of my life, or so the doctor said. It was enough. Next time, they would have to get along without me . . . all of them . . . the lawyers, the agents, the producers and Mother too. Nobody but my husband understood how pervasive in my life was Mother's very existence. I doubted that I could change that, but I was definitely not going to go through anything like this again.

When I walked in the door, Jeremy's only concern was for me. I admitted that the pain had started again and he insisted that I take two pills and go straight to bed. Before I fell asleep, I managed to more or less bring him up to date on all the things that had transpired.

The next day I felt better and took up my normal activities. The day after that, my curiosity got the better of me. I dialed Mother's number. The phone rang . . . so it was back on the hook. After three rings she answered . . . sounding chipper, hale and hearty. I gently replaced the receiver in its cradle. I didn't call Harold. He would probably say, "I told you so," or accuse me of having made things out to be worse than they were. Despite his having been wonderful to Mother over the years, even unto lending her money when she was broke, I wasn't feeling very kindly disposed toward him either just then.

A week passed, then Mother called. "Hi." Very cheerful.

"Oh, hello," I said stiffly. "You certainly seem to be feeling better."

"Yes. It's been rough. I've been through hell!"

"Well, I'm glad you're better. I'll stop by and see you soon."

"I thought you could come over for lunch today."

"Not today, Mother. I've too much to do. Soon, though."

"Oh, I see," she snarled, and hung up. Well . . . to hell with you too, Mother! Business as usual won't work this time. I'm damned if I'll let you pretend nothing has happened.

A day later I found an unstamped letter in our mailbox. It was one of the abject, soul-rending apologies at which Mother was so brilliant, in writing that is. If I hadn't seen so many of them before, I would have been deeply moved. It ended with ". . . I want you to know how grateful I am that you love me enough to have helped me through this. It's been a terrible time for me. All I ask is that you keep on loving me." Isn't it marvelous, I thought, how in Mother's game of life, she could strike out and immediately claim another turn at bat? Oh well, I shouldn't be surprised . . . she would never change. I suppose I kept hoping that she would realize I was a human being, not a fantasy daughter to be pushed, pulled and toyed with as her mood of the moment dictated. It was a foolish waste of time though. For Mother, reality was a script, and her personal script was reality. I called her and made a date for lunch the next day at Bailiwick.

Mother greeted me with a great outpouring of joy and enthusiasm. She was clad in a cocktail dress rather than her normal slacks and blouse. The house was its usual, immaculate self, the dining table was beautifully set and she had gone to considerable pains to prepare a nice lunch: green salad, lamb chops with spinach soufflé, fruit and cheese for dessert. She flitted hither and yon and chatted the while about general topics, the weather, the news and local gossip as though the events of the past weeks had never occurred.

I ate my lunch, letting her run on and marveling yet again at her ability to pretend. When the meal was over and we were having our coffee, I brought the conversation to the point. I began very quietly. "Mother, I want to talk to you and I want you to listen very carefully, please."

"B.D., don't! I don't want to talk about it. Can't you see that I've suffered enough? You were pretty rough on me, you know? But I took it . . . because you love me . . . so let's just drop it."

"No! We will *not* drop it until you clearly understand and acknowledge my feelings in the matter. You say I was rough on you . . . you've no idea what you put me through!"

"That's very sweet, but let's drop it, shall we?" She was getting an edge to her voice.

"Not until I've had my say. If I leave without having it, it will not be on friendly terms." I waited for a response and when she folded her hands in her lap and looked down at them, I went on, "First, I am extremely relieved to find you sober. I sincerely hope that I never see you that drunk again." She shot me an angry look and made as if to start arguing, but I cut her off. "It's no use pretending, Mother. You must face the brutal truth and fear lest it recur. It's over . . . but not forgotten."

"O.K., B.D., that's enough."

"No! It is not enough . . . not by a long shot. I want you to keep one fact firmly fixed in your mind: I will not go through anything like this again. If you pull another of your phony suicides, I'll walk away. To use your own words, you'll no longer have a daughter." She began to splutter a protest, but I cut her off again. "I mean it, Mother. I won't play your sick games anymore. You got away with them when I was a child and you got away with it this time, but never again. I know what it was all about, even if you won't admit it."

I paused, giving her the chance to say, perhaps, something of value, but she didn't. She only glared at me and blurted, "I always knew you were a cold bitch. Jesus! There was nothing phony about it. I wanted to die. I—"

"Bullshit!" I shouted. "All you wanted was for me to feel totally responsible for you . . . to leave my family, like Aunt Bobby left hers, and come home to keep poor Mommy company. I know it and you know it and I won't allow myself to be put into this position again. I can't and won't handle it anymore. You've given me colitis and I wound up at the hospital once, but that's where it ends. It should be enough to satisfy even your craving for attention."

"I didn't know," she stammered, and I thought for a moment that she was actually going to apologize and ask how I felt—but the moment quickly passed. "How can you stand there and accuse me of not trying to kill myself? You deserted me . . . how would *you* know?" God, it sounded lame. How the hell had I let her get me sick? It was beyond me.

"That's a good one," I retorted, laughing despite my anger. "You made your charming phone call, locked all the doors, drew the curtains, took the phone off the hook and hid . . . probably in your bedroom watching television. The only thing you didn't do was take any sleeping pills, try to shoot yourself or anything else. You staged it and it didn't work, so you got bored and pulled yourself together. I knew it stank at the time, but you confirmed it when you answered the phone a couple of days later. I was the one who hung up on you."

"O.K., B.D., you've stated your opinion and I won't say any more about it. I'm just glad that you love me."

"That's another thing," I said. "I may be your daughter, but I'm also a human being and human beings have emotions which they can't control. Right this minute I'm none too fond of you. The love will undoubtedly return but, for the time being, I have no more to give. And I meant what I said . . . don't ever play sick games with me again."

She stared at me and I stared back, neither of us speaking. Then she shifted her gaze and said, "I listened. What else do you want?"

"I had the strange idea," I admitted, "that you might feel some slight remorse for putting me through all this. . . . I see I was wrong."

"O.K., B.D.," she said without a trace of sincerity, "I'm sorry. Can we forget it now?"

"Since that's obviously the best you can do, we'll put it aside. But forget it? Never!"

"Fine, fine," she said impatiently. "Would you like another cup of coffee?"

"No, thank you. I've a lot to do and I'd better get going. Thank you for lunch."

Mother followed me to the door. As I kissed her on the cheek and said good-bye, she said, "I'm glad you were so worried about me. It helps to know that you love me so much."

6

1974–1976

In the summer of 1974, Mother began rehearsals for *Miss Moffat*. Joshua Logan was directing the musical stage version of Mother's 1945 movie, *The Corn Is Green*. The original story about a schoolteacher in a Welsh coal-mining town teaching poor children the three R's was transposed to the modern South with the same poor coal-mining town, but with black children instead of white. A marvelous new young actor by the name of Dorian Harewood played the pupil and Mother had nothing but praise for him. Unfortunately, Dorian was the only person or thing about which Mother had anything good to say.

She and Josh Logan fought tooth and nail from the beginning. She complained bitterly that Logan was working the cast like slaves and claimed they were all dropping from exhaustion. When she called me, she said that Logan expected her to "dance like a young kid," that she would strangle him if she could, and that if he didn't "let up" on them he would kill them all. She predicted a disaster for the show because of Logan's slave-driving.

The usual out-of-town tryouts were scheduled prior to the show coming to Broadway. It opened in Philadelphia on October 7 to very poor reviews. There was the usual frenzy of rewriting and changing and, in due course, Mother's prediction came true . . . she collapsed onstage, unable to move her legs. The show closed on October 17. The newspapers said that Mother had suffered a recurrence of her old back injury; Mother said it was "total physical exhaustion brought on by Josh Logan's horrible and inhuman pace."

Whatever the truth was, the show had closed and Mother was lying in a hospital bed while the production's insurance doctors examined her. They ran tests to determine the cause of her paralysis, kept her in traction and fed her tranquilizers until, one day, I received a call advising me that they were considering exploratory spinal surgery. I had my own opinion of what was wrong with my mother and I screamed like a stuck pig. There was no more talk of any exploratory anything. Mother stayed in the hospital in traction while the insurance people ran test after test and deliberated. Finally, they were satisfied that she was paralyzed from the waist down and the claim for the losses of *Miss Moffat* was settled.

Mother came home to Bailiwick, fully recovered, and had Thanksgiving dinner with us. On New Year's Eve she gave a big party and, while waving good-bye to some guests, slipped on the icy steps and broke her ankle.

In March of 1975 she went to Sydney, Australia, with *An Informal Evening with Bette Davis* and returned laden with sheepskins, kangaroo coats for all and a stuffed toy lamb for Ashley. Almost immediately, she was offered another thriller, *Burnt Offerings,* with Oliver Reed. She was still struggling to avoid such vehicles but, circumstances being what they were, she had to accept it. She went to San Francisco in September to begin work on the film she was later to describe as "a hideous mess" and the worst film she had ever made. On the phone from San Francisco, she told me that she was "cowering in her room, terrified of Oliver Reed," who, she said, ". . . got blind drunk and rampaged up and down the hotel corridors late at night, bellowing for me to come and talk to him."

In October she was off again with *An Informal Evening,* this time to England and Scotland. The show was successful again and Mother loved the applause and her rapport with the audiences. For her, there was nothing like it . . . it was a tonic for her artist's soul.

* * *

Early in 1976, Jeremy and I sold Wildwoods and bought a farm in Pennsylvania. We were eagerly anticipating chickens and ducks and sheep, vast vegetable gardens and wide-open spaces, making our own hay and keeping our horses in our own fields. Also, having two hundred or more miles between ourselves and Mother, and living in a place to which there was no earthly way she could follow us, was not without appeal. Since the Picketts, who built the farmhouse during the nineteenth century, never named it, we called it Ashdown Farm.

Regardless of my constant urging, Mother had made no attempt to find a replacement for Vik and didn't seem to have any intention of doing so. For the most part, despite all my brave talk, she'd got exactly what she wanted from the "suicide." I didn't live in, but I might just as well have. Being only a few minutes away, I was always at her beck and call and had permitted myself to be trapped into spending three or four mornings a week either at her house or running her errands. It had started so innocently, lending a hand until she found a replacement for Vik, that I was fully ensnared before I realized it.

Jeremy and I decided to go to Jamaica for a month before making the physical move to the farm. It would give us a chance to get fully rested for the long siege of farmhouse renovation that lay ahead and which we intended to do ourselves.

I had earlier given Mother a pair of white doves. She squealed with delight upon receiving them, placed their cage in the alcove by her French doors, surrounded them with plants and named them Abelard and Héloïse. Héloïse was a dedicated egg-layer and we had put a nesting box in the cage because Mother kept hoping that they would hatch their own babies. Having first consulted experts, I had told her that the chances were slender, but we had done everything possible to create an atmosphere conducive to success.

When Jeremy, Ashley and I left for Jamaica, Héloïse had been sitting on two eggs for a while. If they were going to hatch, it would be while we were away and Mother intended to keep me posted regarding developments. After we had been at our rented house in Ocho Ríos for a few days, the phone rang. Mother skipped the usual amenities and came straight to the point, sounding utterly distraught. "I don't know how to tell you this . . . but Abelard . . . (sob) . . . well . . . he's . . . (sob) . . . at the bottom of the cage."

"Yes? So?"

"Well . . . he isn't upright . . . he's kind of sideways . . . (sob) . . . what should I do?"

"Is he moving at all, Mother?"

"No . . . his feet are sticking up . . . and he's more on his back than his side . . . oh, B.D. . . . my God! It's horrible!"

"Lying on his back with his feet in the air is not a good sign," I said. "I'm afraid he's dead."

"Oh no-o-o-o-o," she wailed, "I can't stand it. What do I do?"

"I suggest taking him out of the cage and disposing of him."

"Oh, God! How can you *be* so insensitive?"

"Don't worry, Mother, if the eggs hatch you'll have babies to raise. If they don't, I'll get you another male dove."

"You cold bitch! You can't replace Abelard, my sweet Abelard. I have to hang up now . . . I've got to call someone to get this dead bird out of here."

A few days passed before she rang again. "B.D., I had the man from the pet store come and take Abelard away. He was very kind and said he would bury him for me."

"I'm glad, Mother. Do you feel better now?"

"Better? My God! Better? What a question!"

"I thought it was an average sort of a question."

"I figured it out . . . it was Héloïse who killed him. She just sat there . . . she paid no attention to that poor bird at all. No wonder he grew desperate and dropped dead. That *bitch*! I hate her!"

"Mother, please! I'm sure it was unintentional. Who knows why Abelard died? Birds die of all kinds of things. It's not necessary to find a guilty party. Héloïse was just following instinct and sitting on her eggs."

"Did you totally ignore Jeremy when *you* were pregnant? Of course not. Do you think I'm stupid?"

"People have portable pregnancies, Mother. If I'd had to sit on an egg for nine months, I'm sure Jeremy would have adjusted. Anyway, have the eggs hatched?"

"Who cares about the goddamned eggs *now*? I'll call you if

something happens. How's your vacation?"

"Fantastic. We're having a wonderful time and Ashley loves it, particularly the coral reef. He's swimming farther with us every day."

"That's just ducky! You're happy and I'm going through hell!" Click, dial tone.

The following evening, when we got back from watching a polo game in St. Ann, the maid said that Mother had called and wanted me to call her back the second I got in. "Missy Davis sound most upset, most upset indeed." I thanked her and Jeremy and I made wagers on what had happened now.

"Hello, Mother, how are you?"

"How *am* I? Sick! That's how I am."

"Why are you sick?"

"That bitch, Héloïse, managed to hatch her eggs. The first one died. It just lay there like a piece of raw hamburger. God! I couldn't look. I had to put on my dark glasses and draw the curtains. Why aren't you here while I'm living through this hell? You could have taken the cage to your house and *I* could have slept nights. Christ!"

"Was there someone to take it out of the cage for you?"

"The man from the pet store came over again, thank God!"

"What happened to the second egg?"

"It's fine, but it looks like another piece of raw meat. I can't take much more of this, you know."

"Mother, it's all right. Baby birds don't have feathers at birth. You're thinking of chicks, which fluff right out, but most birds are born naked. If the skin is pink, it's normal."

"I'm so *happy* for you that you think it's *normal. You* don't have to face it every day. It's *horrible.*"

"Have you put the lightbulb in the cage like I showed you, to keep the baby warm?"

"Yes, yes"—impatiently—"I've done everything for those damn birds."

"Then they should be fine. Just make sure the baby's warm and free from drafts. And remember to give Héloïse her vitamins."

"I'm so *glad* you can be so *casual* about the whole thing. Well . . . *I* can't!" Click, dial tone.

A week passed without additional bird bulletins. I was beginning to think all was well when Mother called. "Well . . . it's over . . . the baby croaked and so did my darling Héloïse. That son of a bitch, Abelard! How dare he desert her just when she needed him the most?"

"I'm really sorry, Mother. It's a shame."

"Shame? Ha! To hell with birds! I'm sticking to plants. At least when they croak you can just fling them out the door and be done with them. Don't ever talk to me about birds again. Christ!"

Mother at my engagement party at the Bel-Air Hotel,
being kissed by David Niven, Jr.

Dressing upstairs at the church before our wedding

The wedding

At the Plaza Hotel on Easter Sunday during Mother's
first visit to New York a few months after I married.
Left to right: Tom Hammond, Mother, Margot, Michael,
me, Jeremy and Fay

At the World's Fair in New York during the same visit.
Left to right: Fay, Viola Rubber, Michael, Mother and me

Christmas 1969. Mother, me holding Ashley, and
Dorothy Hyman

Thanksgiving Day. Mother, Michael, Josie Hamm, me
and Ashley

Michael at eighteen

Justin and Ashley, 1983

PART III

1

1976–1981

While Jeremy and I were hip-deep in wood shavings and plaster dust, taking apart a century-and-a-half-old, much-neglected farmhouse and putting it back together, Mother spent the summer doing a television movie and the fall making a record album.

The movie was *The Disappearance of Aimee,* in which Mother received equal billing with Faye Dunaway. It wasn't much to write home about but I heard more than enough about Faye Dunaway. Mother seemed to have spent most of the shooting schedule doing retake after retake while everyone waited for Dunaway to get her lines right. Mother's principal comment was "She never eats, just drinks champagne all day long."

She made the record album for EMI and had a ball with it. She performed arrangements of songs from shows and movies she'd done, and a song specially written for her at a much earlier date called "Mother of the Bride." She sang-talked her way through each number and did, in fact, sound on-key and interesting. Mother was very pleased with the album and was both furious with EMI and inwardly hurt when sales proved essentially nonexistent. She even went on *The Johnny Carson Show* and pleaded with people to buy the album, just to prove to EMI that their merchandising was to blame for the failure, not the record itself.

Mother's next step was to move back to California. "Let's face it," she said, "the industry's in L.A." She bought a condominium in Los Angeles and spent several months moving all her furniture in and getting it "just right." It was a great relief to me, for reasons I'll explain later, and would mark a turning point in Mother's career.

In March of 1977 Mother was presented with the Life Achievement Award by the American Film Institute (AFI). There was a gala television coverage of the event, with virtually the entire film industry present, and Mother was genuinely overwhelmed. Henry and Jane Fonda were the masters of ceremonies and countless tributes were paid to Mother's achievements. She looked marvelous on the show and the net effect was that the industry sat up and took notice of her as a vibrant and current star, rather than as a dinosaur left over from the old days of Hollywood. Shortly afterward, offers of quality properties began coming in for top money. Mother could, at last, stop scratching out a living and resume a prestigious career.

The first property Mother accepted after the AFI award was *The Dark Secret of Harvest Home* but, before she went to work on it, there was the matter of my second child to be dealt with. Back in February I had discovered, to Jeremy's and my great joy, that I was pregnant again. My obstetrician's best estimate was a September 1 due date. Mother spent the six or so intervening months telling me all about her plans for her personal participation in the birth of my daughter. The phone conversations were unending and her plans bore a remarkable resemblance to those which had preceded Ashley's arrival in the world.

As she had with Ashley, Mother missed out on the birth of our second son, Justin, who made a sudden, totally unexpected appearance on August 7. Mother was convinced that we had done it on purpose. She arrived at the farm when Justin was five days old and was quite taken with him despite his not being a girl. Jeremy and I had agreed in advance that, since I ought to be taking it easy for a few more days, I permit

Mother to do whatever she wanted, bite my tongue until she left and then clean up the damage. Jeremy found pressing business elsewhere at dawn each day and I watched Mother at work.

Watching Mother work was more tiring by far than doing the work oneself, particularly if it happened to be cooking. When Mother cooked in her own house, one didn't see the production she made out of the simplest things (largely because no one was ever allowed in her kitchen), but now she was in *my* kitchen and pure nervousness forced me to watch her every move. Rather than try to describe her technique in general terms, I'll detail in full her preparation of lunch on the first day.

Stouffer's frozen Macaroni and Cheese—the directions on the box read "Place in oven, uncovered and still frozen, for 35 minutes at 375° and serve." Here are Mother's directions, based on the way she did it that morning:

> Cover a counter with several layers of paper towels and place frozen casseroles thereon; remove covers and allow to thaw.
>
> Cover another counter with several layers of paper towels, slice a large tomato and leave slices on towels.
>
> Sit on stool, smoke nervously and sip from drink hidden behind flour canister while you watch casseroles thaw. WARNING—Do not take eyes off casseroles or they will fail to thaw properly.
>
> When casseroles are fully thawed, get large casserole dish and tip thawed casseroles into it. Thoroughly mush around with forefinger until satisfied.
>
> Sprinkle with bread crumbs and arrange tomato slices around edge.
>
> Hold lengthy debate with interested parties as to exact time dish is to be served. WARNING— Macaroni and cheese is very tricky and must be done just right.

Preheat oven for 45 minutes at 375°, meanwhile moving casserole dish around counter and to different counters to facilitate blending.

Place casserole dish in oven for 35 minutes. Announce lunch loudly and serve, chewing bottom lip in concentration.

Fidget until praised for efforts, then remind diners that macaroni and cheese is *tricky* and requires *some little work*.

So it went for three days. I did the cleaning, with some help from Ashley, now eight, since Mother never had time to leave the kitchen. Jeremy stayed away until dinnertime each day and Mother was deliriously happy. Barely a cross word was spoken during her entire stay.

The Dark Secret of Harvest Home, made late in 1977, was a quality production all the way. Although it was a two-part television movie based on Tom Tryon's book, Mother was as pleased as Punch with it. Witchcraft was the theme and Mother was the head witch who controlled a whole community. The cast was good, the production was good, the direction was good. In fact, the only thing that was bad was the cow, which stepped on Mother's foot when she was leading it out of its corral.

The rejuvenation of Mother's career was the bright side of the coin. The dark side was our personal relationship. Her move back to California had come none too soon, barely in the nick of time if the truth be known. The moment we moved to the farm, Mother had fallen into the habit of announcing visits every three or four weeks. That we were buried in renovations and that the house was a shambles, with torn-up floors, walls and ceilings, were no deterrents. She stayed at a nearby motel and showed up at the farm every morning for three or more days at a time. She always brought someone with her and she always stayed all day, plopping herself down in the house and complaining that I didn't spend enough time with her, that the place was a mess, that she didn't see why "that bastard" had to go on sawing and banging when she was there and so forth. Jeremy's practice later on of disappearing for the entire day whenever she was around couldn't be done during renovation; we were on a very tight schedule to finish everything we wanted to do within the six-month sabbatical Jeremy had granted himself, and we simply couldn't afford to lay down the tools for days at a time.

During one visit, when Mother and I had had a particularly bitter argument about her being there, not only uninvited but unwanted and in everyone's way, she returned to the motel in the evening and got drunk in the restaurant. She sat at a table with a bottle of Scotch and regaled the locals—who increased rapidly in number as word spread through the village of Wyalusing that Bette Davis was in the motel restaurant getting blotto—with her view of my new life-style: "My daughter's a slave . . . that bastard's killing her . . . they're living in filth like pigs . . . how could she let this happen to herself?" seems to have been the essence of her thesis, as reported to me over the ensuing months.

Michael also came with Mother for a couple of visits. He and Chou-Chou had spent two years in Germany while he practiced criminal law, defending United States soldiers charged with civil offenses. Upon their return to the States, he and Chou had taken up permanent residence in Boston and Michael had gone into private practice. Chou liked our wide-open spaces but Michael was discernibly uncomfortable. He and I had seen little of each other since I had got married and, although my love of things bucolic had remained constant, Michael had become a dedicated city dweller. We were always happy to see each other, but Michael felt out of place without skyscrapers while I detested the sight of them.

Early in 1977 when our renovation was completed, Jeremy and I had been on the point of wondering whether moving two hundred miles away had been a ghastly mistake for which there was no cure but to tell my mother never to darken our doorway again . . . then live with the consequences. The latter would be dramatic and continue for a very long time. When word reached us that Mother was returning to the West Coast, it was a fantastic relief. She didn't go peaceably, though.

Before she left we were paid a final visit compared with which all the others paled in beastliness. She stayed for four days, was constantly drunk, dropped lighted cigarettes all over everything, thus keeping me in constant fear that she would set the house on fire (as she had done with her own bed a few times in her life), was rude to everyone and then, and *then,* having tormented me for the entire four days and made it a period of abject misery, she announced, on the morning she was supposed to be leaving, that she had enjoyed the visit so much that she thought she would stay a few days longer. We had as terrible and bitter a fight as we have ever had and Mother left as planned but, once she had actually gone, I had a strange thought: Was it possible that Mother regarded tension, shouting, tears, hysteria and general unpleasantness as the very warp and woof of life? Was what I considered intolerable nastiness, and suffered recurring bouts of colitis over, to her nothing more than boys and girls playing nicely together? It was certainly a question to conjure with.

By the time Mother made *Death on the Nile* in 1978, the problem of her visits was smoothing itself into a tolerable format. She continued to announce her arrival without the least concern for our convenience, but the visits only occurred at four- to six-month intervals. Additionally, and perhaps more important, Mother had found a new friend in New York by the name of Terry Brown and she fell into the habit of bringing him to the farm with her.

Terry was a dead ringer for Truman Capote, irrepressibly effervescent and an indefatigable Bette Davis fan. We all adored him. Everything Mother did or said amused him and, with Terry on her team, Mother never seemed to become more than momentarily irritable. Even when she pounced on him for drinking white wine and other such dastardly deeds, Terry was able to totally disarm her with a retort like "I'm a terrible beast . . . what can I say?"

Death on the Nile was Mother's first honest-to-goodness top-quality theatrical film in fourteen years. She was one of an all-star cast headed by Peter Ustinov as Agatha Christie's Inspector Poirot, and including David Niven, Angela Lansbury, Mia Farrow, Maggie Smith and George Kennedy. The picture was actually filmed on the Nile and the cast stayed in elaborate suites in a hotel that had once been the winter palace. One would have thought that Mother would be as taken with the locale as she was with the picture, but all she talked about was the heat,

polluted food and filthy "natives." She never went near a pyr-
amid and was barely aware of gliding up and down the an-
cient Nile aboard a luxury boat, a treat most people would pay
fortunes for. Her real problem, which didn't become clear until she visited the farm upon her return from Egypt, was her
annoyance over the attention paid Peter Ustinov.

Once when we were having dinner, and Terry Brown was
with us, I brought up the subject of *Death on the Nile* and asked
Mother what being around Ustinov for a couple of months had
been like.

"You," she replied huffily, "would undoubtedly have found
him completely hilarious. Everyone else did . . . though God
only knows why. Nothing but clever remarks and endless anecdotes. Shit! He thinks he's so-o-o-o-o amusing and has to be
the *center* of attention all the time. *Brother*. . . . he's a bore!
And all those Englishmen are just too *charming* to do anything
about it. If I'd had to listen to one more anecdote I'd have
puked right in his face!"

"You're kidding?" I exclaimed. "You didn't find him the least
bit funny?" Mother assumed a very haughty expression. "English actors seem to think they can get by by being witty and
charming. They all make me sick!" Terry dissolved into laughter, but Jeremy maintained a straight face and said, "I doubt
that Laurence Olivier feels wit and charm to be the be-all and
end-all of good acting, and I shouldn't think that even you,
Bette, can argue that Olivier is anything less than the best."
Jeremy was wrong . . . Mother could argue anything she
wanted. She drew herself up and scornfully replied, "Larry
Olivier, my dear, is not an *actor*. He's a *chameleon*. He wears all
that makeup and all those costumes and just *disguises* himself.
Shit! Half the time you don't even know it's him." Terry was
reduced to holding his sides, tears of mirth streaming down
his face, while my husband and I were laughing harder at Terry
than at Mother. Mother, instead of getting into her usual
antilaughter snit, said, "You're right! It *is* funny. Larry Olivier
an *actor*? . . . Ha!"

Mother visited once, having led me to believe that Terry
was coming with her, but she appeared at the farm without
him. When I asked where he was, she answered, "I do love
Terry. I agree he's marvelous and sweet and he certainly loves

your mother, but there's only so much of his silliness I can take. All that laughter gets to me after a while."

Later in 1978, Mother made her first film for Disney, *Return from Witch Mountain*. At first she was reluctant to do it. It was a fantasy and she did not approve of fantasy. She was persuaded to accept the job partly because Disney was a "class" studio and partly because of the top, top money she was being offered but more compelling to her by far was Ashley's reaction to the news. Mother had always been somewhat frustrated that her grandson didn't seem to comprehend her stardom, so his wide-eyed awe upon hearing that his grandmother could appear in a Walt Disney movie, if she wanted to, proved irresistible. She did the film, therefore, with misgivings but, while never admitting it, she thoroughly enjoyed herself. Ashley went to see it with some friends at our local cinema and loved it. When he called to tell his grandmother how impressed he was, she said, "I'm glad. If you hadn't liked it, it would all have been a waste of time. I only did it for *you*."

The next year Mother did another made-for-television movie, *Strangers—The Story of a Mother and Daughter,* with Gena Rowlands. It was filmed on location at Big Sur and Mother complained bitterly about the cold weather there early in the year. Nonetheless, she took great pride in her role and loved the powerful and emotional script. The film was aired on Mother's Day and received nothing but praise. Mother won an Emmy. She even had some nice things to say about Gena Rowlands.

In 1980 it was back to Disney for *Watcher in the Woods*. Mother hadn't changed her mind about fantasy and apparently felt constrained to explain her willingness to work for Disney again. She reminded me of how nice Walt had been to me when I was a little girl, taking me for rides on his miniature train. She seemed to imply that she owed something to Walt's memory for his having been so nice to her daughter, and that the huge paycheck and the star treatment had nothing to do with her making another picture for the studio. In any case, things again went smoothly and Mother had nothing but compliments for the Disney organization.

That year she also made *White Mama,* a television movie

about a poor widow who takes in a black teenage boy as a foster child to gain the extra income. It was totally different from anything she had ever done and was well received by the critics but, for some reason, she never said a word about it, even when I told her I liked it.

Quickly after that came *Skyward;* she had lots to say about that. I imagine that she originally agreed to do it because of the character she would play—a masculine, coarse old pilot who ran a flight school. There's no doubt that Mother knew the names of the producer and director before agreeing to do the film but, when she arrived in Dallas to go to work, she had what her eleven-year-old grandson would have described as a "spaz attack." She had not connected the names of Ron Howard (director) and Anson Williams (producer) with ". . . little Richie Cunningham and that Potsy boy from *Happy Days. They're* going to tell *me* what to do? Jesus! Someone has to be kidding!"

On top of that, Dallas had a heat wave . . . a real, 110-degree heat wave. Shooting was done on a runway at an airport outside Dallas and Mother's costume included sneakers. "This is just *ducky*! *I*'m taking *orders* from Richie and Potsy. *They* haven't the least idea of what they're doing . . . all those *kids* care about is that *dear, darling* little crippled girl. *She* gets to sit in the shade in her wheelchair while *I*'m out on the burning-hot pavement with blisters on my feet and my sneakers stuck to the tar. Shit! If I ever get out of here alive, I'll get even with them." She didn't wait to get even. Her performance was as stiff as a board and she read her lines as though under hypnosis.

Mother was on the second day of a four-day visit to the farm when Fay phoned with the sad news that her mother, Aunt Bobby, had died. She had succumbed to a cancer-induced coronary. Mother dropped the phone to the floor, collapsed into a chair, grasped her face in her hands and began to rock back and forth, wailing piteously. "What am I going to do? What am I going to do? Oh, no! Bobby's dead. I can't go on. I want to die too."

I picked up the phone and told Fay how sorry I was and how much we had all loved Bobby. I explained that Mother was upset and said we would call back as soon as she got hold of herself. Fay said what a shame it was that Mother and Bobby had seen so little of each other in recent years.

Mother, still weeping, withdrew to her room to grieve alone, leaving me to think back over the years and how much Aunt Bobby had meant to Michael and me. It had been a decade since I had last seen her; Ashley had only been two years old on the one occasion she had been to Twin Bridges.

Mother came back into the kitchen. "I shouldn't hide. After all, Bobby didn't leave me on purpose. She was so ill; had been ever since her mastectomy. It's better this way." She sat down and began to rock again. "Oh, my Bobby. What am I going to do without you? Bobby dead. Bobby dead. First Ruthie and now Bobby. Dead. She was so good to you kids. She loved me so much. Oh, my Bobby!" I suddenly remembered that terrible night when Mother so viciously attacked her sister over the roast beef; how I, furious with Aunt Bobby for taking Mother's abuse, demanded an explanation. Aunt Bobby's tearful reply came back to me now, "Underneath it all I know she loves me and that's what counts. . . . I still do love her." Mother continued weeping and rocking for a while, then told me to get Harold on the phone for her.

As soon as he was on the line, she took the phone. "Harold, Bobby's dead. I want you to call Fay right away and make all the arrangements. I'll pay for everything, of course." It was a quarter of an hour before Harold called back and Mother sat in gloomy silence. When the phone rang, she jumped up and answered it herself. "Yes, Harold. . . . She what? . . . *What?* . . . Jesus I don't *care* about any deathbed shit; it's my dough, not hers for Christ's sake. *I'm* in charge of this whole deal. She will *not* be burned up. You tell Fay that Bobby will join Ruthie in my tomb just like I always planned. She's known all about it for years. *Christ!* You tell Fay that *I'm* in charge." She hung up and turned to me. "Can you believe this shit? Fay says that Bobby wanted to be cremated. *Brother!*"

The phone rang again and Mother answered. "Yes? . . . Right. . . . That's more like it. Now, Harold, I don't know how I can go out there. It's impossible with only three days. I'd be crazy to try. . . . You mean you think I should go? I *can't*, I'll be *dead*! . . . Well, of course I want to be at Bobby's funeral, but I just can't. It's too much. . . . Right. *I'll* tell Fay. Send a big wreath from B.D. and me. Make sure there are mums, lots of mums. Bobby loved mums."

Mother called Fay. "Fay, darling. It's all arranged. You don't have to thank me. . . . You're a very brave girl, sweetheart. Now, I won't be able to be there, not with only three days before my movie starts. . . . It is a shame, but life goes on. You know that I'm with you in my heart. It'll be a beautiful service. I love you, sweetheart. Goodbye."

2

1981

Late in 1980 the subject of Ashley having a part in a movie with his grandmother came up again. It had been discussed from time to time and Ashley had always exhibited great enthusiasm for the idea. Now that he was eleven and extremely tall for his age, NBC was discussing a project entitled *Family Reunion*, which had a fair-sized role for a thirteen-year-old boy. Mother was gung-ho.

"Ashley would be perfect for this boy," she enthused. "He'd be playing himself. All he'd have to do is learn his lines and act naturally. Jackie Cooper's going to direct. He loves working with kids and can teach him a lot. It's quite a big part but, knowing Ashley as I do, I'm sure he can handle it if he wants to."

Jeremy and I went into the pros and cons very thoroughly before inviting Ashley into the decision-making process. Basically we were strongly in favor of his doing the movie. Whether or not he had talent and whether or not he would later opt for an acting career were unknowns. The experience would be worthwhile whatever might happen. The problem was Mother and her attitude. She might be all for having Ashley appear in a movie with her now, but had she thought it through? There was no way of telling. The laws of probability dictated that she hadn't thought beyond the imagery of "Bette Davis and her grandson in . . . ," in which event Ashley might be in for a very rough time. This part of the decision would have to be his, since he would have to live with the consequences.

As graphically as possible, Jeremy and I spelled out for Ashley the potential troubles which, in our opinion, might lie in wait for him. We were never fully persuaded that he had given the matter as much thought as he should, but his excitement at the prospect of doing a movie was so great that we simply hadn't the heart to say no.

Now I have to clarify two things—the first, well known to Mother, was the matter of Ashley and clothes. Ashley loved clothes. Forget the toy trains and bicycles at Christmas, just give him a new pair of jeans or a three-piece suit and he was in seventh heaven. There were times when he almost drove me crazy with his "clothing-plex" but, after a little negotiating, we used to come to terms. He could get dressed up for dinner provided that he didn't wear different outfits for lunch and every activity during the day. Jeremy said that he felt sorry if someone were drowning and had to rely on Ashley for help; Ashley would tell the drowning person to hang on for a few minutes while he changed into his new swimming trunks.

The other thing was the use of the word "promise." Jeremy was a great semantic hairsplitter and insisted that the children respect the words "I promise." Ashley had grown up under the interdict "A promise is absolute, so don't make one unless you can and will keep it."

The deal for Ashley to do the movie was made and Mother sent for him to come to New York to meet Jackie Cooper and the producer prior to rehearsals. She seemed to be very excited about his visit and made all sorts of plans for luncheons, dinners, carriage rides in Central Park, a trip to the Empire State Building with friends and a tour of NBC, which Mother liked to refer to as his new boss. Also among the plans was the promise of a trip to Miller's, the riding-apparel outfitters, to buy him a complete western outfit—suit, tie, shirt, boots, the works except for a hat, which he already had. The reason was that before leaving for Dallas to make *Skyward,* Mother had conceived the idea of dressing Ashley up like J. R. Ewing. She worked him into a positive lather of excitement over the prospect of dressing like a Texan, and kept the excitement alive during her many phone conversations with him from Dallas. When she returned from Texas, she visited the farm, but without the western duds. She explained to Ashley that she just hadn't had ". . . the time for all that." He had been terribly disappointed but had taken it like a man. The matter had been laid to rest, and could have been left that way had Mother not called to tell Ashley that she had learned that Miller's had western clothes and that, as soon as he got to New York, she was going to send him down there with her new secretary, Kathryn Sermak, to get outfitted.

Ashley was thrilled at the prospect of meeting Jackie Cooper and all the rest, but the trip to Miller's for the long-awaited western duds loomed as large as the making of the movie. The NBC limousine arrived to pick Ashley up at the appointed time. He looked very grown-up in his dark blue suit but, when I congratulated him on his appearance, he reminded me that I shouldn't be surprised if the English gentleman who was leaving were replaced by a returning J. R. Ewing.

Terry Brown took Ashley everywhere, including a Broadway play. Until his meeting with Jackie Cooper, Ashley was constantly busy doing or seeing something, thanks to Terry, and only saw his grandmother briefly at breakfast and bedtime. The meeting with Cooper went very well and Mother called to say, "That son of yours is incredible. I was *so* proud of him. My dear, Jackie Cooper was completely captivated by him. What a boy! My God, he was just terrific! I can't say enough about the way he behaved in a room full of adults. You should be so proud. Christ! Jackie told him that he could make him a big star and Ashley said, 'I hope so, sir . . . I'll try very hard.' Can you believe it? Well . . . he's the greatest, that's all, just the greatest!" Mother's reports were similarly glowing until the last day of Ashley's visit.

Mother had planned no excursions for her grandson on his last day and by lunchtime he was getting tired of playing cards with Kathryn. Over lunch he asked when they would be going to Miller's for his clothes. Mother had a fit. "Oh, God, Ashley! You don't think we have time for that with all this going on, do you?"

"But, Grandmother," Ashley protested, "there's nothing at all going on and you promised that we'd go to Miller's. You promised! Anyway, Kathryn has time to take me if you're busy. You said this morning that you planned for Kathryn to be with me all day."

"Come off it, Ashley!" Mother exploded. "Haven't I done enough to entertain you for the last few days? Shit! How many boys get the treatment you have? Come *on*! Kathryn has to be *here*! For *me*! When I *need* her! She has no time!"

The first time there had been "no time" for his western outfit, Ashley had been disappointed. This time, rightly or wrongly, he got angry. When lunch was over and the cards were brought out again, Ashley looked at his grandmother and asked, "More cards? If there's time for cards, why isn't there time for Miller's, Grandmother? It would only take about an hour." He was duly shouted at, called a spoiled brat, ungrateful and infantile, and told that he should never mention Miller's again. Being forced to swallow his indignation, he went into a sulk, refused to play cards and just sat and stared out of the window. After a while he broached the subject again. "Grandmother, my father has always told me that promises must not be broken and—"

"*What?*" shrieked Mother. "Your *father*? Shit! Your father is a pile of *crap*! Do you think I care what *he* has to say?" This was too much for Ashley and he shouted back, "You can say anything you like and I know I'm not allowed to argue, Grandmother, but I won't let you say that about my dad! I love him and so does Mom. And everyone who knows him likes him except you. You don't have any right to call him crap and I want you to say you're sorry." He stood his eleven-year-old ground and glared at her.

"You're right, Ashley," his grandmother replied after a moment's hesitation. "I shouldn't have said that about your father . . . even though I'm right." She stormed into her bedroom and slammed the door.

My phone rang. "Ashley's whole personality has changed and he's become a sulky brat. I don't know what to do with him anymore. It's just awful." It took considerable effort and much time to sift the details of what had actually taken place from Mother's disconnected and completely one-sided ramblings, but I finally had them. I was furious and made no bones about it. "How the hell would you feel if someone did that to you? First you go to Dallas telling him that you're going to bring him this great present, which, if I need remind you, was entirely your idea. Whenever you call from Dallas you speak to Ashley and remind him of the impending present and tell him you can't wait to see him in his new outfit. You come back and—"

"That has nothing to do with—"

"It has everything to do with it!" I shouted over her interruption. "Hear me out and then say your piece. You come back and say you didn't have time to get the clothes, and I must say I thought Ashley was a pretty damned good sport about it, considering how excited you got him. Then, when it's all been long forgotten, you call him up and tell him you're sending him down to Miller's the minute he gets to New York and promise him that this time he'll get the clothes for sure. Now you make him sit in the hotel all day watching you and Kathryn do nothing and tell him there's no time to go to Miller's. Frankly, I'm surprised that he's only sulking." Mother tried to interrupt me again, but I shouted her down. "I think you've got one hell of a bloody nerve treating a child that way, any child, and I resent the hell out of your twisting and turning the story in order to disguise your incredible meanness and insensitivity! Now it's your turn."

"I see." She began to bluster. "So it's all *my* fault, is it? You're against me too. How very interesting! Perhaps we should forget this whole thing and all I'm doing for your son, eh? Do you think that managing an eleven-year-old boy is easy? Brother! You're really something."

"If that's the way you feel, Mother, there isn't a doubt in my mind that we should call it off, right now, before Ashley gets tugged in every direction at once."

"Well!" said Mother, changing direction quickly. "Since all anyone seems to care about is going to Miller's, I'll ask Kath if she has time to take him. You and your greedy son have won! Are you satisfied?" Click, dial tone. I tried to call her back but the line stayed busy. It was probably just as well. Had I reached her, Ashley would have been out of an acting job.

When Mother called again, a few hours later, I was still angry but no longer fuming. I just couldn't understand how anyone could be so deliberately unkind to a child they professed to love.

"Wait till you see these boots!" Mother raved. "They're absolutely gorgeous. Ashley picked them out himself and they have birds on them. My dear, I can't tell you what good taste he has. Brother! I'm so glad we waited to do his shopping spree in New York. These are nicer than anything I saw in Dallas. Everything he chose is elegant and I'm sure you'll approve. I'll let you talk to him now. He'll be leaving here at ten in the morning, so you'll see him soon. I'll say good-bye now, darling. I love you. It's been a divine visit."

When Ashley got home the next day, my English gentleman stepped out of the limousine.

"What happened to J. R. Ewing?" I asked. "All that fuss and you didn't wear the suit?"

"I didn't get a suit," he replied. "When we got to Miller's, I found out that Grandmother told Kathryn to get me a pair of boots and a shirt, so that's what I got. The boots are absolutely great, though. Look at them." They were, indeed, nice boots.

After Ashley had unpacked, we sat down for lunch and a long talk. First, Jeremy and I had to satisfy ourselves that Ashley, who had now had three days of exposure to Mother without either of us on hand to protect his flanks, still wanted to do the movie. He admitted that the thought of being with his grandmother endlessly for weeks on end was more than a little frightening, but he was determined to go through with it. With this out of the way, I began to brief Ashley on techniques for survival while under Mother's jurisdiction.

I didn't like doing it. It didn't seem right to be teaching an eleven-year-old to mistrust his own grandmother, be guarded in his every word and deed and, above all, appear to be grateful, subservient and devoted regardless of how much abuse he might have to take. Such lessons were the stuff of a cold, cynical world and a young boy should not have to cope with them. I did it, though; I had to. Unless Ashley were taught the rules, there would be no hope that he and his grandmother would be able to coexist. He had already learned one rule the hard way: "Never accept anything she says at face value, even if it *is* a promise."

After the first day of rehearsals Mother phoned me. "Ashley's brilliant! Jackie's thrilled with him and says he's going to be great. Ashley may call you later and tell you about it." At nine that evening, Ashley called. "I'm sorry it's so late but I wanted to talk to you when I was alone."

"That's all right, sweetheart," I said. "You know I don't go to bed until eleven-thirty or so. I understand from your grandmother that you did very well today and that Mr. Cooper is very pleased with you."

"I don't know, Mom," he said, sounding on the verge of tears, "it was all so mixed up."

"Come on, Ash," I said gently, "it's your first time away from home and you're feeling a bit homesick. Don't worry about it, it'll wear off. The important thing is that you did so well. Concentrate on that."

"That's the trouble," he sniffled. "I don't know how I did. Grandmother shouted at me all day long. Mr. Cooper asked her to leave the directing to him a few times and she agreed, but then she went right on shouting at me."

"Oh, sweetheart, don't cry," I soothed. "You and I discussed your grandmother's shouting. She doesn't even know she's doing it. Do you remember talking about it?"

"Sure I do, but this is different, Mom." He was crying aloud now. "All she did all day long was shout. Shout and call me names and tell me I'm stupid. Mom?"

"Yes," I answered, ready to cry myself.

"I think I want to come home. I listened to everything you said, but I never imagined anything like this."

Suddenly Mother's voice came on the line. She'd picked up the living-room extension of the phone in Ashley's bedroom. "What is this?" she barked. "Ashley? Is that you? What's going on?"

"Mother, it's me, B.D. Ashley just called to talk to us like you said he would, that's all. I'll talk to you when we're done."

"Ashley!" Mother snarled. "I offered to let you call your parents when you went to bed. Why did you wait to do it behind my back, you little sneak? What are you saying, huh?"

Ashley began to explain but dissolved into tears again. Mother went crazy and shrieked at him. "What lies are you telling your parents, dear boy, eh? You and I had a great day! What is this crap behind my back? I don't believe this! Jesus! What the hell are you crying about?"

"He's slightly homesick and didn't want to hurt your feelings," I said. "He called us to talk about it, that's all. It isn't any great mystery."

"Homesick?" bellowed Mother. "He wasn't homesick all day! I suppose he's been telling you that I'm some kind of a monster? I can't take this anymore, I really can't."

"Mother, please," I begged, "may I finish talking to Ashley and then call you back?"

"No!" she snapped. "Ashley's said all he's going to. Hang up, you little sneak. Now! We'll talk more about this when I'm done with your mother." I heard an extension click and nothing more from my son.

I tried to get Mother to stop such paranoid thinking in order to spare Ashley any more grief, but it was no use. She was itching to get at him. I could hear it in her voice. There wasn't a doubt in my mind that she had behaved just like the monster she had accused Ashley of calling her, and now she wanted to grill him about what he had said to me, just as she used to grill Michael whenever he got back from a visit to Gary. The phone conversation ended with me feeling impotent and worried to death.

I waited half an hour and called Mother again. "How's Ashley?"

"Fine," she answered very unconvincingly, "just fine. We had a long talk and worked out all his problems. You have nothing to worry about, dear girl, nothing."

"What did you work out?" I asked, getting more concerned by the second.

"Ashley and I are chums again"—then to Ashley, who must have been in the room with her—". . . aren't we, Ashley?"— then back to me—"Don't worry, B.D., I really am a good dame, you know. I'll take good care of your son. Ashley now knows he has to be *honest* with me. He and I will call you tomorrow, after rehearsal. Everything will be fine. Tell me how much you love me, I've had a rough day." I received a letter from Ashley a few days later telling me that Mother had grilled him until 2:00 A.M. My phone call had interrupted her attempt to make him admit that he had told me she was "a monster."

The next day went well and Ashley recovered his poise. Mother gave a small dinner party in her suite, after which Terry Brown took Ashley to see *Brigadoon* on Broadway. Before they left, however, Ashley found himself the center of a lot of adult attention. The ham in him took over and he told an off-color joke which he had memorized after having heard his father tell it. Apparently he told it well and got a big laugh, or so Terry informed me later. Thus encouraged, Ashley pulled out an entire repertoire of jokes, not one of which was overly imbued with socially redeeming features, and entertained the assembled company until he ran out of material. That an eleven-year-old is out of line doing what Ashley did is beyond dispute, but I have to admit that I would have loved to have been a fly on the wall while he was doing it.

Mother phoned the following morning. "B.D., I have to tell you that I am horror-stricken!"

"Hello, Mother. Why are you upset now?"

"Your son, naturally. God! Last night, with a room full of elegant people, including the producer, Jackie Cooper and Harold Schiff, for Christ's sake, Ashley sat there spewing out one dirty joke after another. No one could stop him. Christ! It was a nightmare. What can I do? I can't have this sort of thing going on while I'm trying to make a movie. Shit! I don't know if I can go through with it after last night. I'll just have to think about it."

"Mother, let's take one thing at a time. First of all, are you trying to tell me that with all those adults in the room there wasn't one, let alone you, who could tell an eleven-year-old child to put a sock in it? Why didn't you simply march him out of the room and read him the riot act? This is the silliest thing I've ever listened to. Something tells me I'm not getting the whole story."

"You don't understand, B.D. He has a very forceful personality. I asked him to stop but he ignored me."

"Mother," I said, laughing aloud, "do be serious. In my entire life I've never known anyone who could ignore you. I ask you again, if he was behaving so terribly and everyone was so aghast, why didn't you stop him? You were perfectly able to if you'd wanted and you know it."

"Let's just drop it," Mother flared. "I can't stand this! Don't you dare give it to me! Christ! I'm telling you there was nothing I could do, that's all. Since you won't believe me, there's nothing more to say. I'll just have to give this whole movie thing some more thought. I just don't know."

I knew two things, one probable and one certain. The probability was that Mother had sat back during Ashley's little performance, enjoying his stage presence if not the jokes themselves, and had only become "stricken" when somebody, perhaps Harold, had evinced dismay. The certainty was that Mother wasn't going to play on-again-off-again-Finnegan with Ashley and this movie. I had had enough of her threats.

"Mother," I said, measuring my words, "listen to me carefully. I have no idea what your problem is, but I want you to understand one thing. I will not stand idly by while you play yo-yo with my son. This is far too important for the playing of games. Now, you either decide that you're doing the picture with Ashley or you don't. Whatever you decide, it's final. No more 'I'll just have to think about it' whenever you feel bitchy. If your decision is not to go ahead, that's fine with me. I'd rather explain that to Ashley now than explain a lot worse to him later on."

"Don't do this to me," Mother whimpered. "I can't stand it, B.D., not today. That boy of yours is a rough customer and I just don't know if I can deal with him at my age, that's all.

"Don't do what to you? It's not a question of what I'm doing to you. It's a question of what you're trying to do to Ashley. He won't even be your responsibility once the movie starts shooting, except to the extent that you're his grandmother. Kathryn is being paid out of the budget to be his companion and surrogate mother, there will be the tutor to take care of his schoolwork and Jackie Cooper to direct him on the set. If you leave him alone to do his thing, there won't be a problem in the world for you. Why do you have to interfere with everything? Hell, you won't even let the poor child speak to his mother without getting on his case about it!" Mother hung up on me.

That evening she called again and gushed, "Of course Ashley will do the movie. I'm not a monster, you know. I wouldn't hurt that boy for the world; we're chums. So don't be angry with me, please don't. Everything will be fine." Nothing about staying off his case, of course, but that speech was a waste of time anyway. Mother had never stayed off anyone's case.

"I'm glad to hear that, Mother," I replied, "but let's not have a replay. I want your word that you won't threaten to call it all off again."

"You bitch!" she snapped. "Shit! All right, B.D., Ashley will do this movie whatever *hell* I have to go through. Does that satisfy you?"

"Yes, it does. Thank you, Mother, you're most gracious."

"So are *you*! Brother! You should run the Mafia."

"As long as we understand each other, Mother, that's all I ask.

Commencement of principal photography was delayed by all the usual problems plus the departure of Jackie Cooper from the director's slot. No reason was given me and, not knowing Mr. Cooper personally, I couldn't ask him, but I had strong suspicions. Shooting finally began in January and Ashley's part, which was supposed to have entailed him being on the set for three or four weeks, wound up keeping him there for the entire twelve-week schedule. He loved the actual work and had no trouble keeping up with his schooling. His tutor stayed in touch with his sixth-grade teacher in Camptown, Pennsylvania, to ensure that he kept up with his classmates. There were no more threats regarding Ashley being in or out of the movie, but there were plenty of other problems.

There was Ashley's underwear. Even though he had his own living expenses and his own paid companion, Mother decided one day that it was an insupportable extravagance for him to send his socks and underwear to the laundry. Since Kathryn did Mother's lingerie for her, Kathryn could also do Ashley's socks and underwear. As anyone who has done laundry knows, there is a significant difference between washing lingerie, which is light, rinses quickly and dries almost immediately, and doing a boy's white gym socks and underwear. Add to that the fact that bleach is not used for lingerie and, therefore, wasn't used for Ashley's things, and what do you get?

"Ashley!" Mother shouted. "I don't know why you can't take better care of your clothes. They don't look dingy and gray at home. Why do you do that to them here?" Try as he might, and did, he was unable to convince his grandmother that there was any correlation between the dingy grayness of his socks and underwear and the fact that they were not being properly laundered. She came up with a novel solution to the problem: She forbade him to change his socks or underwear without her permission. Thereafter, he had to smuggle clothing in and out of the bathroom in order to change and hide the dirty items in a bottom drawer, whence Kathryn would have to retrieve and launder them when Mother wasn't around. All because the very same woman who once thought nothing of sending a bottle of nosespray across New York in a limousine professed to believing that Ashley sending his underwear to the laundry was a waste of money.

There was also the matter of food. Ashley was growing very fast indeed. When he left to do the movie, he stood five feet six; when he returned three months later, he stood five feet nine. He ate like a horse three times a day and accepted anything offered to him in between. Even though Ashley had his own living expenses, Mother became irate over the amount of food Ashley ate and "took charge." The extraordinary thing was that she didn't change the amount he ate, only what he ate. She ordered for him in the dining room every week for a full week ahead. He had been happily choosing his own meals from the menu, but now he had to eat what his grandmother chose for him. That alone wouldn't have been the end of the world. The problem was that his grandmother could only be bothered to think about it once a weak and instructed the headwaiter, who obeyed her orders to the letter, to give Ashley the same thing at every meal until she chose something else for him.

The real problem, which I had failed to foresee and which underlay all other problems, was that Mother's love of all the attention Ashley was receiving, and her satisfaction with the role of proud grandmother, had worn thin very quickly indeed.

"No one is paying nearly enough attention to *my* performance!" she complained to me on the phone one day. "Jesus! All Fielder seems to care about is rehearsing Ashley. I guess I'm all on my own. Brother!" Fielder Cook had replaced Jackie Cooper as director and, apparently, was very supportive of Ashley.

"Since you keep telling Mr. Cook how to direct Ashley, perhaps he thinks that he'd best leave you alone as far as your own performance goes," I suggested.

"I do not keep telling him how to direct Ashley!" she blustered. "Maybe a helpful suggestion now and then, but that's all." I could well imagine her "helpful suggestion now and then." "Anyway," she went on, "that isn't the point. All anybody around here seems to care about is Ashley. God, it's boring! 'Isn't he marvelous?' 'Great, Ashley, you got it in one take.' 'Terrific, Ashley, you're a natural!' Jesus! It's all I hear. It's getting on my nerves. *My* performance is the crucial one. Brother!"

"They're only trying to instill a little confidence in a newcomer," I said soothingly. "You've been at it for fifty years and have every award known to man to prove that you know what you're doing. I think it's just that simple."

"You're right!" she exclaimed. "That's all it is. They're being nice to him because he's my grandson. God knows I don't need any direction. Shit! I direct half the films I'm in anyway."

Although that particular conversation ended on a satisfactory note, the attention paid her grandson continued to irritate Mother throughout the schedule. Had Ashley's part been finished in three weeks as originally planned, things might well have been all right, but three months was far too long. It wasn't much consolation for my motherly instincts, but at least I knew that Ashley understood why he had to finish the picture no matter what. The law suits that would have arisen had he breached his contract would have been horrendous.

Mother phoned frequently, a commonplace occurrence, but each time now she told me that she had ". . . offered to let your son talk to you but he declined. I don't know why." I did. The first few times he had tried to talk to us with his grandmother present, she had hovered over him and virtually dictated his every word. Since he wasn't allowed to talk to us in privacy and, even with his grandmother present, wasn't allowed to hold a normal conversation, he preferred to communicate his circumstances by not talking to us at all. This was nothing new. Mother had always resented anyone trying to exercise their right to privacy, decrying them as "sneaky," "dirty" or "dishonest." The thought of Ashley being left alone to say whatever he liked to his parents horrified her. "He'll make up all sorts of lies about me," she said when I challenged her on the subject. "Don't think I don't know it. Brother! Why else wouldn't he want to talk to you with me in the room?"

"Perhaps because you won't let him talk. You dictate every sentence to him."

"You're both against me. Jesus! I can't stand it." Click, dial tone.

Kathryn had been instructed to make sure that Ashley didn't call us when Mother wasn't around but, one day when Kathryn was out too, Ashley called. For the first time in weeks we enjoyed a family chat. He told us that he was thoroughly enjoying the work and only wished that he had more of it to do instead of sitting around so much of the time. He asked about the farm, his brother, his horse, dog and favorite cats and then, suddenly, his voice became frozen as he said, "I've got to go now. See you soon," and hung up. As I found out later, Mother had returned unexpectedly.

"What were you doing behind my back?" she yelled at Ashley.

"I was—"

"You were calling your mother, weren't you? I know everything that goes on, Ashley!"

"Yes, I called Mom, just to say hello and chat."

"What did you tell her, eh? That I'm a monster? That things are real tough? What lies did you make up that you couldn't say in front of me?"

"I didn't say anything except that everything is fine and that I like acting. I—"

"Oh-h-h-h, I can just imagine. You're a damned liar, just like your mother always was!" she ended in a shriek, thrusting her face into his and almost deafening him.

"My mother?" Ashley asked, dumbfounded. "You've always said that she's the world's only perfect person. How can she be a liar?"

"You're the liar, not your mother!" she screamed. "You leave her out of this!"

"But you said that I was a liar, just like my mother. Now you say that I'm the liar, not my mother. Well, I'm not a liar either."

"Oh, so you think you can trick me, do you? Well, isn't that interesting? Let's just drop it, shall we? Just keep in mind that if I ever catch you sneaking another phone call to your parents, you're off this picture. Got it?" She stormed out and slammed the door behind her.

Ashley didn't try to call again. Whenever I called to speak to him, Mother said that he was "unavailable" but that she would have him call me later ". . . if I can convince him. I just never know with him." Occasionally he was in her room when I called and we got to exchange a few pleasantries before Mother snatched the phone away but, whenever I tried to call him directly, I was told that on Miss Davis's orders no calls could be put through to, or placed from, his room. I kept my cool for Ashley's sake, figuring that he had enough troubles without my adding to them but, one day, Mother phoned me and said that the switchboard had told her that a woman identifying herself as Ashley's mother had tried to call him several times.

"I want it stopped, right now!" she stormed at me. "I'm in charge here and Ashley will call from my room when he wants to talk to you."

"Mother," I said, struggling to stay calm despite my rising bile, "Ashley's expenses are sufficient to cover a few phone calls to his parents. I don't know why you're so obsessed with this. It's really most unfair."

"Unfair? Unfair?" she shouted. "That boy of yours is a rough customer. He's not to be trusted for one second. What did he say to you the day he sneaked a phone call to you alone, anyway? What did he say, eh?"

"If you're referring to the time he called me from his room, we chatted about the farm and Justin and his animals and so forth. And since you seem determined to keep on with this unpleasantness, why, may I ask, are you playing Gestapo with this switchboard nonsense?"

"Nonsense, huh? Let me tell you something, dear daughter, I'll manage this boy as I see fit! I'm sorry I ever agreed to this whole thing, I'll tell you that, right now."

"It was your idea, Mother, and I've never regretted anything so much in my life. It won't happen again and that's a promise."

"Just what does that mean, may I ask?"

"Just what it says. I made an error in judgment and I won't repeat it. Amid your enthusiasm and Ashley's excitement, I forgot the lessons of my childhood. I made the mistake of thinking that you would treat Ashley like a human being, a co-worker even, but I couldn't have been more wrong if I'd tried. You talk of him and treat him as though he's a criminal. I won't forget it, not ever."

"You better watch it, B.D.!" she bellowed. "You'd just better be careful!"

"What are you threatening me with, Mother?" I asked menacingly, fighting to control my temper. "I'd really like to know."

"God!" Mother suddenly wailed. "Don't do this to me, not today! Can't you tell how dead I am? I beg of you, on my knees, to lay off."

"Oh, for Christ's sake, spare me your dramatics!" I finally exploded. "Even if you're utterly lacking in the milk of human kindness and can't treat your own grandson decently, at least don't try to convince the world that he's a liar and a sneak. I'm not going to tolerate any more of it."

"Oh, boy, are you a bitch! I treat your son like a god-damned *king*, for Christ's sake! Do you know that?"

"Kings can make phone calls, Mother!" She hung up.

She called again the next day. "Ashley's acting is just incredible. He's so conscientious and industrious. Well, he's too much for the people and you should be very proud." It was warming to hear that at least for a few minutes Mother was feeling kindly disposed toward Ashley. I would have been far more convinced of her sincerity, though, had she told me she would let him call me from the privacy of his own room.

About halfway through the filming of the movie, I received a call from Harold Schiff. "You've got to do something, B.D., and quickly. Your mother and that friend of hers are getting drunk together during the day. Your mother's been drunk on the set and has been wandering around in public bumping into things." He went on for a while and I got the clear impression that he considered it all to be the result of Mother having to cope with Ashley.

"I won't dispute that Ashley has a bearing on it," I argued, "but it's not *his* fault. Mother's *competing* with him, just like she did with Gary, me and everybody else. She's jealous of all the attention being paid him and won't leave him alone for a second. She won't let him send his underwear to the laundry, she won't let him eat what he wants, she won't leave the director alone to direct him, she's blocked all calls to or from his room and won't let him talk to me unless she's monitoring the conversation and God only knows what other little tricks she's up to. Ashley's doing his best to get along with her, but how can an eleven-year-old be expected to deal with Mother's neuroses?"

"Listen, B.D.," Harold said, "once in a while your mother needs your help. She knows better than you what she's doing and doesn't deserve your criticism. I would think that, considering how much she loves you and how generous she's been to you, you would be happy to help her when she needs you rather than presume to judge her." It wasn't the first time Harold had read me his version of the riot act and I should have expected it. He seemed to see everything from one point of view only, Mother's, and this usually left me speechless with frustration. But, as I reminded myself at such times, he was *Mother's* lawyer, not mine, and he served his client well.

"Given all the circumstances, Harold, I don't think there's anything I can do this time. I'm certainly not going to say that I heard through the grapevine that she's drinking during the day. She'll accuse Ashley of telling me and then I shudder to think what she might do to him."

"Well, B.D., you've got to do something," he said. "You're the only one who can. I've been getting calls and the situation is serious. I haven't received any threats to remove your mother from the picture, but it's crucial that the situation be remedied before it deteriorates any further. Perhaps you could convince your mother that people are talking about her friend's drinking and suggest that she stay away from her until the picture's finished."

"That's a possibility," I conceded. "If she's encouraging

Mother to drink while she's working, which has never happened before to the best of my knowledge, getting rid of her
might cure the problem. Can you think of anyone else to keep
her company, though? You know she hates to be alone when
she's working. If you don't, there really isn't much I can do
about it except go there myself." There followed a long silence
from Harold, to which I quickly responded, "Oh, no! Not for
anything will I be her nursemaid! I couldn't stand it when I
was single and I'm certainly not going to do it now. Poor Aunt
Bobby wound up in an asylum a couple of times being Mother's nursemaid. Count me out!"

"Be that as it may, B.D., you've got to do something."

"Why don't *you* talk to her about her drinking?" I was suddenly inspired to ask.

"I have," he replied, "but she won't listen to me. You're the
only person she ever listens to. Anyway, it's not her fault. It's
her friend's fault."

"Oh, come off it, Harold," I exclaimed. "She's been a drinker
all her life, even though you won't admit it. The only difference now is that she's letting it interfere with her work." I waited
but Harold didn't reply. After reflecting for a moment or two,
I said, "Look, she's sounded like she's been drinking the last
few times I've spoken to her. Next time she sounds like that,
I'll jump her about it, but she's got to give me the opening.
Unless you want me to call her up and say that you told me to
stop her drinking, that is."

"No," he said quickly, "I don't think that would be produc-
tive. Wait for your opening, or manufacture one, but be sure
to do it soon. I'll wait to hear from you."

The opportunity presented itself when Mother called the
following day. Her speech was decidedly slurred and I jumped
in with both feet. "It's only lunchtime, Mother, and you sound
like you're plastered. What's going on? You've never hit the
sauce while you're working before. Why are you—"

"Christ! Don't you start too! It's not drink! It's my cold
medicine, it makes me woozy. I have the worst cold in the history of man."

"I sure hope so," I said, deliberately making my voice sound
as skeptical as possible. "If you start wandering around the set
drunk, your whole career could go up the spout." The balance

of the conversation consisted of Mother shouting at me, calling me a liar just like the rest of them and generally denying that she'd had a drop to drink in years. When it was over I called Harold and reported the gist of what she had said, ending with, "She sounded angry enough to remember the conversation. She'll either get better or worse. We'll just have to wait and see which way it goes."

I didn't hear from Harold again and Mother sounded normal on the phone thereafter. I assumed that shouting at me had had a beneficial effect on her. I did hear from other sources, though, that the weather on Long Island that winter was the coldest on record. The camera operators and other technicians not only had trouble with their equipment but carrying a flask in one's hip pocket was not uncommon on the set. Mother had fallen into the habit of carrying a flask "to help ward off the cold" and I suspect that that was the real beginning of the problem, not the much-maligned friend.

I grew increasingly upset as time marched along. I had been dead wrong in thinking that Ashley would be able to get along with Mother in some sort of harmony. I had forgotten all the games she played, had swept them under a mental carpet as it were. I had done my best to prepare him for coexistence with Mother, and Kathryn, bless her, did all she could to keep him out of trouble. She not only ran occasional interference, kept him updated on the "rules" of survival and was an all-around friend, but also, as I mentioned earlier, washed his underwear for him on the sly. I should have foreseen that Ashley would be miserable and feel like a prisoner with a power-mad warden. I had grown up with her and had learned how to fight at an early age; Ashley had been thrust under her control at eleven years old. He had had no preparation. He had been taught to be polite and considerate of other people, to be a gentleman, not good schooling for survival within Mother's orbit. I thought more and more about accepting Harold's implied suggestion that I join them on Long Island, but I knew that I would be doing it only for my own sake. My presence wouldn't solve anything, might even make things worse. There was no doubt that I could take the heat off Ashley at the hotel, but Mother would have no trouble in finding new ways to torment him on the set. There was no quick fix available. It was far too late to bring him home; there were contracts and lawsuits would follow if I did that. Ashley, Jeremy and I had no choice but to grit our teeth and hope for the best until it was over.

Until Ashley committed his great crime against humanity, Mother continued to call me frequently. Her reports were essentially meaningless, however. One day Ashley was "difficult and terrible, a rough customer," the next day he was "fabulous, an extraordinary young man." The only real information the reports conveyed was her mood of the moment and whether Ashley had had a day of peace or a day of torment. He had always been inclined toward moodiness but, with constant help from his father and me, had been getting over it. Now he was moody all the time and it was my fault. I had blown it, and blown it big. I could only hope that three months wasn't long enough to make any permanent change in Ashley.

Ashley's last great crime was actually very funny. Mother, of course, saw no humor in it at all and jumped at the opportunity to mete out punishment for a heinous offense. One day my phone rang. "B.D.," Mother began, a peremptory edge to her voice, "something terrible has happened." I froze, horrifying possibilities tumbling over each other in my mind. "I have to let Ashley tell you about it. It's so horrible, I can't bear to speak of it. I can't believe that he did such a thing." I relaxed.

"Hi, Mom," came Ashley's voice.

"Tell her what you did and forget the 'hi' bullshit!" roared Mother in the background.

"Hi, Ash," I said. "Who've you killed?"

"Well," he began, unable, with his grandmother hovering, to respond to my attempt at humor, "I'd taken my shower and had a towel around my waist. I went into the bedroom to get dressed, but I couldn't find my jacket or white dress shirt. Kathryn said she'd taken them to Grandmother's room to press them and went to get them for me. It seemed like she'd been gone a long time, so I went down the hall to find her. It's off-season and there aren't many people in the hotel besides us and I forgot that I was only wearing a towel."

"Did anyone see you?" I asked.

"No. There was no one around."

"Give me that phone and go get dressed!" I heard Mother yell. "Not in your dress clothes either. Oh, no! In your cords and sweater . . . you'll eat in your room tonight."

Mother came on the line. "I've never been so humiliated in my entire life! Your son was invited to dinner tonight by a very elegant old lady who lives here. He will not be allowed to go now. Christ! Mrs. Whoozy-poo's been very nice to him and he looks forward to his dinner with her once a week. I hope he's miserable. It serves him right!"

"Good grief, Mother! The titled heads of Europe have jumped naked into fountains with less of a to-do than you're making of this. Why don't you calm down and get it into perspective?"

"Calm down?" she howled. "I heard what you said to your son on the phone. You think the whole thing's funny, don't you?"

"What Ashley did isn't funny but your performance is. How the hell can you say you're humiliated when nobody even saw him? It's only the kind of thing that kids do when they aren't thinking. It's not as though he flashed a state dinner. Don't you think that a simple reprimand might suffice?"

"Certainly not! It's fortunate that I'm in charge, not you. I'll take care of it my way."

I kept on trying, but it was quite obvious that Ashley was not going to have dinner with "Mrs. Whoozy-poo" that evening. The truth of the matter, undoubtedly, was that Mother had been looking for an excuse, which Ashley had now provided, to mess up his dinners with the old lady.

The day finally arrived when it was all over. Ashley came home, whooping with happiness to be done with it and dumping a mountain of dirty laundry in my lap. He was thrilled with the experience of being in a movie and even thought that he might like acting as a career, but not if it involved being with his grandmother again. Once was enough to last him a lifetime. I kidded him about having spent only three months with her while I had spent sixteen years. His only comment was "I don't know how you survived it, Mom. She's nuts, stark raving loony-toons! How *did* you survive it, anyway?"

Mother, of course, raved about how close she and Ashley had become and how grateful she was to have had the chance to spend so much time with her darling grandson. For a long time afterward, she referred to Ashley as "my co-star" and by no other name. She was convinced that they had become "chums for life" and that Ashley had enjoyed every minute of his time with her.

3

1982

At the beginning of 1982, Mother made another television movie, *A Piano for Mrs. Cimino.* If she had said little about *White Mama,* she said even less about this one. I didn't even know she had done the movie until she called one day to tell me to watch it on television that night. I was slowly gaining the impression that Mother was embarrassed by doing television movies, as though television were an inferior medium, and even if the work turned out to be first class, like *Strangers—The Story of a Mother and Daughter,* it didn't really count.

As she had done several times before, Mother spent Christmas with us before returning to the coast to do *A Piano for Mrs. Cimino.* She simply couldn't get the hang of our Christmas Eve parties. The very idea of people being invited to come and go at random was anathema to her. She wasn't comfortable unless someone was "in charge" and people arrived and departed precisely as instructed. Since live and let live was not in Mother's vocabulary, she found all sorts of interesting ways to make known her discontent.

At one Christmas Eve party she appointed herself custodian of the ice bucket. That it was a huge bucket which held virtually enough ice to last the entire evening was unimportant. She kept popping out from corners, waving madly at me and shouting, "B.D.! Ice! Now!" Ignoring her only made her shout louder, so I kept going to the ice bucket, never less than three-quarters full, and putting a few more cubes in it. Each time I topped up the bucket, I tried to convince Mother that there had been nothing to worry about. She, in turn, persisted in advising me that "a proper hostess never let's the ice get low." By the third or fourth time we went through this routine, the guests were getting the hang of it and took turns at grabbing my arm and imitating Mother's "Ice! Now!"

On another Christmas Eve, at 9:00 P.M. when a few people were about to leave for church but most had just arrived, Mother gathered up a huge armful of coats, stomped into the living room and dumped them on the sofa. When all eyes were on her, she declaimed in her best stage voice, "My daughter has slaved her guts out preparing this beautiful party for you all, which was her great pleasure. Now, she is tired and it is time for you to leave." A few people accepted my assurances and stayed for another half hour or so, but most discovered that they "really ought to get an early night anyway."

Mother's crowning achievement in absurdity and bad taste, however, was the occasion upon which she went to bed without a word as the first guests were arriving. She waited until there was a full complement before taking up a stand at the top of the stairs in her see-through shorty nightie and calling loudly for someone to tell me that she wanted some warm milk. A friend by the name of Tony Lohman was closest to the stairs and undertook to deliver the message. He did so thusly: "I hate to tell you this, B.D., but I think you better do something. Your mother is standing naked at the top of the stairs, hollering for milk."

When Mother visited the farm again that spring, it was during the time of the Emmy Award presentations on television. She spent the day bitching about how absurd the TV awards were. "It's fine to give awards to movies, but to give them to series is ridiculous. It's the same every year, year after year, and I'm damned if I'm going to sit through another few hours of that crap." Mother was one of those who, for some reason, won't admit they watch television. No matter what show was mentioned, she would announce that she had never seen it, had no intention of doing so and that it was probably "crap like everything else on television these days." I told her that I planned to watch the Emmys that night. She said that she would go to bed and read a good book, ". . . which anyone with a grain of sense would do."

In the middle of dinner, Mother suddenly jumped up from the table and began running around the house, checking the time and searching frantically for the *TV Guide* to find out what time the Emmys began. "We can't miss them. Christ! They're a big part of the industry." I managed to convince her that the show wouldn't begin until eight and that there was plenty of time to finish dinner, it being but seven-fifteen at the time.

Well within the time limit that had suddenly become so critical to her, we were comfortably ensconced in the living room, drinking our coffee and awaiting the awards show. As soon as the preliminaries were over, the presentation of technical awards began. Mother immediately jumped up and began to pace about the room, irritation written all over her. "Shit! Why the hell they have to bore us with all this crap is beyond me. It used to be just the insiders who watched the technical awards. Who cares who lit what or who accomplished the best sound mix or who was the best photographer, for Christ's sake? It's just plain stupid! The whole show's stupid!"

By the time the technical awards had all been presented, Mother had smoked a half pack of cigarettes and almost worn out my carpet with her spastic pacing. "Thank God that's over!" She sat down with a great sigh of relief.

For the next few moments, categories were announced and lists of nominees read out. As each list was completed, Mother said, "See? What did I tell you? All the same damned people, over and over, year after year!" From time to time I pointed out that one show or another was a newcomer and Mother replied, "Oh! Right . . . at least *that* one's a good show." When I asked how she knew that, since she never watched television, she explained that she had had to watch that particular show because of some young actor or actress in it whom she had been told to watch as a possibility for some part or other in some project or other that she couldn't right at that moment recall. Each time we went through this routine, I simply said "Oh" at the end of her more and more complex explanations. Mother eventually awoke to the fact that I was making fun of her and informed me in no uncertain terms that my sarcasm was ". . . inappropriate and unappreciated. Stop being so rude . . . you know perfectly well what I mean." I said it was very clear.

A seemingly endless stream of categories came and went and then the soaps arrived. Soaps are shows in which I have no interest; even when trapped in a hospital room once, I found staring at the blank walls preferable to watching the afternoon soaps. I made mention of these feelings to Mother. Her indignation was quickly voiced. "Soaps are the only things on TV that are *worth* a shit! If you knew *anything,* you'd know *that!* They're *brilliant,* the scripts are fantastic, the actors really *act!* If you don't like the soaps, then what in hell *do* you like?" I mentioned a few shows I liked—*All Creatures Great and Small, M*A*S*H, Hill Street Blues.*

"*M*A*S*H?*" she roared. "That junk! I don't believe it! It's horrible, pointless crap." I asked if she ever watched it.

"Of course I don't watch it. I already told you I don't watch TV." I asked how it was possible to hate something she'd never seen.

"I just know how bad it is. After fifty years of experience, I know what I'm talking about."

She felt the same way about the other shows I mentioned, so I suggested that our tastes were so far apart, we had best try not to convince each other of anything.

"How many times have you watched a soap?" she asked suddenly.

"I've sat clean through one a couple of times. Why?"

"That's not a fair test," she charged angrily.

"What do you mean, not a fair test? You condemned all the shows I like without ever having seen them."

"Of course I've seen them! I just can't bear to recall them."

We heard an announcement that the movie awards were coming up and Mother was greatly relieved. During the commerical break, she vented what appeared to be a major anxiety. "God! In the *old* days, time was *really* spent giving the *important* awards . . . the cameramen, lighting people, sound mixers, all the *really* important people. Now . . . no one cares about them. It's just *awful!*"

Awards were presented to an assortment of movies and Mother watched in silence. Then she became bored with those also and proclaimed how thrilled she was not to have been nominated for anything this time. "I'm so *sick* of getting awards. Shit! I can't *begin* to tell you. Every time I turn around I get an award for some goddamned thing or other. It's really horrible. Brother!" She mused for a moment, then continued, "First I have to pay a hundred bucks for the makeup man, and a few hundred more for a new dress. Then I have to hire a limousine to haul me there so I can sit like a stuffed pigeon on a dais all night. I can't have a goddamned drink because by the time it's my turn to speak, I'd make a bloody fool of myself. Christ! So I sit there all night, *dying,* being gawked at and bored to death, so that I can *finally* get up and thank everyone present for the *great* privilege of being there and for the simply *incredible* honor being paid me . . . thinking all the time that I'd give *anything* for some comfortable clothes and a *drink.* Then I go home with another piece of *crap* that goes on my shelves which are already too crowded, so I'm soon going to have to hire a carpenter to build more shelves to add to the cost of the makeup and dress and car. They're usually brass or silver and have to be polished all the time. I shudder to think how many hours of labor I pay for each week, just keeping the tarnish off my awards. Probably while I'm out receiving one, the rest are turning black and I have to start all over again. Jesus!"

When I had more or less recovered from the convulsions of laughter into which this diatribe had thrown me, I suggested in all sincerity that she put her awards, except for the really important ones, in a closet. That way, I pointed out, it wouldn't matter if they tarnished. Mother stared at me in blank astonishment and replied, "I can't do *that!* In this life, one has to *respect* the honors one is paid!"

Mother had long had it in her head that summer in California was unbearable. She also thought that summer in the east was unbearable when she lived there, but now she was living in the west. Consequently, she had developed the habit of going to a hotel in New York in the summer to escape California's blazing sun by holing up in New York's smoggy humidity. She would visit friends in Connecticut and come to see me, to be sure, but most of her time was spent in the air-conditioned hotel, complaining about the humidity outside.

This year she had a better idea. After leaving the farm, but before returning to the West Coast, she determined to rent a house on Long Island for the summer. She and Kathryn took up the search and looked at a dozen or so houses. The first was too small, so the real estate lady headed for larger game, but that was too far from the water. They were too elegant, too big, too small, too old, too new, too close to the neighbors, too far from civilization, too this or too that. Mother had to return to California, so she left the search for the perfect house to Harold, who found one without much trouble and described it to her over the phone.

Mother was very excited about doing *Right of Way* with Jimmy Stewart. Although it was not a film for theatrical release, in her mind there seemed to be a difference between HBO, which financed *Right of Way,* and free television. Pehaps the fact that HBO viewers have to pay a fee made the difference. Mother was unable to resist Jimmy Stewart's charm and she approved of the story about two elderly people fighting for the right to end their lives as they saw fit. It was one of those rare instances when Mother was as happy with a project at the end as she had been at the beginning.

Late in May, Mother arrived at, and saw for the first time, her summer rental. It was too huge, too elegant, too close to the water, etc. She immediately had "the sweats," became very depressed and averred that she would never be able to "make it work." She said that the upholstery on the furniture was too elegant and that the collections of china and glassware were priceless and a terrible responsibility. The house was so enormous, she said, that she would need a staff to maintain it, and the garden stretched to the horizon.

By the middle of June, Mother and Kathryn had moved all the furniture around several times and, having placed everything exactly where it was at the beginning, Mother proudly announced that she might "make it work." She sent Michael and me invitations to a family reunion over the Fourth of July weekend. Phone calls flooded Pennsylvania, several a day, wanting to know all the children's favorite snacks, drinks and desserts, as well as what Jeremy and I liked to drink, what time we were used to having meals, what my diet would and would not permit me to eat and endless other details, all for the purpose of enabling Mother to be the perfect hostess. She was very excited about it all and talked endlessly of the fabulous meals she was planning and all the activities that were available.

Her rental was part of a large estate and she had permission to use the tennis courts. In addition, there were a croquet court, mussels just waiting to be harvested and endless clam beds. I kept my fingers firmly crossed, expressed unbridled enthusiasm and assured Mother that I wouldn't forget to bring plenty of tennis rackets, balls and appropriate clothes for all these sporting activities. I mentioned that we didn't have a clam rake, there not being a pressing need for one in Pennsylvania. Mother said she would get one. This entailed countless more phone calls before she was satisfied that Kathryn had found the right weapon.

It was eight o'clock on Friday night when we pulled into her driveway. She must have been watching out of the window for, before the car had even rolled to a stop, she was hopping up and down on the front steps letting out cries of *"God,* you must be famished . . . *no,* you probably ate on the way . . . I told you not to . . . I've spent hours getting a meal ready for you." She paused to catch her breath and I almost, but not quite, managed to say hello before she continued, "Anyway, dinner's probably ruined because you're so late!"

"Hi, Mother," I said, getting out of the car, "how do you like this for punctuality? I said we'd be here at eight, give or take, and it's eight on the button. No, we didn't eat on the way. Yes, we are hungry, but mostly though, I think everybody's thirsty."

"Thirsty . . . right . . . Kathryn! Where the hell are you? Oh . . . there you are . . . everybody's thirsty . . . no . . . wait a minute . . . let's go in the house."

Jeremy and the boys got out of the car and we all followed Mother indoors, deciding to leave the bags until later when they would be less likely to create tension. A few more hellos were said and Mother turned to Ashley, "What would you like to drink?"

"Whatever you have will be fine with me, thank you," he

replied, knowing from experience that to be specific was to court disaster.

"I have every goddamned thing there is!" Mother cried. "Orders from your mother."

"Oh, great," said Ashley. "In that case I'll have a root beer, please."

"What? Christ! I don't have that . . . why the hell don't you ask for something I have? Your mother said you loved Coke . . . why don't you have that?"

"Terrific," he said. "I'd love a Coke."

Next came Justin, now almost five and very perceptive. "I'll have a Coke too, please, Grammas."

"Shit!" Mother exclaimed. "Your mother said you liked apple juice. I don't know what's going on around here. I guess I can't please any of you." Justin maintained his composure with some difficulty and said, "Apple juice will be fine, thank you, Grammas."

"Well . . . you should have thought of that first. I've poured the Coke now and I'm damned if I'll waste it just because you've changed your mind." While these exchanges were taking place I mouthed "gin and tonic" to Kathryn who quickly produced one each for Jeremy and me.

Next on the agenda was the grand tour. It was a charming little house with cozy rooms, situated right on the bay. At high tide the water lapped halfway up the seawall on which the house sat. The garden was neat, with a long lawn running up a gentle slope to the main house about a hundred yards away. Except for occasional strollers on the beach at low tide, it was nicely secluded. The contents which had thrown Mother into such a tizzy turned out to be nothing more than cotton slipcovers on the furniture, Victorian tables and incidental pieces and assorted collections of strictly pedestrian bric-a-brac, any or all of which could, if necessary, have been replaced in a trice.

Jeremy and Ashley brought the bags in and the four of us moved into the loft. It had been converted into one largish bedroom and barely managed to accommodate us all. It had its own tiny bathroom and, being removed from the rest of the house, it offered the kids somewhere to hide in moments of stress. We unpacked, washed up and rejoined Mother.

There was still no sign of Michael and family, so Mother

served dinner before everything became totally spoiled. I wasn't expecting much since I had agreed with her that it would be best if she kept it simple the first evening. She did . . . macaroni and cheese.

After we had enjoyed a sociable cup of coffee, Kathryn repaired to a nearby motel. The house which Mother had earlier decried as too huge and too elegant only had a master bedroom and the converted loft, plus the tiny servant's room into which she had moved for the weekend. Michael still hadn't shown up when we went to bed.

There was a clear threat of rain the next morning, so Jeremy and Ashley armed themselves with a bucket and the clam rake and set off in search of the much-touted clam beds. Justin and I took stock of the beach toys which Mother had provided and went hunting for interesting shells and rocks. Mother was busy in the kitchen, preparing lunch and ordering Kathryn around.

Jeremy and Ashley returned after about an hour, looking thoroughly disgusted. Even with the tide near dead low, they hadn't found so much as an empty shell, let alone a bounteous clam bed. Mother went bananas and dragged Jeremy around the house to the front garden to show him the empty clam shells with which the owners had edged some of the flower beds. "Where do you suppose all these came from?" she demanded.

"I haven't the faintest idea . . . but certainly not Huntington Bay," he responded. "If it'll make you feel better, though, we'll give it one more try."

"Make me *feel* better? Shit! The whole damned bay is full of them . . . and I bought a clam rake just for you. Christ!" Satisfied that she had dealt properly with my husband's ignorance, she stomped back into the house and slammed the door.

When Jeremy came back to the bay side of the house, he had that gritted-teeth, furious look with which I had become so familiar whenever he was near my mother. "I heard," I said, taking his arm and strolling with him toward the beach. "What are you going to do?"

"Leave the clam rake in the bushes and go for a walk. At least I'll be away from her for a while."

"I'd like to come with you . . . but I better not. Why don't you ask the locals whether there are any clams around here?"

"I intend to . . . and if I'm right that there aren't any, I'm going to get a geologist's survey and then stick the clam rake—"

"We have two more days to go and then we should be O.K. till at least Christmas. Keep reminding yourself of that." He gave my hand a squeeze and took off with Ashley along the beach.

I wandered about aimlessly and watched Justin build sand castles. It wasn't much fun because the weather was chilly and overcast, but it was better than being in the house. Mother had been in the kitchen since breakfast, ostensibly getting lunch ready, and whenever I went indoors she darted in and out of any room I was in to tell me how hard she was working and how exhausted she was. It got on my nerves.

Another hour or so passed before Jeremy and Ashley returned. My husband had an evil glint in his eye that did not bode well for my mother. I followed him into the house.

"*Well?*" Mother challenged. "You were looking in the wrong place, weren't you?"

"Absolutely the wrong place." Jeremy couldn't suppress his grin of satisfaction. "A quarter of a mile up the beach we met a man who's lived here for forty years. He says the bottom's all wrong for clams. Nobody's *ever* found any in Huntington Bay."

"Then where the hell did all the clam shells in the garden come from?" Mother squawked.

"The fishmonger. The guy up the beach knows the people who live here. They buy clams from the fishmonger to make chowder." It made Jeremy's day when Mother, speechless, spun on her heel and stormed back to the kitchen.

Michael and his family arrived shortly before lunch which, I learned, was when he had told Mother to expect him. She, as usual, hadn't been listening. Michael took their bags to the master bedroom while Chou introduced us all to their year-old son, Matthew. Mother barely took time to say hello before dashing back to the kitchen. Lunch was announced and I got ready for the first of the much-discussed and publicized culinary masterpieces.

Cold cuts.

A normal pattern developed. Mother pursued her regular

habit of drinking vodka all day long, but hid her glass behind the sugar canister on the kitchen counter and put a little orange juice in it just in case anyone should see it; then she would dash in and out of the kitchen, clad in an endless array of aprons embroidered with cutesy sayings, for the unvarying purpose of criticizing Chou-Chou, Jeremy, the children or all of them at once. Michael and I, being her children, were perfect and therefore immune. If Chou picked Matthew up to keep him out of trouble, she was blasted with "For Christ's sake, Chou, leave him alone! What can he hurt? Let him follow me around . . . I'm great with kids." Whenever Chou left him to toddle around, however, she heard "Why the hell doesn't Chou keep track of that damned baby? Jesus! These aren't my things."

It was obvious that, despite the adverse weather, we had to get out of the house. Someone suggested tennis and we were galvanized into action. I stuck my head in the kitchen door to tell Mother where we were going.

"Why?" she asked.

"Why not?" I said.

"Well . . . I just don't know if you ought to." She wrung her hands and looked nervous. "The people in the main house and I are not on very good terms. They had the nerve to walk across *my* lawn to get to the beach . . . they were staring over here. Brother! I threw them out."

"Don't they own the property?" I asked.

"No . . . shit . . . their parents do, but they're in Europe. Just their teenage sons of bitches are here. They wouldn't respect my privacy, so I threw them out. Christ! Under the circumstances, I just don't want to use their tennis court. Jesus! They might start up again and I'd be in terror for the rest of the summer."

Mother had, indeed, set up a croquet course near the house and, since tennis was out, we decided to play croquet. Mother had laid it out in much too small an area, so Michael and Jeremy pulled the far peg and all but the starting hoops and paced off across the lawn what looked like normal distances for the game. We were in the middle of our first game, and having fun at last, when Mother bolted out of the house in full cry. "Jesus! What's going on? What are you doing?"

"We're playing croquet."

"But you've messed it all up!"

"No, we haven't. We've simply made the course the right size."

"What do you mean? My course was perfect. Jesus! I slaved over it for hours."

"We appreciate that, but unfortunately you had everything cramped into too small a space. Anyway, what's the problem?" Mother fidgeted, muttered a few ers and ums, then went into her hand-wringing routine, just as she had when the subject of tennis had been brought up. "Well . . . *Christ* . . . you've gone onto their part of the lawn." She flapped her arms and looked in all directions. Jeremy bridled. "For God's sake, Bette, the frigging lawn is a hundred yards long and we're only play-ing on the thirty yards nearest your house! What possible harm can that do?"

"*Harm?* How can you ask that? Brother! We're discussing privacy! If they won't respect mine, at least I'll respect theirs."

The subject of what to have for dinner on Saturday night had required several phone calls from Long Island to Penn-sylvania. Mother had felt constrained to say many times, "You're always cooking what that husband of yours likes. Jesus! I'm going to cook what *you* like." We had settled on cold poached salmon with mayonnaise, pickled cucumbers and boiled new potatoes. Not only did Mother and I both love this meal, but none of it was greatly in violation of my perpetual diet. Mother was doubly happy with my choice because the fishmonger was willing to cook the salmon in advance. When Kathryn disap-peared in the car for half an hour, shortly before dinner, I assumed that this time at least all was going according to plan.

Great goings-on in the kitchen followed Kathryn's return and I was only slightly unnerved by an overheard conversa-tion relating to oven temperature . . . it probably had some-thing to do with dessert. Dinner was announced and we eagerly took our seats.

Reheated lasagna . . . solid starch and twice as greasy.

Fortunately for all of us, Sunday morning brought bright, hot sunshine. We sunbathed, played on the beach with the children and swam. The sole remaining authorized activity, gathering mussels, was scheduled for that afternoon, so we lazed about on the beach and indulged in idle chitchat. I gleaned from Michael that Mother hadn't spent hours on the phone with him, as she had with me, discussing what to have for each meal. She must have felt that he didn't need the dangling of that particular carrot since he didn't, as Mother believed I did, spend his life in the kitchen slaving his guts out. He didn't care what we ate, as long as it wasn't barbecued. My brother is the only person I have ever known who can't stand the taste of barbecue sauce . . . couldn't even as a child. Lunch was served.

Colonel Sanders's Kentucky Fried Chicken . . . barbecue style.

After lunch, Michael and Chou played with Matthew on the lawn, close to the house to be on the safe side, Justin and I played on the beach, and Jeremy and Ashley set out after mussels. Mother had given them a big bucket saying, "Bring back a mess. God, they're good . . . we all love them." A "mess" to Mother was a definitive term meaning enough to more than adequately fill the needs of everyone present without her having to figure it out in pounds, quarts or whatever. It frequently created problems in communication, particularly when the person to whom the order was given was on the other end of a telephone and had no idea of how many people's needs he was trying to adequately fill.

My men returned with the bucket spilling over with mussels. The harvest patently constituted a "mess" and, believing that this success might make Mother forget the clam fiasco, which she regarded as a conspiracy contrived by her son-in-law for the sole purpose of getting her, Ashley and I delivered them to her with some optimism. She stared at the brimming bucket, clutched her head in her hands and wailed, "Oh, no! How do you expect me to clean all those? It's just not fair." I said that I'd had enough sun for the day and would cheerfully scrape and wash the mussels. Mother left me to it but, half an hour later, when I had finished scraping and was going out to the patio to rinse them off, she reappeared and grabbed the bucket. "Give me that. *He* may sit around and let you do all the work but *I* won't. Get back in the house and have a drink . . . now!" It couldn't have been more than a moment or two before Michael, who had showered and dressed for dinner, wandered out onto the patio. Mother, who had barely begun to do any rinsing, leaped at him. "Oh, Michael, thank God you're here! Finish washing these goddamned mussels for me. I'm *killing* myself out here! It's just too much, too much!" Michael, without comment, did her bidding and was finished in about two minutes. He delivered the mussels to the kitchen and came to join the rest of us at the bar.

A little while later, Mother emerged with a huge bowl of steaming mussels and placed them on the table as hors d'oeuvres. *"Well,"* she said threateningly, *"you* wanted them . . . *I* did it for you . . . *now* you can damned well *eat* them!"

"With pleasure," I said, trying to sound as though I were responding to a polite invitation rather than a do-or-die injunction.

"You'll never eat all those . . . I'll tell you *that*, right now! It's just *awful* that you would give me a project like this while I'm trying to cook a huge lobster dinner for you. I can't believe that you would actually do this to me. Christ! Well . . . they're here . . . so eat them!" They were delicious. Justin had two heaping bowls and everyone else was on a third or fourth when I called to Mother in the kitchen, "Mother? Would you like some mussels? I'll bring you a plate."

"Shit, no! They're for you kids. Anyway, I couldn't look at them anymore."

"Are you sure?"

"Yes!"

Kathryn wanted one bowl, so we set it aside for her. The serving bowl was about empty when Mother flew out of the kitchen, poked the few remaining mussels around with her forefinger and actually began to cry. "If any of you gave a shit about me, you'd have left me some. I *adore* mussels . . . you know that!" Without a word, we all dumped what we had left on our plates back into the bowl and left the table. Mother sat down and began to eat, muttering to herself about rude, ungrateful people. We had intended to gather more mussels to have for lunch before we left the next day, but they didn't seem that appetizing anymore.

Kathryn tried to restore the situation by going to the bar and offering drinks. She asked Justin what he would like.

"I'll have some apple juice, please." Exit Kathryn's good intentions. Mother appeared from the kitchen, teary-eyed and mouth full of mussels, shaking an empty apple juice jar. "Je-

sus! I had tons . . . how can he possibly have drunk it all up?"
Justin finally succumbed to the atmosphere and began to cry.
"Because when we got here you were mad at Mommy because
I asked for Coke when you'd bought apple juice specially
for me."

"Right! And you've gone and hogged it all. Now I've got
all this Coke and you want me to go out and buy more apple
juice for you!"

Ashley had heard perpetual mutterings about ". . . what
I'll do with this *mountain* of Coca-Cola if it isn't drunk . . . got
no other use for it . . . bought it specially for this weekend . . ."
and had been assiduously applying himself to the consump-
tion of it. Seeing help in his task, he said, "Why don't you have
a Coke with *me*, Justin?"

"Yes, Justin," Mother snapped, "stop being so damned fussy
and have a Coke with your brother." Kathryn fetched two Cokes
in the mistaken belief that another crisis had been overcome
and turned her attention to the adults. Jeremy, Michael and I,
remembering that a "mountain" of tonic water had also been
purchased "specially for this weekend," had gin and tonic. Chou
tried to help Ashley with his Coca-Cola problem. "I'll have a
rum and Coke, please."

Kathryn vanished into the kitchen to emerge a moment later,
empty-handed. "We're out of Coca-Cola." Mother went nuts.
"What?" she screamed. "I don't *believe* it! How the hell could
you do this to me? *Ashley* . . . how much did you drink, anyway? I had enough for an army! *Kath,*" she bellowed even
louder, "go out and find one of those twenty-four-hour mar-
kets and get some more Coke! We're out! Get a *mess* of it . . .
and maybe, Ashley, this time you'll have the decency to leave
some for the rest of us. Jesus!"

Chou protested that she would as soon have a gin and tonic,
but Mother would have none of it. "You wanted a rum and
Coke and you shall have it! This weekend is for you kids. Ashley! Christ! I don't understand you!"

A lifetime later, for so it felt at the time, dinner was about
to be served when a voice was heard from the beach. "Hey,
Bette!" Jeremy stepped over to the window and called down,
"Bette who?" Mother shrieked at Jeremy, "How *dare* you talk
to those people? Don't you know they make my life *hell*, how

Ashley, Mother with Justin at five days old, and me

Ashdown Farm

The Hyman family at Ashdown. I'm on my Arabian, Pasha. Justin is riding his pony, Chocolate.

they *upset* me? How can you encourage them like that when you know what it does to me?" Jeremy lost his grip on civility despite himself. "Bette, please stop screaming. I'm not overly fond of it." Mother burst into tears again and wailed, "How can you *do* this to me? I've worked so *hard* to give you a lovely weekend. *Brother,* you're nasty!"

"You aren't being so all-fired nice yourself, you know," Jeremy grated, glaring at her. Mother became wide-eyed with astonishment. "Oh! I was only *charmingly* explaining to you that I'd prefer it if you ignored those awful people out there." She struck her sweet southern belle pose, hands extended from her sides in supplication. Jeremy stared at her for a moment in disbelief, then said, "In that case, I apologize for taking offense. It would be helpful, though, if you'd announce ahead of time when you're charmingly explaining something and when you're screaming hysterically. It's tough to tell the difference."

Mother watched, speechless, as my husband turned on his heel and walked out of the house, closing the door behind him with ostentatious quietness. I was sure that he wouldn't be gone for long, wanting only enough time alone to regain his composure. To the best of my recollection, it was the first time over all the years that he'd permitted himself to say what he wanted to. It would be interesting to see how Mother took it. I tried to get her back on track by telling her that the "awful people" had continued on down the beach. She insisted that that had nothing to do with anything and retired to the kitchen. "Well . . . I might as well serve the lobsters. I got them specially for you . . . God knows I won't enjoy them . . . not after what Jeremy has done to me."

Jeremy returned and joined us at the table seconds before Mother bore the platter of lobsters out of the kitchen. He did an excellent job of behaving as though nothing untoward had occurred, while Mother put on a fabulous performance of the ill-used, pathetic heroine, shuddering and giving vent to extravagant sighs and hiccupping sobs. She maintained the pose for the rest of the evening and also changed tactics for the balance of the weekend. Instead of being critical of, and rude to, both Jeremy and Chou, she ignored Jeremy completely, which suited him perfectly, and became syrupy sweet toward Chou, who found herself smothered with solicitous attention and thus was more uncomfortable than she was with Mother's usual rudeness.

As full dark descended, the fireworks at Huntington Bay began. Mother had carried on for weeks about them. Apparently the owners had told her about them and how the house was the greatest spot on earth to watch them. It *was* an extraordinary sight and the owners had not exaggerated. There were groups of people setting off displays all around the curve of the bay, the Bay Club next door was mounting a display from a raft offshore, and all along the Connecticut coastline, a few miles across Long Island Sound from us, we could clearly see the rockets being fired up at all the coastal town displays. We drove each other crazy by pointing in all directions at once and insisting that he or she had seen something outstanding which all the others had missed.

Back in the house, Mother was demonstrating. A peek through the window discovered her to be seated in an armchair, arms folded and foot tapping, staring fixedly away from the windows. It was obvious that she was waiting for someone to beg her forgiveness, convince her that she was loved and plead with her to come see the fireworks. Unfortunately for her, we were all delighted to be spared her presence for a while, so she was forced to abandon the pose. She finally wandered out to join us on the seawall, skulked about for several minutes and then said, "This is no big deal. We had fireworks like this in Maine all the time. What do you mean? It's mostly noise anyway. Brother! You enjoy it, my dears, go right ahead!" Under another burst of rainbow colors overhead and sprays of Roman candles from the raft, she swept stiffly back indoors.

Shortly after midnight, although the festivities were still going strong, we found that we had had enough. As I carried a sleeping Justin toward the stairs, Mother popped out from a dark corner. "I don't know why you bother to try to sleep with all that noise out there. Christ, it's horrible!"

At breakfast Mother was in great fettle. "I'm so *proud* that I could have you kids here to see such an amazing sight! I told you this was the greatest place in the world on the Fourth of July. *Boy,* was I right! Jesus! We'll probably never see anything like it again. God! I'm so *proud* that I could show it to you! I only hope that you fully appreciated it!"

We stayed out of Mother's way until the farewell luncheon, and then faced the inevitable. Cold cuts had been laid out on the dining-room table and we were to fix our own sandwiches and carry them out to the umbrella table on the lawn. Mother had provided wicker plates to be used for support under the paper plates, and precisely one each of these was also laid out. When everyone had helped themselves and taken their seats, Mother suddenly charged at us, brandishing before her a wicker plate. A glance at the table disclosed the culprit. "Jesus, Ashley! What the hell is wrong with you? Why do you think I bought these, you thoughtless bastard?" Ashley gazed blankly at his grandmother, mumbled something under his breath and slid the cause of his debasement beneath his paper plate. All things considered, he did a fair imitation of his father in like circumstance.

Mother was only in the kitchen for moments before she rushed at us again, this time brandishing two milk containers in a visibly threatening manner. "Someone has to drink this up! Christ! I bought it specially for this weekend." Receiving nothing but "no, thank you" to her gracious offer, she moaned, "At least Coke will keep forever, but milk? I'll just have to pitch it, that's all."

"Why don't you leave it on the table?" I asked. "One of us will take it off your hands."

"Both jugs? Christ! What'll I do for milk if you do that . . . I'll have to buy more."

It was, at long, long last, time to depart and, as Jeremy was loading our bags into the car, he asked me if I was sure that we had everything. I said that I'd take one more look to be on the safe side. As I dashed back to the house, Mother was at it again, obviously thrilled at the opportunity. "Shit, Jeremy! Of course B.D. has everything. She was packed and organized while you were still lying in the sun, for Christ's sake! She's the most organized dame on earth. Brother! Come off it! I don't know how she stands it."

I emerged from the front door, Justin's favorite storybook in hand. "Thank heavens I checked . . . I found this under the bed. Justin would never have forgiven me." Mother whirled around and stalked off, undoubtedly convinced that Jeremy had hidden the book.

She went to the foot of the steps and called out that she would make her farewells from there. This crafty piece of stage management positioned her on the passenger side of the cars as they went by. Knowing that Jeremy and Chou were driving our respective cars, she was able to kiss her children fondly while ignoring the in-laws and the grandchildren. She was so thrilled with herself that we could still hear her cackling as we turned into the lane.

Looking back on that weekend visit from the perspective of a few days' remove, I realized I wasn't much better off than I had been while it was unfolding or during the postmortem in the car on the way home. I had fully expected Mother to phone me a day or so later and rave about the wonderful time we had all had, and she hadn't disappointed me. She did, in fact, try to have another "reunion" over Labor Day weekend, but both Michael and I pleaded prior, unbreakable commitments.

There was no longer any doubt in my mind that my old "thought to conjure with" was a fact: that Mother thrived on high drama, that what I considered to be abject misery *was*, to her, nothing more than boys and girls playing nicely together. What I couldn't figure out, no matter how hard I tried or how many directions I approached it from, was how she could delude herself so thoroughly.

Prior to our arrival for the weekend, I had been sure Mother believed, as Jeremy and I had, that we were really going to have a pleasant time. We had reasoned that, in her house with Mother at liberty to "be in charge" and none of us caring what she did or how she did it, she would be as close to happy as she ever got. She had had a field day making plans and changing them without let or hindrance. She had discussed meals and activities and fully indulged her self-image of perfect mother, mother-in-law, grandmother and hostess. As zero hour approached, however, all of her elaborate plans went out the window as the work involved overshadowed her intentions. She simply forgot all the plans, all the phone calls and all the promises as the reality became too much for her to cope with. Then, when we, the family, arrived, she came face to face with the actuality, us, whom she didn't really like. She didn't even like me . . . I wasn't who she wanted me to be . . . and her disillusionment, the collapse of her fantasy, turned her to irritability, anger, and rudeness.

Early in our marriage I had thought her behavior toward Jeremy and me was the result of a new mother-in-law's jealousy, but it wasn't that simple. Nor did attributing everything to her craving to be the center of attention account for everything. These things unquestionably contributed to her behavior, or lack thereof, but they didn't complete the picture. They did not explain why she treated Chou as she treated Jeremy. Michael had never been the only thing she loved. Every time Chou was out of the room Mother would mutter that Chou pushed Michael around and Michael had better learn to stick up for himself. It was the same as her saying that Jeremy had taken me over. Michael and I were her children and therefore expected to be the bosses, even if there was nobody in need of bossing. Michael and Chou had a very loving partnership, just as Jeremy and I had. Michael was easygoing and they got along splendidly, just as Jeremy and I did. Perhaps that was what so infuriated Mother. Perhaps she found a happy marriage upsetting . . . a threat to the validity of her lifelong views on the subject. Coupled with her love of high drama, this would account for some of her behavior but failed to explain why she was so unpleasant to all our children. Why did she pounce on Justin to the point of frightening him, shout at Ashley for every little thing and find fault with baby Matthew? I was undoubtedly missing something but I just kept coming back to her love of nastiness, tension and hysteria. It was *possible* this was at the root of it all and the rest just followed, but somehow I wasn't satisfied. There was something else . . . something that I would get close to once in a while but which always slipped away from me. Somewhere beneath all the fire and smoke was the original spark. Fires begin from a spark and Mother, in full histrionic eruption, was a forest fire destroying everything in its path. There had to be a cause. The trouble was that, cause or no cause, I was finding it increasingly difficult to ask my husband and children to tolerate my mother.

4

I received a call from Harold at Thanksgiving. He told me that Mother was suffering severe anxiety because I had not been to California to see her new home. I found this rather odd in that Mother had no more than casually mentioned that she wished I could see the condominium. Harold insisted, however, that it was a real and pressing problem and that Mother was suffering deep depressions because of me. "Your mother isn't getting any younger, B.D. She needs you to go to the coast and see her and, more important, her home. You know that she can't spend Christmas with you at the farm this year due to her work schedule. She'll be leaving the country to make a movie at the end of January. I wouldn't ask you to give up Christmas with your family, so you'll have to go in January. I cannot overly stress how important this is to your mother."

"Harold," I said, "hold on just a minute. Is there something I ought to know that you're not telling me? If there is, let's get it out in the open."

"I'm not hiding anything from you, B.D.," he replied with some asperity, "but at your mother's age anything can happen. She needs you to see her apartment. It's preying on her mind."

"I hear what you're saying, Harold, but I have to admit that it sounds like the same old Mother to me. I really don't see why I should have to go galloping off to California just because she's lonely."

"I thought that I had made myself perfectly clear, B.D. I think that you should fly out there right after Christmas for at least a week. Tell her now that you're going. Her spirits will be lifted and she'll be able to concentrate on her work without this upsetting her as it now does."

"If this has nothing to do with business, Harold," I asked impatiently, "why is it so all-fired important to uplift her spirits now? Why don't you just admit that she's trying to weasel out of something and you want to use me again?"

"I don't understand you, B.D. Why do you think you're being used just because your mother would like to see you?"

"Oh come on, Harold! My mother always wants to see me. It's when you get involved that I start being used."

"That's extremely unfair. You're the one who creates all the problems. Your mother loves you, as you well know, and asks very little of you. She's a great lady, an international symbol and, with the world at her feet, you're the one to whom she's devoted. Your happiness is always foremost in her mind and she's always been more than generous with you. You haven't visited her at home since you moved to Pennsylvania and your reaction to being told that she would like to see you is that you're being used. As I said before, I don't understand you, B.D."

"Of course you don't, Harold. It doesn't suit your purposes. And as far as visiting her goes, it was only a few months ago that we spent a few days with her on Long Island. It was an agony. She—"

"Look, B.D., I've heard what you have to say about being with her and frankly I'm unmoved. She's not just your mother . . . she's Bette Davis. She's entitled to special consideration and you should have the decency and moral fiber to show her that consideration. She understands *your* needs . . . why can't you understand hers? You sit up there on your hill and dictate the terms under which she's permitted to visit you. Why are you so unwilling to give just a little?"

"Harold," I blurted, feeling like crying and screaming all at the same time, "you're deliberately twisting everything around. I do my best but you've no idea what it's like for me to be with her."

"That's not important, B.D. What's important is that she needs you and you have an obligation to her which must be met. She's not getting any younger and I would hate to see you regret your selfishness for the rest of your life."

"All right," I sighed resignedly. "I can't argue anymore. I'll go out and see her for a couple of days right after Christmas."

"A couple of days isn't good enough. You must go for at least a week or it won't do any good."

"That's asking *too* much," I protested. "Do you really expect me to leave my family for a week or more in the middle of the Christmas holidays? I won't do it. There wouldn't be time for us to take a winter vacation together. You'll have to settle for a couple of days or wait until later in January when the boys have gone back to school."

"Later in January is no good. You have to go as close to Christmas as possible. Why don't you take your winter vacation in California? Your family could stay somewhere else and you could be together when you're not busy with your mother."

"That won't work and you know it, Harold. The minute I set foot in Mother's apartment she'll own me. I'll never be able to see my family without a massive argument. Apart from that, Justin would have to stay with me."

"If you care anything for your mother you'll figure it out. Make up a schedule of things you're going to do with your family and send it to your mother. Arrange it any way you want to, but arrange it. I hope for everyone's sake that you can be a little more understanding."

Harold had succeeded and I didn't understand why. My common sense was screaming that I was being used again, but my emotions betrayed me. Guilt, obligation, love, call it what you may, I fell for it again.

Jeremy agreed to go out of consideration for me, provided that he and Ashley see Mother only when absolutely, unavoidably necessary. We studied the boys' vacation schedules and decided to fly west on December 27 and stay through the fifth of January. We made up a schedule of things we intended to do, like visits to Marineland, Disneyland and assorted friends, and carefully left open New Year's Eve and January 4, our anniversary, so that Mother could give a party on one or the other date as she would inevitably insist on doing.

As Harold had instructed, I called her to let her know we were coming and she certainly sounded as though her spirits were uplifted. She immediately pounced upon January 4 and filled the next several days with phone calls to discuss guests for our anniversary party. I also sent her our schedule indicating when I would and wouldn't be with her and I even got her to acknowledge that she understood its significance.

It had been agreed in advance that we would all have dinner with Mother on the first evening. There were the usual shrieks of joy at our arrival and several repetitions of "This is the greatest present you could have given me, Jeremy. I know how difficult it is for you to be separated from B.D." We took the guided tour of the apartment and found it large, comfortable and airy with a fantastic view of the city from the balcony. The furniture was all familiar.

The agony began when Mother brought out an hors d'oeuvres tray before dinner and continued, almost without surcease, until we left nine days later, essentially a replay of the Fourth of July weekend with variations. At dinner the first night, Mother served Justin a pint tankard of apple juice and said that he had to finish it before he left the table. When I interceded, she took the tankard away and brought him a liqueur glass holding a few sips. She refused to give him a normal glass, screamed bloody murder if I so much as appeared to be going to the kitchen, insisted that it was her great pleasure to fetch Justin however many refills he might want, but always told him not to be so greedy when he asked for more. She gave Justin helpings of food that would have tried the appetite of a lineman and did her "That's not the way my children were brought up, I'll tell you that much right now" number whenever I told him that he need only eat as much as he wanted. She was rude to Jeremy at every turn, picked on Ashley for everything and yelled at Kathryn a few times.

Jeremy and Ashley left immediately after dinner and at 8:00 P.M., Mother sent Kathryn to bed and turned off all the lights, stating that she was dead and that I should go to bed to rest up from my long trip. I didn't bother to argue the first evening, but after Mother had spent all of the second day in the kitchen, where I was never allowed to enter, and again headed for bed at eight, I made so bold as to ask why I had traveled all the way to California to see her if she was going to spend all day in hiding and then go to bed at eight each evening. I knew that asking was a waste of time but, from the moment she had started up the night before, I had been getting angrier and angrier at Harold and at her . . . but most of all at myself for having been duped again. Her response, naturally, was that she was "dead" and that I shouldn't be ". . . so mean as to do this to" her when all she wanted was to give me a beautiful vacation.

Like the mountains of food on Justin's plate and the apple juice in a liqueur glass, Mother's hiding in the kitchen all day and going to bed early were also the pattern for the entire visit. I was a prisoner in my room every night and bored to tears every day, except for watching Justin play and the days I was with my family.

The following morning at seven, after Justin had climbed into bed with me and was playing with his E.T. doll, Mother barged into the room and said accusingly, "I *thought* I heard voices." To my response of "We just woke up," she said, "Why are you hiding in here? You're only going to be here for a few days and it would be nice to see you once in a while. Justin! Get out of your mother's bed! You're too old to be cuddling with your mother." Justin didn't move. He sat wide-eyed and pale while strange emotions flitted across Mother's countenance. I couldn't read them. Anger was dominant, but the rest eluded me.

"He should *not* be in bed fondling you," she suddenly spat, face almost contorted. I was surprised to find myself far more embarrassed than anything else. "He's not *fondling* me, for heaven's sake! We're cuddling and playing . . . there's a significant difference."

"Fine! Fine! Have it your way," she sneered, mouth twisted in an ugly, frightening fashion, "but don't be surprised when he turns out to be a goddamned faggot!" I stared at her, bemused; things people had insinuated about her at one time or another and recollections of similar outbursts at Michael when he was little flashed through my mind. I didn't want to think

298

about it, let alone discuss it further in front of my five-year-old son. "This conversation is ended, Mother. We'll see you in the dining room when we're dressed." Eyes squinted and mouth compressed into a tight slit, she spun around and marched from the room.

Later, as we were driving to Disneyland, Ashley and Justin in the backseat, Justin suddenly asked, "Mommy, what's a faggot?" Ashley burst out laughing and tried to explain, but I cut him off. "I'll field this one if you don't mind, Ashley." Jeremy took his eyes off the road for an instant to glance at me with raised eyebrows. "How did this one come up?" I told him about our early morning conversation with Mother.

"That's pretty warped, even for your mother," he observed.

"I know," I agreed. I turned sideways to look at Justin, who was patiently awaiting an answer. "Justin, I'm going to try to give you an answer you can understand. A fag, or faggot, which is slang for a homosexual, is a man who doesn't like ladies and never gets married. He prefers to only be with other men." I waited while Justin processed this new information. "Why did Grandmother say that I would turn out not to like ladies? I like Kathryn and Suzanne and Bonnie and lots of ladies. I'm going to marry a lady when I grow up."

"Of course you are," I said, "and what your grandmother said doesn't relate to you."

"Then why did she say it?" Jeremy and Ashley waited expectantly for my next response.

"Because she's eccentric," I answered.

"What's eccentric?" asked Justin. Before I could reply, Ashley chimed in, "It means, Justin, that Grandmother's weird . . . loony-toons."

"Is it because she's eccentric [Justin loved big new words] that she does all the things she does, like shouting at everybody all the time?" Justin asked.

"It accounts for some of the things she does," I said, "but most of them are the result of neuroses."

"What are neuroses?" asked Justin.

"It means she's loony-toons," said Ashley.

Jeremy laughed so hard that I had to grab the steering wheel to assure myself that he wouldn't weave off the highway. Justin, however, was unmoved. Since his father found Ashley's answer so funny, Justin suspected that he was still lacking a proper definition for neuroses. He waited for the uproar to die down and said, "You said that when I asked what eccentric meant, Ashley, so it can't mean neuroses too. Mommy said neuroses means something else, so don't be dumb."

"I'm not being dumb, Justin!" Ashley stated indignantly. "That's what it means." Jeremy stepped into the breach for me. "Ashley . . . keep quiet for a minute. Justin, I'll answer this one for you if you promise not to ask for any more psychiatric definitions, including the definition of psychiatric." Justin looked at me to see if he could get a better deal.

"What your father said," I said.

"O.K., Dad, I promise," he conceded reluctantly.

"Neuroses," Jeremy began, "is the plural form of neurosis. A person afflicted with any form of neurosis, and there are many, is a neurotic. One of the meanings of neurotic, and there are several, is a person of unbalanced judgment." We all waited for Justin's reaction. After mulling it over for a while, he said in deadly earnest, "Mommy, you keep using different words, but they all mean the same thing. Grandmother is loony-toons."

Apart from visiting Disneyland and Marineland and friends in Malibu and Lake Arrowhead, there were two bright spots. The first was a cocktail party, which Mother gave one afternoon and from which Jeremy, to his great relief, was excluded. The other was the anniversary party on January 4. New Year's Eve was a nightmare.

On the day of the cocktail party we had been to Marineland and were running a little late. The guests had been invited for four and, when Justin and I had changed and entered the living room at 4:05, most of the guests had already arrived. Mother introduced me to those I hadn't met before and I said hello to the ones I had. Kathryn fixed me a drink and gave Justin his liqueur glass of apple juice. I sat down on the big chaise longue, Justin beside me with the ever-present E.T. tucked under his arm. I didn't notice that he promptly fell asleep and no one mentioned it. No one, that is, until Mother materialized at my elbow. "B.D.! This is disgraceful!" Justin jumped half out of his skin and I asked, "What is?"

"That elegant boy sleeping in the living room like a vagrant!" she bellowed. "You were not brought up with such lax standards, I can tell you that much. Jesus!"

"Aw, look at that adorable little tyke," said a bystander, causing everyone nearby to smile as they gazed at my sleepy little boy.

"He'd be more adorable if he were in bed!" Mother snapped. "That's the proper place for a tired child."

"Poor little guy," said another bystander, "he looks exhausted."

"Yes," I said, getting up to rouse Justin and take him to our room for a nap, "he—"

"Poor little boy?" Mother cut in. "Brother! There's nothing poor about *that* boy. He's terrific. He's had a fabulous day with his parents at Marineland after going to Disneyland yesterday. You think that's so rough? Jesus!"

I gently led Justin, weaving sleepily, back to the bedroom and laid him down under a quilt. He was asleep again in an instant. I stood beside his bed for a few minutes, smiling down at him. I treasured his extroverted, joyful spirit and wanted to nurture it, not let it be suppressed by the likes of my mother. His natural, inquisitive outlook and enthusiasm for life were what Ashley frequently referred to as "the family sunshine." I was thankful that Mother wouldn't be able to cloud it for long.

When I returned to the party, the only nonarrival was Betty "Boo" Lynn, a dear longtime friend of Mother's. Mother took Kathryn aside to dispatch her on some previously discussed errand. "The only person who hasn't arrived is Boo. Go now and be back as fast as you can." A young man called Tom, whom I had just met and who was young, attractive and had once lived in the building, said, "Kathryn's leaving? Why?" Quite understandably, he looked slightly stricken. Kathryn was a bright, slender, strikingly attractive woman in her late twenties, about five feet five, with long black hair, big brown eyes and a naturally cheerful personality. I had frequently wondered why she put up with Mother's abuse. Toward the end of our visit, I learned that Kathryn had had substantial training in psychology. I chuckled inwardly at the thought that she might be working on her Ph.D. thesis.

Mother glared at Tom. "It's none of your damned business! Kathryn will go *where*ver I want, *when*ever I want. *I'm* in charge of Kathryn, not you. Christ!" Tom was undaunted. "I just wondered where she was going. Will she be back before I leave? I hardly ever get to see her."

"You are here to see *me* and my daughter, *not* Kathryn!" Mother trumpeted.

"I'm delighted with both of you, but I want Kathryn too. Can you blame me?"

"Shit! You really are a bastard . . . do you know that? If you can't live without Kathryn, then go with her . . . but don't bother to come back!" Mother stormed off to the kitchen, from whence she could clearly be heard talking to herself about insufferable people who would never again be invited to her home.

Kathryn had vanished on her errand during the exchange and, unable to ignore Mother's offstage rantings, Tom commented, "She says that every time I'm here."

"You must be doing something right," I quipped. At that moment Boo Lynn arrived, overflowing with apologies for being late and blaming it on heavy traffic. I said hello and Mother said, "That's no excuse . . . it's just damned rude! You'll have to get your own drink!"

"I'll get it, Mother. What would you like?" I asked Boo.

"You will *not*! *I'll* fix it," said Mother. Boo asked for a Scotch and turned to me. "Where's Justin? I'm dying to meet him."

"If you'd been here on time," Mother bellowed triumphantly, "you'd have seen him! Ha! Anyway, what is all this? All anyone wants is to see Kathryn and Justin. Jesus! You people are really something."

Muttering to herself again, she swept back into the kitchen.

Conversation resumed until Mother reappeared with an opened bottle of beer. She set it down next to Tom's half-full tankard. "Here! If you want any more, you'll have to get it yourself. I can't spend the entire afternoon worrying about your damned beer."

"Thank you, Bette." He was completely unruffled. "You don't have to worry a bit. I haven't finished my first one yet. Anyway, I know where the refrigerator is."

"You aren't kidding, you do! Brother! Last time you were here, you cleaned me out!"

"She loves me," Tom said as Mother vanished again.

Mother was her usual fidgety-hostess self, never sitting down, just flitting in and out of her beloved kitchen and taking shots at people. *This* time I was having a ball though. This was *her* house, *her* party, *her* friends, all there, one would assume, of their own free will.

The conversation was mostly about my life in general: marriage, children, life on the farm, how Jeremy and I met, how we came to "drop out," how one has a successful nineteen-year marriage in this day and age, etc. Mother had lost control of the situation. She darted in and out of the kitchen and prowled around looking for something to get excited about. It took her an unusually long time to find an excuse, but Tom finally came to her rescue . . . he used the wrong ashtray.

As he leaned forward to use the ashtray on the table in front of him, he failed to notice the one on the table at his elbow because it was slightly behind him. Mother had been bored and frustrated for half an hour but now, thanks to Tom, she could take charge and liven things up. "You stupid idiot!" she shrieked, startling the hell out of everyone as she charged across the room. She picked up the "correct" ashtray and shook it viciously in Tom's face, spraying him with ashes and a few cigarette butts. "What do you think this is here for? I put an ashtray next to *every* chair so my guests will be comfortable. How dare you ignore it?"

"I'm not likely to forget again," Tom replied, calmly brushing himself off. "Why don't you sit down and relax?"

"How *dare* you?" screamed Mother. "That's the worst thing anyone could *possibly* say to a hostess. I can't believe you would say such a horrible thing. Jesus! It's *work* being a hostess, or haven't you noticed?" Back to the kitchen she went, muttering loudly all the way and even louder when she got there.

At Mother's next emergence, several people stood up to leave. Mother decided that it would be appropriate for each guest to have a photograph of him- or herself, posed with me, to immortalize the joyous occasion. Kathryn, who usually wielded Mother's instant camera, had not yet returned. Mother polled the crowd and Dori Brenner, an actress friend of Mother's whom I had met for the first time that afternoon, accepted the task.

Mother was very fond of Dori and had spoken of her often.

She, like Kathryn, was a woman whom Mother referred to as "one of my adopted daughters." Dori took the camera. She had a little difficulty with the flash but, despite some delays, the pictures were coming out all right. After three pictures, all of which were fine, Mother jumped at Dori and snatched the camera away. "We'll just have to wait for Kath. Shit! You don't know what the hell you're doing." Dori and I and a few others developed the giggles over Dori's peremptory dismissal from her first photographic assignment. Mother was not amused by our amusement and went to the kitchen.

There was still no sign of Kathryn when, at Mother's next appearance, a guest apologized and said that she couldn't wait any longer. Mother thrust the camera back into Dori's lap. "*You'll* just have to do." Dori had as good a sense of humor as Tom and I was fast becoming fond of both of them.

"Thank you for the expression of confidence, Bette," said Dori.

"A new career in the making," quipped Tom.

"Shit!" yelled Mother. "None of you bastards takes *anything* seriously!"

Tom and Dori, for some reason, were unendingly curious about my life with Jeremy and continued to ply me with all sorts of questions. Every time Mother joined or even walked past our little group, she heard nothing but details of my married life and, worse than that, the frequent mention of my husband's name. Her anger at having to incessantly hear glowing reports of love among the pots and pans, not to mention barn chores, finally reached critical mass.

She flopped into a vacant chair, a sure indication that she meant business, and bellowed, "Christ! What can be so *wonderful* about that English bastard is beyond me. He's made a goddamned *slave* out of you, as he would *all* women if he could. He's a selfish *shit*!"

"Since it agrees with me so well," I said, "I guess I was just cut out to be a slave."

"Happiest slave I ever saw," said Tom. "I'd like to meet your husband . . . I think I'd like him."

"I'd trade places with you in a second," said Dori.

"You all make me *sick*!" screamed Mother.

"Seriously, Bette," Tom said, "if you could have chosen

B.D.'s husband for her, what kind of man would you have picked?"

"Now . . . there's a really good question," I said eagerly. "Whom would you have selected, Mother? Do tell."

"Well," she began, looking truly thoughtful and directing her response at Tom, "I'd have preferred it if she'd had a string of lovers and no husband at all. *Women,* my dear, would be much better off with that arrangement. Brother! Men would have to treat them better if they didn't have the security of a commitment to hang their hats on, I'll tell you that much right now."

"But . . . if you *had* to choose a husband for her," Tom persisted, "I'd really like to know." Mother frowned, gazed at the ceiling for a while, then stood up, placed her hands on her hips and, with feet widespread, announced, "I don't really know, but *certainly not an Englishman!*"

Tom, Dori, I and a few others who had been listening, literally, as the English say, "fell about" with laughter. Mother roared, *"Oh,* so you think an Englishman is such a goddamned *picnic,* do you?" She then gave her impersonation of Jeremy, affecting an exaggerated, Hollywood version of an Oxford accent. *"Sweetie,* how about a nice cup of tea? *Sweetie,* how about a snack? *Sweetie,* do something, the baby's awake. *Sweetie,* what's for dinner? Shit! It's just *ducky!"* This time, we didn't just fall about . . . we rolled on the floor.

When I finally recovered, sides aching, I said, "Let's face it, Mother, you and Jeremy will never get along."

"What!" shrieked Mother. "I get along perfectly well with that bastard. Jesus! I've always been an ideal mother-in-law. You and Jeremy should appreciate how hard it's been for me not to interfere in your lives. Brother!"

"Mother," I said, "it's difficult for anyone to respond warmly to someone who hates them."

"I've *never* let Jeremy know how much I dislike him," she blurted defensively, "so how the hell could he be offended? Shit! He's simply an objectionable man who hates all mothers."

Kathryn returned, looking particularly beautiful in a gray wool suit, black high heels and a very feminine black Derby hat with a small black veil.

"Wow!" Tom exclaimed.

"Are you going to start again?" Mother complained. "Leave Kathryn alone, for Christ's sake!"

"You look incredible!" Tom went on, jumping up from his chair and ignoring Mother completely. "That hat is fantastic."

"Thank you," Kathryn replied, setting down her purse and hanging up her jacket. "Is there anything you want me to do, Miss Davis?"

"Yes!" Mother blared. "Get that hat off and fix drinks. The snack trays need replenishing too." Kathryn did Mother's bidding with her usual good grace and, shortly thereafter, Mother ended the party in her typically abrupt fashion by starting to empty ashtrays and shouting at Kathryn to start washing glasses.

The anniversary party was held in the Magnum Room at the La Scala. It was a beautiful evening and Mother was on her absolutely best behavior since, among the notables, were Rock Hudson, R. J. Wagner and Jill St. John, Roddy McDowall, and Dorian Harewood. It was lovely renewing some old acquaintances and I might even have managed to leave California without *too* bad a taste in my mouth had it not been for the events of New Year's Eve a few days earlier.

On the afternoon of December 31, a crew from *McCall's* magazine had come to take pictures for a layout on famous grandmothers and their grandchildren. Mother had been particularly impatient with Justin, whose poor little nerves were stretched as tight as a drum. Jeremy would be calling for me at six and Justin asked lots of questions while I got ready. He wasn't seriously upset that I was going out for the evening with his father and leaving him and Ashley at Mother's, just apprehensive about being with her while I was gone. He wanted to know why I had to stay away all night. I explained that we would be out very late and that I was spending the night at the hotel with Daddy. His expression became increasingly agitated as six o'clock neared but I assured myself that as soon as I was gone, he would be fine. It would be difficult to change plans now despite the knot growing in the pit of my stomach. Mother had pleaded so strongly for the chance to spend the evening with her grandsons. If she only had *them* to focus on, I told myself, she would be the typical doting grandmother and all would be well. If I could just be strong and push aside my fears. I had to . . . if I changed plans now, all hell would break loose. Anyway, I told myself, I was letting my imagination run away with me. I was being silly. I smiled reassuringly at my little boy, reminded Ashley to take especially good care of his little brother, as he did at home when he "brother-sat" and, with a last pat to my hair, took my suitcase and headed for the living room.

Mother told me how ravishing I looked. I thanked her. Justin held my hand and stared up at me. I tried to ignore the look in his eyes. Ashley was telling Justin what fun things they were going to do. The buzzer sounded; it was the doorman announcing that Jeremy was waiting, double-parked. Justin's face began to crumple and he hung on to me tighter. I started to say good night to both boys. With sudden violence, Justin began to scream hysterically and grip me with desperate strength, begging me not to leave him. Mother was furious at his reaction, yelling that he loved her and that she would not be insulted like this. I tried in vain to calm him down but he was beyond reason. He was gripped with terror. I felt as if I were drowning. Everything took on an air of unreality and I felt as though I were in a black vortex. Mother was screeching, "Just go!" Justin was begging me not to leave him, Ashley was looking on, helplessly. Feeling as though I were watching myself from outside, I lifted a frantically struggling child and handed him to his brother, wrenching his little hands as gently as I could from their hold on my dress. There were no words possible. I told Ashley to hang on to him. As I left, Ashley was clutching a kicking and screaming Justin who was crying, "Mommy! Mommy!" desperately, with his arms outstretched. Mother, still furious, virtually pushed me through the door.

I felt physically sick. I stood in the hall waiting for the elevator to arrive, with the sounds of my son's anguish ringing in my ears, I loathed myself. Why was I standing here? Why didn't I throw open the door to the apartment and reclaim my child? I stood there, tears coursing down my cheeks, until the elevator doors opened. I stepped in like a zombie. God, I loathed myself! How had I let her bring me to this? I was no better than she . . . she had won. I had deluded myself for all these years that I was my own person. What a joke! I was so filled with self-revulsion that I was almost unable to stand. Yet there I stood, going farther and farther away from my terrorized child. All right, Mother . . . you've won them all till now . . . but it stops here. Ashley will take care of his brother for this one evening. I've done it now . . . the worst is over. Jeremy's waiting for me . . . it's New Year's Eve and I won't spoil it for him too. I'll find the strength to put a good face on it, bury my self-recrimination for a little while and comfort myself with the promise that it will never happen again.

I stepped out into the lobby and paused before the mirror to repair my face. Oh God, I was a revolting hypocrite! I went out to the car and Jeremy came around to open the door for me.

"Hi, darling," I said, a bit too brightly.

"Are you all right?" he asked as he kissed my cheek.

"I'm fine, thanks. Why?"

"Oh, I don't know. You just look a bit off."

It was early the next morning when we arrived at Mother's to pick up the boys. I knocked on the door and, instead of Kathryn greeting us, there stood Ashley and Justin. Justin ran to me, threw his arms around my waist and hugged me wildly, jumping up and down for joy. Ashley said quietly to his father, "Wait till I tell you what happened last night."

"Not until we're outside, you jerk!" Jeremy hissed under his breath. Mother and Kathryn stepped out of the kitchen and the amenities were superficially observed. Then Mother blurted, "Well . . . you wanted them ready early . . . they are. Why don't you go?" Ashley's suitcase and Justin's satchel were standing by the hall bench. We picked them up and went.

"Now," Jeremy said to Ashley as we headed west on Sunset. Ashley told us his tale.

"Well, actually it was horrible. The minute you left, Grandmother grabbed Justin from me and started shaking him, shouting that he should stop his infernal noise or she would do something about it. Justin howled louder and Grandmother put her hand on the back of his neck, bent him over and spanked him. She only hit him three times, but I know it was as hard as she could. The expression on her face was vicious. Justin screamed at the top of his lungs . . . you know how loud he can scream when he's really upset. Well, that's what he was doing, and flailing his arms at Grandmother and trying to get away from her. She didn't let go of him . . . she dragged him by the arm to the back bedroom, gave a huge yank and threw him through the door. She slammed the door and shouted at him that he better damn well stay in there and not try to come out till he'd learned his lesson.

"She came back to the living room and started on me, saying it was all my fault and that if I hadn't been coddling him, none of this would have happened. I told her that's what you'd told me to do and I was going back to the bedroom to take care of him. She screamed at me like she was crazy or something. She said I wasn't to go back there, that I wasn't to talk to Justin at all without her permission. She shouted that she was in charge, not me . . . and certainly not my mother who'd gone out and left us.

"I didn't know what to do, so I just sat down and felt rotten. I don't know how long I sat there . . . ten or fifteen minutes . . . I don't know. But then it suddenly dawned on me that I'm a foot taller and a lot stronger than Grandmother . . . why was I just sitting there instead of doing what you'd told me? My poor little brother was back there, scared out of his wits and crying his heart out. If I really wanted to do something about it, there was nothing Grandmother could do to stop me. Kathryn certainly wouldn't help her. She looked as upset as me. I got up and headed for Justin's room. Grandmother yelled where was I going and I yelled back that I was going to take care of my baby brother. She yelled even louder that I better not and I yelled louder still that I was going to and she couldn't stop me. I went back, picked Justin up and sat down with him on my lap, just the way I've seen you do, Mom. Boy, is Justin strong when he squeezes you round the neck! Grandmother followed me and stood there, shouting and yelling and screaming and shaking her fists at me. I don't remember what she said . . . most of it didn't make any sense anyway. When she finally shut up and left the room, all I knew was that she seemed to have gone completely nutso and that Justin and I were going to stay right where we were until you got back, if we had to.

"Justin started to quiet down a bit and I remembered the piece of paper with the hotel phone number which Dad had given me. I found it in my pocket and Justin and I went to the phone next to the bed to try to call you. I was in the middle of dialing when Grandmother sort of jumped at me out of nowhere. She shouted something like you were having a wonderful evening and she wasn't going to let me wreck it for you. She yanked the phone out of the wall and said that I should stop being sneaky and trying to go behind her back. She said, and she really did say it, Dad, that I'd fucking well learn to behave myself or she'd really let me have it. She took the phone out of the room and was gone for . . . oh, I don't know . . . five or ten minutes. All of a sudden, she came back with this great big smile on her face and said, as nice as can be, that dinner was ready and since she'd gone to all the trouble of making Justin's favorite, the least we could do was come and eat it while it was still hot. She went away again and Justin and I . . . he was still sitting on my lap but wasn't crying anymore . . . sort of looked at each other and shrugged our shoulders and said why not? So we went and had dinner and then went to bed. We messed around this morning and had breakfast and then you guys showed up."

It had taken Ashley five minutes to tell his tale and then there'd been another couple of minutes of embellishment from Justin. Then there had been only the noise of the car engine and the traffic flowing the other way. The sun was pouring down and the sprinklers were going about their unending battle for the preservation of lawns of grass not native to the climate. The palm trees marched by in their rows and the incredible homes and mansions of the unbelievably rich floated by like ghosts from a dimly remembered past. Inside me, all was black and cold. My husband continued to drive in silence, his knuckles white on the steering wheel. Ashley pointed out to Justin the mansion of the Shah's sister, now all blackened and boarded over after a terrorist torching. It reflected my mood.

I thought I needed time to think, time to sort things out in my mind . . . but then I realized I had been thinking and sorting for nineteen years and it hadn't made any difference. All right, Mother . . . you've finally done it, I thought. I've tried to understand your needs and fulfill my obligations, but you've gone too far. I don't know what demon drives you, not for sure, and after last night, I don't care anymore. When the battle was between the two of us, or three with Jeremy's involvement, you were picking on people your own size. My children aren't. They can't make their own decisions and walk away if they want to. My husband could, but he stuck by me. Why my children too? You've blown it this time, Mother. They can't defend themselves, so I'll have to protect them . . . against their grandmother, for God's sake. Living legend you undoubtedly are, but I won't play games with my children. I may have obligations to you . . . God knows I've been reminded of them often enough . . . but I'm a mother too. My obligations to my children transcend any I may have to you.

Ashley was telling Justin that the road leading off to our right, between a pair of stone pillars, led to where I had lived years ago.

"Justin," I said, "you have my word. You'll never have to visit your grandmother again. I'm sorry for what happened, but I can't explain it . . . please don't ask me to. All I can do is make sure it never happens again."

"Why don't we go home now, Mommy?" Justin asked. I spelled out my reasoning, that having gone this far with the visit, the worst was over. Of the remaining five days, today was being spent with friends in Malibu; tomorrow and the next day we would be with friends in Lake Arrowhead. The day after that would be the anniversary party. Grandmother would spend all day getting ready for it. The following day we would be packing to leave at dawn the next morning. To throw in the towel now, I said to everyone, would cause more problems than it would solve. Apart from anything else, we had to consider the people who were coming long distances to the anniversary party. Dave and Andi Keeler, for instance, friends from Wyalusing, had already left there and were visiting Andi's mother in San Francisco on their way. No . . . we couldn't get on the next plane home.

Jeremy looked at me and nodded grimly, his meaning somewhere between "thank you" and "it's about damned time." Justin was more or less reassured. He and Ashley were chattering much more normally in the backseat. I was still cold inside. It was comparatively easy not to visit Mother again . . .

and if I had to, I could always go alone . . . but what about her next visit to the farm? I hadn't realized it at the time, but this trouble had begun two years ago, with Ashley during *Family Reunion* . . . it had continued with both boys at the Fourth of July gathering . . . now this. I was afraid that worse was yet to come.

5

1983

At the beginning of 1983 Mother was signed to do a cameo as the grande dame of the Vanderbilts in the television show *Little Gloria—Happy at Last,* but before she was due to come east to do it, I received a call from Harold. A deal had been made for Mother to do an upcoming television series called *Hotel.* Even though the script for the pilot was perfectly acceptable to her and there were more than adequate assurances that subsequent scripts would be of at least comparable quality, and even though she would be getting one hundred thousand dollars a day for seven days' work each year, Mother was trying to bug out. Harold wanted me to talk sense into her immediately.

We went through the usual discussion of how I was to initiate a phone call and then bring up the subject of a series about which, ostensibly, I had never heard. Harold reiterated the urgency of the matter but left me to figure it out, reminding me as usual that he and I hadn't talked. As it turned out, I was spared the need to contrive a conversational opening with Mother. She phoned the next day to tell me how depressed she was about her new commitment.

"I need to talk to you, B.D. I've signed to do a part in a

series called *Hotel*. I play the owner and have to appear in seven episodes a year. It's at Fox Studios on a sound stage instead of location all the time and I only film for one day per show, but I hate it. I'm broke and I have to do it for the money. Shit! They're paying me a hundred thousand bucks for each show and I can do more than seven a year if I want to, but I'm doing this for Harold because I need the dough. Christ! I'm sick about it."

"First of all," I said, "I read the book and enjoyed it. I think it'll make a great series."

"You would!"

"Come on, Mother! Seven days a year for seven hundred thousand dollars and you expect *sympathy*? That's a bit much, isn't it?"

"I detest doing things for money. You know that."

"Mother, we've been over this countless times before. People work for money . . . you get paid a bit more than average, that's all. You don't work for free on projects you like . . . far from it. You get paid for everything you do. You don't mind getting paid when you start out liking something and wind up hating it, do you? You like spending money well enough. Why do you resent making it? Why is *Hotel* such a problem for you? You liked the script, it's not on location, it's on a sound stage in a studio right down the road from your home, the money's—"

"That's it! Keep talking to me . . . convince me. I need to be convinced! *Harold*, as you might imagine, is *thrilled* . . . I can tell you that much right now."

"I don't blame him for being thrilled. It's a great deal. You hate being on location, you hate being away from home when you're working, you're constantly complaining that the movie scripts you see stink and half the things you do want to do fall through for lack of financing. I really don't understand what you're complaining about with this *Hotel* deal."

"O.K., B.D., but I'll be stuck like a rat in a goddamned trap in California for the summer. I hate it here. I wanted to come east to see you."

"I just spent two weeks with you last month. Anyway, I thought your objection to California was the persistent sunshine. It's been raining out there for a month now. I'd have thought it would have earned a special place in your heart by this time."

"Christ! This isn't rain . . . it's monsoons. Shit! I can't stand it anymore . . . I'm beginning to mold."

"Have you forgotten that you're spending two weeks on the French Riviera in May and then coming back through New York and Pennsylvania for another couple of weeks? That's not exactly stuck."

"You would twist it all around. I used to think we were twins. Christ! We're opposites! No matter what you say, I hate working for the dough. It makes me sick!"

"Oh, for heaven's sake, Mother!" I said, nearing complete exasperation. "Most people work five or six days a week, fifty weeks a year to earn a lot less than you're earning in one day, and *you* have the gall to insist that you resent the money. It makes me nauseous, it truly does. Do me a favor and grow up . . . please?"

"I know what I'll do!" she suddenly exclaimed. "I'll marry some rich old fart and retire."

"Spare me, will you?" I groaned. "You've had your chances to do that too and passed them up. What the hell does that have to do with playing an elegant lady in a classy series a few days a year? Where's the hardship? It doesn't make sense."

"Let's drop it, shall we?" she snapped. "I'll put in my sweat labor like a pro and shut up. I can see I'll get no understanding from you. Shit! I'm just delighted with the whole stinking mess . . . all right? By the way, are you watching *The Thorn Birds* on television?"

"Oh, yes."

"Did you read it?"

"Twice."

"What do you think of it?"

"Fabulous! I think Richard Chamberlain is magnificent!"

"Yagh! He's not even vaguely believable. He's totally sexless. And *Stanwyck*! God! She was awful! She wasn't the least bit sexy. Mary Carson was supposed to be a sexy broad, for Christ's sake! *I* should have played Mary Carson. You know I wanted to. Brother! *Then* the audience would have known about sex appeal!"

"Mother! Mary Carson was seventy-five years old and had delusions of sex appeal, not the attributes. That's what it was all about . . . her jealousy of Father Ralph's devotion to Meggie, even as a little girl. I liked Barbara Stanwyck tremendously."

"Oh, you did, did you? Traitor! Well, anyway, all Chamberlain's Father Ralph seems to think about is sex. He's supposed to be a priest, for Christ's sake!"

"Make up your mind, will you? You just finished saying that you thought he was sexless. He can't be overtly sexy . . . he's a priest. The point of the whole thing is his torment between Meggie and his love of the Church. He's living a kind of hell."

"I'll tell you who could really have played Father Ralph . . . Burt Reynolds! Of course he's ruined himself with all that crap southern comedy he does, but—"

"Burt Reynolds? The same of *Smokey and the Bandit* fame? I adore Burt Reynolds, Mother, but surely you can't see him convincing a fly that he's a tormented priest. I can picture him choking with laughter at the suggestion. And he's hardly ruined himself . . . he's probably the most popular male star in the country. He's a good actor but, good grief, not Father Ralph!"

"Well, I can see we're not going to agree on anything today. We'll talk soon."

As the beautiful days of spring passed gloriously by, the memory of Christmas dimmed. I had no illusions about what lay ahead of me, but my concerns became less and less imperative with the passing of time. When I permitted myself to contemplate it, Mother's next visit did have me worried. Jeremy had tried to discuss Mother's future visits with me, but I had put him off by saying there would be time enough to worry about it when it happened, and asking him not to make things worse for me than they already were. When Mother came east and announced that she would visit the farm in mid-May, I faced up to Jeremy.

"What are you going to do?" he asked.

"It'll only be a short visit," I replied. "I'll just make sure that everything's kept under control." My husband's eyes hardened. "How, pray tell, do you think you're going to manage that?"

"I'm simply not going to let her push me around anymore. You'll do your disappearing act, Ashley will be at school and I'll be super careful that Justin's never left alone with my mother. Trust me . . . I know what I'm doing."

"For heaven's sake, listen to yourself! We've been telling each other garbage like that for nineteen years and we've never been able to keep her under control. Have you forgotten New Year's Eve?"

"No . . . of course not, sweetheart. I haven't forgotten anything. That was at *her* house though. I promised that we'd never go to *her* house again . . . I *meant* it. This is different."

"Quite frankly, Sweetie, I see very little difference. In fact, I think this is worse. It would have been easier for you to walk out on her at Christmas than it'll be to throw her out of *here*. You weren't willing to take a walk *then* . . . are you telling me that you *are* willing to throw her the hell out of here if she behaves like that again?"

"But I won't let her . . . that's what I'm trying to tell you."

"Oh, come off it, Beed . . . you can't predict what your mother's going to do or how you're going to control her any more than you can fly to the moon. Maybe you can fool yourself, but your argument leaves me cold. I think—"

"Stop! Be fair about this . . . *please*! You're telling me that I have to shut my mother out of my life completely. I can't do that . . . I just can't. When your mother stayed with us and drove me crazy with her incessant complaining, I didn't tell you *she* would never be welcome again, did I?"

"There's a slight difference, Beed, and you know it as well as I do. My mother can be pretty damned aggravating, but she doesn't presume to clobber or threaten other people's children, let alone frighten her own grandson half to death."

"But it won't happen again," I pleaded. "I won't let it happen again. I told you . . . I'll never leave Justin alone with her."

I was becoming more and more distraught and tears were forming in my eyes. Jeremy, angry as he was, suddenly relented. "I'm sorry, Sweetie. I didn't mean to pick on you. This is tough enough on you without my making it worse." He paused while I sniffled a bit, then said, "Wouldn't your mother be thrilled if she knew we were fighting about her?" I managed an agreeing chuckle through my tears and he went on, "I'll tell you what . . . I'll make a deal with you . . . I'll do my disappearing act, as you call it, and leave the rest in your hands if you'll make me a promise."

"What's that?"

"If your mother ever again lays a finger on Justin, or even threatens to, it's all over. He's my son too and I love him just as much as you do. I want you to remember that if my mother had done what your mother did, there wouldn't have been a need for this conversation." I knew he was right. He wouldn't tolerate such behavior in his own mother, so how could I go on finding excuses for it in mine? I had no choice but to accept his offer. "You have my word. If she goes after Justin again, it's over. But don't worry," I added bravely, "it'll all work out. I'll be able to keep it under control . . . you'll see."

"I'll be rooting for you and I'll do anything I can to help, but I think you're kidding yourself." Unfortunately, I tended to agree with him. I didn't feel nearly as brave as my words. The sense of foreboding which had begun on New Year's Day grew heavier and heavier as Mother's visit drew closer.

6

Little Gloria—Happy at Last was filmed in and around New York; Mother's part of the show was done at The Breakers, the old Vanderbilt mansion. The morning that Mother was due to arrive at the farm, for what would turn out to be her last visit, I discovered that Justin had a high fever and a rash all over his body when I woke him for school. I dosed him with liquid Tylenol and sponged him down until Doc Pete's (Dr. Karl Peterson) office opened at eight-thirty. He told me to get Justin down there on the double because it sounded like a form of strep rash that was going the rounds.

While I dressed Justin, I asked Jeremy to try Mother's number at the Lombardy Hotel in New York. There was no answer from her suite . . . it was too late to head her off. One of us would have to stay behind at the house and, since children invariably cling to their mothers when they're sick, it fell to Jeremy to wait for Mother. There was a chance I would be back before she arrived but, from what Pete had said, there was an equal chance that I would have to take Justin to the hospital.

Pete decided that, provided I watch him very carefully for the next two days and obey instructions to the letter, Justin would be all right at home with antibiotics. With this type of strep virus, his temperature could spike and bring on convulsions . . . keeping his temperature down was of the essence. Pete also told me not to give Justin any medicine until we got home, it might make him car sick. I phoned Jeremy, gave him Pete's diagnosis and said I would be home as soon as I picked up the prescriptions at the pharmacy.

Poor Justin was absolutely miserable and very grateful when his daddy carried him into the kitchen and put him down in the big reclining armchair. Mother had arrived but minutes earlier. I followed Jeremy into the house, said hello to her and Kathryn and explained that I needed five minutes to get Justin settled and give him his medicine before I would be able to focus.

While I was seeing to my sick little boy at one end of the thirty-foot, L-shaped kitchen, Mother was messing with bags and boxes at the other end, around the corner in the L. Kathryn, who was going on with the car to visit her sister in central Pennsylvania, came over to me and asked how Justin was doing. I told her that his condition was borderline; if his temperature were to rise above its present 105 degrees, I would have to rush him to the hospital.

Mother suddenly loomed at my elbow and thrust a large, cold, raw salmon in my face. I jumped back and she poked at it with her forefinger. "Isn't it the most incredible salmon you've ever seen? Just look at this fish!" Jeremy stepped around her and, on the shelf of the bay window, placed the bowl of ice water I had asked him to get. I pushed past Mother and her fish and put two washcloths into the bowl, wringing one out and placing it on Justin's forehead. Even as I was bending over him, Mother again thrust the fish in my face.

"Aren't you going to look at this? Jesus! It took some little effort to find the perfect size salmon."

"Mother, please!" I pleaded. "I have a very sick little boy and I only need a few more minutes. As soon as he's comfortable and I've given him his medicine, you'll have my undivided attention. Put the salmon on the counter and leave everything where it is until I can focus." She strode off and angrily slammed the salmon down. I went to the table and opened the bag in which I had brought home Justin's three medicines. As I was measuring out the proper dosage of the first one, Mother again clamored at my elbow, "What do you think of the size of these artichokes?" This time she thrust an artichoke in my face.

"Terrific," I said, "just terrific. I'll be with you in a minute." I administered two of the medications but had to get a different measuring tube from the cabinet over the sink for the third one. As I was reaching for it, Mother jabbed at me with a live lobster and asked indignantly, "What are you going to do about these lobsters?"

"Nothing until I'm finished with Justin's medicine," I replied.

"Fine," she sneered, "let them die! What's the difference? They only came all the way from Maine and cost a fortune." I returned to Justin, gave him the last of his medicine, replaced the cloth on his burning forehead with a cold one and straightened up to find Mother standing right behind me, still holding her lobster.

Even though her total lack of interest in the welfare of her grandson came as no surprise, her absolute absorption with herself and the food she had brought rankled. "Lobsters die a lot faster when you carry them around," I said. "Why don't you put it back with the others and leave them alone? They'll be fine in the chest you brought them in if you leave it closed."

"Don't blame me if they croak," she snapped.

"You can relax now," I said. "You have my undivided attention." I looked around for something to enthuse about which hadn't already been shoved in my face. "What a pretty basket the artichokes are in!"

"Oh, so you noticed? I didn't think you cared."

"Will you kindly come off it, Mother. I stated quite clearly, I thought, that my first concern was for Justin. It's pure luck that I'm not at the hospital with him instead of here. It could have gone either way."

"Christ! That would have been just *ducky*. I wouldn't have come if I'd known Justin was sick. Jesus! This is some visit!"

"I tried to call but you'd already left. Now that you're here, however, you might show a bit of concern for your grandson. He's very sick, in case you haven't noticed."

"Why? What for? *You're* fussing enough for an army. He's

fine! Brother! *I'm* the one no one gives a shit about."

"Oh good grief!" I spun away from her in exasperation. "Do you ever listen to yourself? You're utterly pathetic."

"Oh, I am, am I?" she shrilled. "Why isn't precious Justin up in his room if he's so sick? Shit! That's the way my children were brought up."

"I remember . . . but I have to bathe him constantly and take his temperature every half hour. There's a chance it could spike and bring on convulsions. He's staying right here where I can take care of him."

I walked angrily away and went over to Justin, took a fresh cloth from the bowl of ice water, squeezed a few drops onto his parched lips, and put it on his forehead. I took his temperature; it was still 105 degrees. I sponged him again with cool water, as the doctor had instructed. Jeremy came in from giving Kathryn directions and seeing her off, took Justin's hand and asked how he was doing.

"He's *fine*, my dear, just *fine*!" Mother blurted. Jeremy ignored her. I told him that Justin was the same and it would be a big help if he could spell me with the sponging every so often. We kept at it and after two hours, Justin's temperature inched down to 104 degrees, a good sign.

For the rest of the day we concentrated on keeping him cool and giving him liquids. Mother paced angrily about the house, smoked like a chimney and wandered in and out of the kitchen to tell me that Justin was ". . . *fine*, my dear, just *fine*," or to say, on one occasion, "I find it *fascinating* that Justin was well enough to go to the circus yesterday, but can't so much as sit up today." I didn't bother to reply. By dinnertime, Justin's fever was down to 102 degrees. He felt alive again and was managing to smile.

The lobsters were still fresh and healthy and were finally put out of their misery. I had recently heard Gary's voice both in TV commercials and as a cartoon character. In the attempt to find a topic of conversation, I asked Mother why, in all her years, she had never done the voice for a cartoon character.

"It's not that it hasn't come up," she replied. "They've been after me forever to do a voice, but I've always told them to go to hell. Only people who can't get a decent job do that shit.

Look at Gary . . . he does them all the time because he's too lazy to work. It would be humiliating."

"I don't know," I mused. "I'd have thought it would be great fun."

"*Fun?* Christ! Do you know what *work* that is? It's hours and hours of looping. They pay *peanuts* for the sweat that goes into it."

"Well . . . now I know why you've never done a voice."

"Right! Gary's done practically nothing else for years. He's made a *fortune* out of it."

"You just said that it didn't pay much. How could he—"

"I *hate* cartoons. I hate *commercials* too. Jesus! They make me sick. Anyway . . . no one ever asked me."

By Saturday morning, Justin was definitely on the mend. His temperature was hovering between 101 and 102 degrees and he still had to stay quiet and drink a lot of fluids, but I could at least devote more attention to Mother than to him. It didn't make much difference, though. The only acceptable topics that morning were how good the lobsters *had* been, how good the salmon *would* be, what to do with two extra artichokes and how incredible it was that Mother had brought all this food. Whenever I was ministering to Justin in any way, she came and stared at him, much in the way one stares at a foreign object in one's soup. She didn't speak to him . . . just stared for a while and then walked away.

At lunchtime Justin expressed a desire for some canned peaches. This was good news indeed and, coupled with his new temperature reading of 100 degrees, was reasonable evidence that the worst was over. I opened a can of peaches, fixed him a bowl and told him to leave what he didn't want on the table to nibble at when he felt like it. I left him sitting at the table and went to the bathroom. Within two minutes at the most, Justin was screaming and sobbing and pounding on the bathroom door. I rushed out and he flung himself into my arms, clinging to me with all his might.

I finally got out of him that the moment I left the kitchen, Grandmother told him that if he didn't finish every single bite, she would give him a spanking. He still remembered New Year's Eve too vividly not to panic. Leading him by the hand, I went to the kitchen to confront Mother. "What's your excuse, this time?" I demanded angrily. She struck a belligerent pose. "What's my excuse for what? What's that little liar been telling you, eh?"

"Shit, Mother!" I exploded. "Spare me the little liar crap! You know perfectly well that you threatened to spank him if he didn't finish his peaches. It's the same garbage you were handing him in California and I want to know why." Her eyes narrowed to a squint and her expression became venomous. "You coddle him too much . . . he'll be a sissy when he grows up . . . you'll see. A good whack now and then will do him good. Shit! You're just too much of a lily-gut to do it."

"Mother," I said, restraining myself with great difficulty, "listen to me and listen very carefully. . . . I'm never going to tell you this again. You keep your whacks and your spankings to yourself, and don't you dare threaten Justin again. I'm giving you fair warning . . . one more time will be your last."

"Fine," she sneered, face contorting with emotion. "Justin deserves better than that, but have it your way!" She stormed upstairs, slammed the door of her room and wasn't seen again for hours.

Justin had clung tightly to my hand and half hidden behind me during my altercation with Mother. I took him to his chair and sat down with him on my lap. "I'm sorry, sweetheart, I really am. I didn't think she'd behave like this in *our* house."

"I knew she would," he stated simply, lower lip quivering. "She hates me."

"I wish I could disagree with you, but she certainly behaves as though she does."

"She hates everyone. I told you that before."

"I know you did, but she's leaving in the morning. We'll worry about it after she's gone." I stood up, gave him a big squeeze and put him down in the chair with a kiss on the forehead. As I straightened up he said, "I love you, Mommy. It's not your fault." I turned quickly away. I didn't want him to see the tears in my eyes.

When Mother came downstairs in midafternoon, I had difficulty maintaining even a semblance of civility. She began to place a series of phone calls, the routine for each being the same. She was trying to use her new telephone credit card and didn't know how. It took her three or four tries with each call before she got a connection and, each time she messed up, she slammed down the receiver of my antique kitchen wall phone. By the time she was making her third attempt at her third call, I'd had enough. Not only was she getting on my nerves, but I feared for the life of my lovely old phone. "Why don't you let me do it for you, Mother?"

"I know how to run this machine," she snarled, placing her hand possessively on top of the phone. "Leave me alone!"

"Then why do you try so often with each call?"

"There are a lot of stupid operators, that's why! Now leave me alone!"

"Mother, please! You're slamming the phone down so hard you're going to break it. Let me act like your secretary and place the calls for you. It'll be easier." She spun around on the barstool and screamed, "Get off my back! I can dial the phone myself! You can't tell *me* what to do!" That did it. I leaned forward until my face was mere inches from hers and hissed through clenched teeth, angrily clipping each word, "Don't you bloody well scream at me, Mother. Do . . . not . . . scream . . . at me. If you know what you're doing, then do it . . . but stop crashing my phone to bits every time you screw up." She squeezed her eyes into narrow slits. "You'd better just watch it, B.D. You'd better be damned careful."

"What exactly am I being threatened with this time, Mother? Are you going to give me a spanking?" She slid off the stool and headed for the stairs again. I followed her. "Well? What are you going to do if I don't watch it? I'd like to know, Mother. I guess you only hit children, so what are you threatening *me* with? You've done it often enough . . . you must have something in mind." By this time she was at her bedroom and I was at the top of the stairs. She turned in the doorway. "I don't know . . . I just don't know. Leave me alone! Jesus! I can't stand any more! Don't do this to me!"

"Do what?" I demanded. "I'm not doing anything except try to clarify what I'm being threatened with." She slammed the door in my face.

Mother didn't appear again until dinnertime. She went to the bar, poured herself a big one, then went to the kitchen ta-

ble and sat down without a word. Justin was asleep in the re-
cliner at the far end of the room. I was at the counter, preparing
the trimmings to go with the salmon, which I had already
cooked and placed in the refrigerator to cool. Mother belted
down her drink and went for another, taking mincing little-
old-lady steps, shoulders all hunched forward. If she wanted
games, two could play . . . I would serve and eat dinner in
silence before I would speak first.

Hearing waking-up noises from Justin, I went to him and
helped him down some juice. When I asked if he felt like eating anything, he said he'd like half an English muffin, if we
had any. It was the first solid food he had wanted since taking
ill and I was delighted. I fixed the muffin and he took a seat
at the end of the kitchen table, as far from Mother as he could
be. Without thinking . . . and why should I have? . . . I went
to the dining room to set the table for dinner. No sooner was
I out of the kitchen than I heard Mother's voice. "You better
damn well finish that muffin or your mother's going to whack
your ass and boot you to your room. She's had enough of your
insolence." I was back in the kitchen before Justin had even
had time to react. I said, "You eat as much as you want and
no more, Justin. Then, I think, it would be best if we put you
to bed. Your grandmother seems to have a problem." I gave
Mother, an "Open your mouth and I'll close it for you" type
of look and she glanced away. I sat with Justin until he finished, made sure that he didn't want any more and led him
upstairs.

I put dinner on the table as soon as Jeremy came in. I can't
speak for anyone else, but I didn't taste a mouthful. Conversation was limited to how good the salmon was, how much effort it had taken to find it and how much it had cost. Mother
went to bed as soon as we were finished, again affecting mincing little steps and hunched shoulders. It was quite obvious that
she took it as her God-given right to say or do anything she
wanted to anybody, anywhere, at any time . . . then she expected me to apologize for resenting it. I suppose I had always
been aware of the fact but swept it under my mental carpet,
along with so many other things concerning my mother.

The next morning Justin's temperature was normal and he
was feeling fine. He had eaten a good breakfast and the prob-

lem now was to keep him from running around too much and bringing on a relapse. Mother was late in emerging from her room. As soon as Justin heard his grandmother's footsteps on the stairs, he asked if he could go up to his room to play. I said that he could but reminded him to take it easy.

Mother went directly to the kitchen to make herself a cup of coffee and boil an egg. I was in the den and had seen her pass through the dining room, moving quite normally but, as soon as I set foot in the kitchen, her shoulders slumped forward and she started the mincing little steps again.

"Good morning, Mother," I said formally.

"Good morning," she whimpered in a frail little-old-lady voice. I went to my chair at the end of the room and sat down to read a magazine. A full thirty minutes passed before she came over to my chair and stood before me, still hunched forward, but now her arms were hanging straight down before her, fingers curled inward, and she was tapping her nails together in a most peculiar fashion. In the tiniest of tiny voices, she said, "I'm sorry we argued, B.D. We mustn't argue. I can't stand to have you angry with me. . . . I just can't bear it." She reached toward me, arms apart, as though expecting me to leap straight out of the chair and embrace her. "I only want you to love me . . . just love me a lot." I remained seated. "Arguing is the least of my concerns, Mother." She dropped her arms and began to take little steps back and forth in front of me, alternately sighing and wringing her hands. "What? Then why—"

"It's your treatment of all of us, Mother. I don't know why you even come here. You drive my husband out of the house by being as rude and unpleasant as you possibly can. You provoke endless arguments with me by consistently doing things you know will annoy me. You're furious when I won't let you mess about in my kitchen, but you got hysterical when I even walked *toward* yours to get Justin a glass of apple juice. And, as far as Justin is concerned, I'm absolutely at a loss. It's inconceivable to me that you could be so jealous for my attention that you would treat your own grandson so bizarrely. I don't know what you want, Mother, and worse than that, I don't think you do either. You say that you just want to be with me, but you don't. I was with you for days in California, not to mention most evenings, and you never spent any time with me. You hid in the kitchen all day, drinking no doubt, and went to bed early every night. And don't tell me that you were tired . . . you stay awake watching television in your room every night of your life. You don't want to be with me . . . you want to *own* me. You want to have me sitting in a chair like one of your trophies on a shelf. You didn't want a daughter . . . you wanted a doll to play with . . . a toy which you could wind up and have perform for you when you were in the mood, a cute fantasy being to unquestioningly do your bidding. Perhaps this is all my fault. Perhaps I should have gone on strike years ago. Whatever the case, Mother, I can't take any more."

She stopped pacing and faced me, frantically wringing her hands. "I don't know what you mean, B.D. I love you . . . I love all of you. Please let's stop this. All I want is that you love me back. Let's not fight when I have to leave . . . you know I'm sad when I'm leaving. Just tell me you love me." It was no use. I'd had to try though, one more time. I rose wearily to my feet. "O.K., Mother, I love you. Does that make you happy?"

"Oh, *thank* you, B.D.," she whispered. "I can't *stand* it when we fight. I need you to really love me."

"Right," I said, heading for the stairs to check on Justin. We hadn't even had an argument, not a voice had been raised in anger, and I was completely, utterly, to the marrow of my bones, emotionally drained.

Kathryn arrived while I was still upstairs and took Mother's bags to the car. When I came down, Mother and I went through the now-farcical ritual of hugs and kisses. She reiterated how much she loved us all and how grateful she was that I loved her so much.

"Right," I said for the second time, and she was gone.

For a few days after Mother left, I kept postponing the inevitable. Jeremy knew, of course, everything that had happened during his absences. Whatever details I had omitted in the telling had been more than filled in by Justin. My husband was being very patient with me, permitting me time to come to terms inwardly with what I had to do. I knew that I had to confirm to him my intention of doing it, but I was having trouble saying the words. I kept picturing myself saying to my mother, "You can't say I didn't warn you, but you're no longer welcome in my house."

I was two people. I was a wife and mother who couldn't knowingly do anything to harm her family, and a daughter who could only make her mother happy by permitting her to be cruel to that same family. I loved my husband and my children and they loved me. That should make the choice very simple, but it wasn't. My mother loved me more than anything else in the world and whether I loved her or hated her at any given moment in time, I had never really doubted that love. I might not understand her kind of love, let alone want it, but I couldn't convince myself that it didn't exist.

I had tried for nineteen years to combine the two roles, to permit this woman who was my mother to come and go as she pleased and, at the same time, be myself a loving wife and mother. Somehow, through all of it, the love between my husband and me had grown and deepened, but seeing Mother trying to victimize little Justin was another matter.

I told Jeremy I would like to go for a walk with him in the woods. We strolled up the field behind the house, bathed in the warmth of spring, his arm around my shoulders and mine around his waist. The meadow grass was fresh and springy beneath our feet, the air smelled sweet and all about us life was renewing itself. Great swaths of lacy ferns edged the path through the woods, the birds chirped and sang and squirrels chattered. Two deer jumped out of the path ahead of us and a grouse started in fright and winged away through the fresh budding leaves. The courage that had been so elusive flowed into me from God's wonders.

"Sweetheart," I said as we strolled slowly along, "I know you don't want me to apologize and I won't. You've been angry many times over the years and the other day I made a promise. I couldn't bring myself to listen to you and I couldn't face the truth. Now I have . . . it's done. I'll have to live with the knowledge that I'm turning my back on a mother who loves me . . . and please don't say she doesn't . . . but I've finally come to terms with the knowledge that her kind of love will destroy me if I don't shut it out of our lives. The only thing I ask is that you permit me to do it my way and at the time of my choosing. I'll probably wait until next time she announces a visit. Don't worry that my continuing to talk to her on the phone will weaken my resolve . . . it won't. I've finally made my decision and I'll stick to it."

We stopped walking. Jeremy folded me in his arms and said, "I'll never mention it again unless you ask for help. I love you . . . just remember that you're not alone with this unless you choose to be."

7

Mother returned to California and did the pilot episode of *Hotel*. In June she called to tell me that she had gone for a physical to Vincent Carroll, her lifelong physician and friend. A breast lump and a vein dysfunction behind her eyes had been discovered. At Harold's urging, she came east to have the lump removed and her circulation checked. Harold wanted her in a New York hospital because he thought that it would be easier to maintain secrecy and keep it out of the press.

She arrived on June 24 and checked into the hospital on the twenty-seventh under the name of Barbara Bailey. The cyst was removed but was found to be malignant. A mastectomy was performed the following day. Mother cried a little but basically behaved stoically. I was terribly shaken and very worried about her. There is something about cancer that is different from any other affliction; even the word itself is terrifying.

Tests were run to isolate the problem with Mother's veins, but her recovery from the operation was going very well indeed. It was intended that Mother stay at Harold's apartment for her recuperation, again in the interest of secrecy, but everything went wrong at once.

On July 2, the day before she was due to be discharged, the sedatives and pain killers were discontinued. On July 3, Mother suffered a mild stroke. When I spoke to her late in the day, she told me the doctors didn't know what they were talking about; they kept telling her that the stroke had been very mild and that there were no aftereffects when, in fact, she was itching all over. On July 4 she suffered another stroke and again I spoke to her late in the day. This time she was absolutely incensed with the doctors; the itching had become overwhelming and being touched was painful. On July 5 she had a third stroke and I managed for the first time to exchange a few words with Kathryn. While Mother was distracted by a therapist, Kathryn took the phone into the bathroom to talk to me. The itching, she said, had become so acute that Mother was scratching herself raw; she screamed when anyone touched her, claiming that it was painful beyond bearing; she couldn't sleep, she was hungry but couldn't eat. Kathryn said it was horrible to watch and no one seemed to have the faintest idea what was causing it. Apart from everything else she, Kathryn, was exhausted from lack of sleep since Mother screamed all night from the itching and the pain and shouted continually that she was being starved to death, even though she was unable to eat anything offered her.

Vincent Carroll called and said he was unable to reach Harold and, therefore, didn't know where or how Mother was. I told him the cyst had been malignant and that a mastectomy had been performed with complete success. I told him about the strokes and described the itching, the pain and the hunger as best I could. Vincent became very agitated and asked whether I knew the names of any of Mother's doctors; he wanted to get in touch with them to apprise them of certain facts of which they might not be aware. I told him I didn't know, that Harold was running a complete mystery show and the best I could do was give Kathryn his number and have her call him. I asked whether he had any idea what the itching, pain and hunger were all about and whether they were stroke-related. He said that was precisely why he wanted to talk to Mother's doctors; she was going through alcoholic withdrawal and would have to be handled carefully. He also said that Mother's strokes were the direct result of many, many years of alcoholism and that he had been begging her for just as many years to cut down on her drinking.

I grasped the first available opportunity to ask Kathryn to call Vincent. She said she would but stressed that she had been instructed to speak to no one without first obtaining Mr. Schiff's permission. She also agreed to try to have one of Mother's doctors call Dr. Carroll. I called Harold and told him of my conversation with Vincent Carroll. Harold said that he had spoken to Vincent, that Mother was under the best care available anywhere in the world and that, in essence, I should mind my own business.

I made one more attempt. I called Mother and told her that Vincent was most anxious about her welfare and greatly wanted to speak to her; would she call him or accept a call from him? She raved, ranted, called me names and said she never wanted to hear Vincent Carroll's name again. Within the hour, Harold called and said that I had gravely upset Mother and was impeding her recovery with my interference.

My family and I went away for the weekend and I left the phone number where I could be reached with both Harold and Kathryn. I spoke to Mother before we left on Saturday morning. Harold called on Monday evening, just after we got home, to tell me Mother had had another stroke at midday on Saturday, this time serious. Her left arm was paralyzed, her face was sagging and there was weakness in her left leg.

Mother was now suffering hallucinations in addition to the itching, pain and inability to eat. She told me she was constantly being given different medications to relieve the itching. Kathryn told me Mother had become so abusive toward the nursing staff and the therapists that they were turning over daily, refusing to return after one or two sessions. She was making so much noise, screaming and throwing tantrums, that the hospital had had to move her to a room in the tower structure at the side of the building and set up a soundproof screen in front of the door.

On the fourteenth, despite Mother's continuing protests that she didn't want visitors, I went to see her. I took many deep breaths in the elevator on the way up to her floor, determined not to permit any reaction to her appearance to show on my face. She looked frighteningly small and sad and my heart went out to her. Kathryn, very tense, was keeping herself busy with Mother's mail on a card table and seldom looked directly at me. When she did look my way, it was to comment on things like the flowers in the room or the view of the river from the corner window. The room was huge with a very high ceiling, a private bathroom, a large couch, upholstered armchairs, bureaus, a coffee table and a tiny kitchen facility in one corner. It was decorated brightly in green, yellow and white. There were paintings on the walls and even the curtains were lovely. If it hadn't been for the hospital bed and the equipment around it, I would have thought myself in a hotel suite.

While we waited for lunch, I asked Mother why she was chain-smoking. She screamed at me to mind my own business and claimed the doctors had said it was perfectly all right. She constantly dropped ashes all over herself and the bed and frequently dropped the lighted cigarette itself into the confusion of her rumpled nightgown and bed linens. Each time she did so, Kathryn or the nurse rushed to retrieve it and make sure all the sparks were out.

Kathryn and I had chef's salad. Mother pushed her lunch tray off the bed and onto the floor for the nurse to clean up. Conversation when I arrived, despite my best efforts to be warm and caring, had been rendered stiff and stilted by Mother. Now it was limited to her complaining about the nurses, complaining about the doctors, complaining about the food and complaining about the therapists. Once in a while, she interrupted the litany with a comment on how nice it would be to be ". . . staying at the farm with her beautiful family." After lunch, a therapist arrived and I was witness to a scene straight from hell.

The therapist was a charming lady who was endlessly patient with Mother. She carefully explained, over and over again, why Mother had to move her leg a certain way and her arm a certain way and say certain words. She repeated in a sweet, even tone that the doctors had to know if there was any improvement. Mother screamed profanities at her. Everytime the therapist did or said something, Mother screamed profanities. "Don't touch me, you bitch! . . . Jesus! I'll kill you if you touch me again! . . . You fucking idiot! . . . None of you are worth a shit in this place! . . . Get your fucking hands off me! . . .

You don't know what you're doing! . . . Keep your filthy hands to yourself! . . . Get the fuck out and leave me alone! . . . Shit! . . . Christ! . . . Jesus! . . . Fuck! . . ."

My consciousness faded out and I was back in another time . . . back at Honeysuckle Hill in my early teens. Mother was in bed with a cold. Aunt Bobby was trying to get her to eat some hot soup.

"Jesus, Bobby! Can't you see I'm going mad with hunger? I can't eat that! I'd choke on it! Don't you know *anything*? Can't you see I'm sick? I've got the worst cold in the history of man. Christ! You've no idea the agony I'm in. You don't care. Shit! All you care about is your precious soup. What's wrong with you? Leave me alone! Get the fuck out of here! If I want you, you stupid bitch, I'll ring for you! Now get the fuck out of here!"

Poor Aunt Bobby, she was such a sweet lady. She wouldn't harm a fly, and I really think she loved her sister despite everything. Marriages messed up. Life messed up. Having to park her daughter all over creation because Mother wouldn't have Fay in the house while Aunt Bobby worked for her. Wouldn't let her own niece live in because it would have distracted Aunt Bobby. Poor Aunt Bobby . . . she's gone now. Why did she do it? Why did she let her sister convince her she was useless, that she'd starve to death without Mother's benefaction? Aunt Bobby worked her heart out for Mother. She was loyal and good and nice . . . and what did she get for it? Abuse, abuse and more abuse.

I was brought back to the present by the lack of noise around me. The therapist had gone and Kathryn was helping Mother into an upright sitting position in a chair. Then she brought out hair brushes and makeup and helped Mother get spruced up. I was completely at a loss. A few minutes ago, Mother had been a helpless invalid who couldn't stand to be touched, who spewed filthy invective at the therapist and screamed that she wanted to die. Now this—hair brushing and makeup and no complaints at all while Kathryn moved her to the chair. It didn't make sense.

Minutes after Mother was robed, slippered, lipsticked, seated and had her hair arranged, the mystery unraveled itself. A handsome young doctor strode through the door. He was very charming and, as he sat down to chat, he explained that he had nothing to do with Mother's case but liked to stop by each day during his rounds. Gone the vicious, crumpled, foulmouthed invalid . . . enter the wide-eyed, gutsy star. If I hadn't seen it, I wouldn't have believed it. She smiled bravely, she joked with him, she told him about my beautiful farm and how she wished she were there instead of in the hospital. No wonder Harold was so smug and complacent whenever I spoke to him. This must be what he saw when he visited his client every evening. When the young doctor left, so did the wide-eyed, gutsy star. Within seconds, the surroundings were disgusting, the doctors and nurses were trying to kill her and she wished they'd succeed.

I stayed a short while longer and then stood up to leave. Mother was lying flat on her back, eyes squeezed shut, muttering to the nurse who had just come in, "Why won't anybody help me? None of you give a shit. Jesus! Just keep away from me!" Kathryn walked me to the elevator. She said it was the first time in sixteen days that she had been outside the room. She was telling me again about the nurses and therapists refusing to work more than one shift each when we heard Mother screaming, "Kathryn! Kathryn!" Kathryn looked at me wanly and said, "See?" I asked if she had explained all this to Harold. She had. I told her to keep a stiff upper lip and assured her that I would have a long talk with him as soon as I got home.

I did have a long talk with Harold that night. I told him Kathryn needed some time off regardless of Mother's tantrums. I related the incident of the handsome young doctor. I mentioned the smoking. I again suggested that he talk to Vincent Carroll. I told him what Kathryn had said and everything I had seen for myself. He said he didn't know why Kathryn would say such things, that he had no intention of speaking to Vincent Carroll again and that I didn't know what I was talking about. He said he saw Mother every day and that she was being quite remarkable. He suddenly changed the subject and said that he and I had to make a decision about where to put Mother. I suggested that since he and I were discussing two different people, he had better make the decision on his own.

Vincent continued to call me frequently, despite the fact that my efforts to have someone consult him had come to naught.

Harold phoned one day and said that the hospital had released Mother as a surgical patient and wanted her to leave. A
month later, she was still there. Harold called many times during the intervening weeks to enlist my help in convincing
Mother that she was well enough to move out of the hospital.
I tried, but all she did was argue that the doctors were incom-
petent idiots and that she was the only one who would know
when she was well enough to leave. When I pressed the matter, she hung up on me.

I volunteered to go to New York and move Mother, whether
she liked it or not, to any place designated by Harold. He didn't
like my attitude and told me to leave it to him. Finally, late in
August and only a few days before the date upon which Harold had told me the hospital was going to evict Mother, she
moved to the Lombardy.

For the next couple of weeks, Mother was irritable and rude
whenever I asked how she was coming along. She said there
was no improvement and that the therapists came every day
to torment her for nothing. Harold said she was making a miraculous recovery. She was walking, her face muscles had almost returned to normal and her face and arm were improving
daily. I told him that Mother had not admitted any of this to
me and he said that I must have misunderstood her.

At the very next opportunity, I told Mother what Harold
had said. She grunted and replied, "It's just *fascinating* how
everyone in the world knows how I am better than I do."
Whenever I volunteered to go see her which, I have to admit,
I was not overly anxious to do after the first time, she said she
didn't want me to just then.

On September 2, Mother called. "B.D., I'm going back to
California on the thirteenth and I have to see you before I
leave."

"That's terrific," I said. "I know you'll be much happier in
your own home."

"I know that's what *you* think," she retorted sharply. "Christ!
You've said it often enough. Anyway, when are you coming in?"

"Why don't you tell me what days are convenient? I'll check
with Jeremy and see which is best for him."

"Jesus! You mean you can't drive yourself yet?" She was

referring to my back ligaments, about which she had inquired virtually every time I spoke to her, which I had ruptured a few years earlier and which became inflamed if I drove a car for too long.

"Of course I can't," I replied. "We've discussed it often enough."

"Shit! How are you going to get here then?"

"The same way I got there last time," I answered patiently. "I just told you. Tell me what days are good for you and I'll check Jeremy's availability."

"I don't *want* that bastard to bring you in. I don't want to owe him any favors."

"Mother," I said, having trouble with the concept, "I don't know where you got the idea, but you don't owe Jeremy any favors. I can assure you he doesn't bring me to see you as a favor to *you*. He does it because I ask him to, that's all."

"You mean that's the only way you can get here?" she yelped. "If *he* doesn't bring you, *I* can't see you?"

"That's right."

"Christ! I'll have to call you back." Click, dial tone.

It was a revelation. I had been to see Mother only once in all this time because every time I mentioned coming, she had got upset. It had been a far cry from the demand that I become a New York commuter which I had expected. I hadn't been sorry, just puzzled. Now I had the answer.

Mother called again. "B.D., I'm going to call Josie and ask her to go get you and bring you in to see me."

"Are you out of your mind?" I exploded. "Josie is two hundred miles from here and I'm two hundred miles from you. By the time she came here, went to New York, came back here and then went home, she'd have driven eight hundred miles. That's the most ridiculous thing I've ever heard."

"She'd do it for *me*," Mother stated imperiously.

"I doubt it very much . . . but even if she would, I wouldn't let her . . . so forget it."

"Jesus! I'll have to figure something else out." Click, dial tone.

The phone rang, "B.D., I'm sending a car to pick you up." The hell with it, I thought, at least it would save Jeremy a drive to the city and back. I realized something. I had started out feeling terrible that Mother had cancer, then relieved at the outcome of the mastectomy, then shocked by the serious stroke, then mortified by her behavior in the hospital, then fed up with the nonsense about whether she was recovering or not—and now it was business as usual. My sympathy had completely evaporated. The board was wiped clean. All I wanted was to get this over with as soon as possible and have her go back to California and leave me alone. She and Harold both.

"Fine," I said, "when will it be here?"

"What day would you like?"

"Wednesday would be best."

"That's no good. There'll be costume people here."

"How about Tuesday? I have an appointment, but it's easily changed."

"That's no good either."

"Look," I said impatiently, *"you* pick the day. Any day between now and the thirteenth is fine except Thursday. I have an appointment at the dentist to have my gums scraped and I'd rather not postpone it."

"Let me see . . ." she mumbled, ". . . yes, that's what I thought. Thursday's the only day I have open. It'll have to be Thursday."

"Right," I said.

"What time do you want the car there?"

"Seven-thirty A.M."

"Why so early?"

"So that I can be back in time to see Justin before he goes to bed."

"Jesus! That won't give us any time together."

"We'll have four hours. I'm confident we'll be able to say all we have to in four hours."

"God, you're a cold bitch!" Click, dial tone.

Kathryn called to confirm that the car had been laid on. She said that Mother had instructed her to say to me: "Your terms have been met. It won't give us much time together, but it's better than nothing."

The limousine and Justin's school bus arrived at the same time. Ashley wasn't returning to school until the following Sunday and, after we all waved Justin off, Jeremy and Ashley saw me into my gilded chariot and wished me luck.

It was an interesting visit. Mother commented on how much she liked my long, layered haircut (Jeremy liked my hair long and Mother had been complaining for years that I only looked well with it tied up in a bun), how beautiful the farm was, how wonderful Jeremy and the children were, how grateful she was that I was so indispensable to my family and what a marvelous feeling that must be. She told me about a phone conversation she had had with Aaron Spelling, head of the company producing *Hotel*. She had called him and said, "I never did want to do your lousy show. Now I'm not up to it anymore . . . and don't let anybody tell you I am . . . you can take your show and shove it!" She laughed uproariously as she told me about it, but laughed even harder while mimicking Harold trying to convince Aaron Spelling that she was really just fine and would be back to do another episode any minute now. Then she said, "I'll tell you one thing . . . Aaron Spelling knows who the fighter is now." She said that Kathryn was unofficially engaged to a Frenchman and commented that she seemed to lose all her daughters in France. She extolled the virtues of Englishmen and Frenchmen. She cried copiously over not being able to return to the farm with me and apologized for having been so boring all afternoon.

The drive home took four hours and I used every minute contemplating the events of the afternoon. Prior to today, Mother's parting sentiment would have been a paradox. I had been tempted to tell her that, far from being boring, it had been the most pleasant few hours I had ever spent with her; that if she would only be boring *all* the time, we wouldn't have a problem in the world. I didn't tell her because I knew the few pleasant hours had been nothing more than a coincidence . . . the fantasy daughter and myself coinciding in place and time. I finally had the missing piece of the puzzle and I hadn't even been looking for it anymore. Mother had handed it to me on a silver platter when she recounted her call to Aaron Spelling.

She had triggered my memory of a long-forgotten conversation, one between a despairing woman and her eight-year-old daughter in a gazebo behind a stone cottage in Brentwood. I wondered whether it would have made any difference if that conversation had taken place when I was a little older and more able to understand its import; or whether it would have helped if I had simply remembered it sooner. Perhaps, but why waste time on what-ifs? I had, at last, remembered it . . . and now I understood.

Now that I had my finger on the answer, it seemed so obvious. Here I had been racking my brain all these years searching for whatever it was that drove Mother to do the things she did, and I had known all the time. She had told me herself . . . twenty-eight years ago. I thought back over unforgettable incidents in my life with Mother, both before and after my marriage, and tested the newly found missing ingredient against the facts. It fit in every instance. Although not the sole cause of all her actions, it *was* that hitherto unidentifiable "something else" that had eluded me for so long.

This discovery was not triumphant but, rather, extremely sad. It was sad for all of us because the revelation came years too late. As the limousine rolled smoothly and noiselessly through the mountains and valleys of Pennsylvania and along the winding Susquehanna, I knew what I was going to do. I had thought of one way, the only way, of doing something which could make a difference at this late date. I wanted to get home and see what my husband thought.

The house was empty when I arrived. Jeremy had taken the boys out to dinner so that I wouldn't have to start cooking the minute I walked in the door. I glanced at the clock, seven-thirty, and knew that they wouldn't be long. By the time the coffee water was boiling, I heard gravel crunching in the driveway.

We hugged and kissed each other as though I had been gone for a week and Justin narrated the details of an earth-shaking school event involving a boy called Moosey Otis. I made coffee for Jeremy and me and gave the boys each a soda. Then I sat them all down in the kitchen to listen to my revelation.

I began by explaining that I had found the elusive missing ingredient that drove my mother to do inexplicable things all the time. "She was telling me about a conversation she'd had with Aaron Spelling. Apparently she called him and told him to take his show and shove it. She was delighted with herself for having done it and didn't seem in the least concerned that she was throwing away a fortune. All she cared about was that Spelling now knew who the fighter was.

"It triggered my memory of a conversation she and I had when I was eight. She told me her view of her father and men in general, and her philosophy of how to deal with life and the world as a whole. Lots of what she said was about fighting. Oh, don't get me wrong, I know she's always talking about her fights, but what I was missing was that fighting is done for its own sake; not just to win an *argument,* but to prove who's *strong* enough to win. Fighting has its own justification and *is* its own reward. And I was supposed to be just like her; I was supposed to fight with everyone to prove that I was one of the strong ones too. You see? At the end of that conversation years ago, she said everything would be fine because we'd fight the world together, she and I.

"The disparity between me and the fantasy daughter we all talk about derives from my unwillingness to fight. I don't fight with you guys, I don't fight with my friends, I don't fight with strangers at cocktail parties. To make it worse, I do occasionally fight with *her,* the one person I'm not supposed to fight with at all. She and I are the dominant ones and on the same team, while the rest of the world, particularly husbands and children, must be made to toe the line. You guys, I'm sorry to tell you, are the Lilliputians who'll devour my soul if I don't slap you around a bit and dominate you.

"That's how Mother views it. The weaklings allow the Lilliputians to climb up their legs and devour them; the strong fight them off. It's a round-the-clock battle and everyone and everything is a Lilliputian trying to get her. She despises weaklings and the difference between the weak and strong is as simple as how hard and how often they fight. When she and I are apart, she convinces herself that I'm a fighter just like her, but the moment she sees me in the bosom of my family, she realizes that I'm one of the contemptible weaklings who spend their lives being considerate of other people. Being considerate and being dominated are the same thing to Mother and it sends her right off the deep end.

"I really think she'd like you, sweetheart," I said to Jeremy, "if I were rude to you and pushed you around and you groveled and submitted like a wimp. The same with you two," I said to Ashley and Justin. "If I hit you with a hairbrush from time to time, told you to stay out of my presence most of the time, and refused to answer your questions any of the time, your grandmother would consider you properly brought up and would stay off your case. It has nothing to do with how you behave, it's how firmly I dominate you that counts.

"When I'm in the kitchen cooking dinner, though, and Ashley asks what we're having and I tell him, or Justin runs in wanting a toy repaired and I repair it, or Dad wants a bowl of salad to tide him over and I fix it for him, it's all proof to Mother that I've been taken over by the Lilliputians and have no will of my own anymore. She can't tolerate it and it makes her mean. I've let her down, I've blown her fantasy daughter out of the water. All her carrying on about how brilliant and wonderful and extraordinary I am is to convince herself that it's so. The moment she sees me as I really am, she begins to boil. When she sees me happy and content and deferring to my husband, living as much as possible in harmony with my chosen world, she becomes driven to change the image which then poses a threat to everything she's ever believed or held dear; and she does it the only way she knows how . . . she starts a fight. If *I* won't keep my image properly polished, then, by golly, she'll shine it up *for* me.

"It's become worse with time instead of better, because the longer I stay happily married, the more her frustration grows. It was at critical mass just before her operation. Not just her threatening Justin when she was here, but that business of calling that friend of hers in Chicago, Laura Abelson, and saying that I'd been hypnotized and she had to set me free. Remember? Then there were those other people who phoned to tell me Mother had called them to say that I was being held against my will, that I'd been brainwashed and needed help to escape from here.

"We figured it was because she was drinking more than ever, and that may well have been the case, but still the missing ingredient was needed to fully explain it. *All* the pieces fit now. No one facet of anyone's character accounts for everything they do, and it's no different with Mother. No one neurosis, obsession, character trait or what-have-you accounts for all the weird things she does, but no explanation of anything she does is complete unless one understands the importance she attaches to fighting for its own sake.

"On the way home this evening, I thought back over Mother's favorite heroines, the ones who occupy a special place in her heart, the ones she always contended were 'good dames': Jezebel, Aggie Hurley, Mildred and so on. Most revealing, though, is the role she *didn't* play. The greatest disappointment in Mother's life was that she didn't get the role of Scarlett O'Hara in *Gone With the Wind*. It meant more to her than I did, any of her husbands did or any role she ever played did. She often said that she and Scarlett were twins. There's no doubt in my mind that she was absolutely right.

"Except for you, Justin, we've all seen or read *Gone With the Wind* at least once. It's a direct peek into Mother's soul. Scarlett had no use for men except for strictly selfish purposes. First she married Charles, who was one of a flock of suitors about whom she cared nothing, because she was in a snit over her failure to talk Ashley Wilkes out of marrying Melanie. Then she married her sister's boyfriend, by lying to him that her sister didn't love him, in order to get at his money to pay the taxes on Tara. Then she married Rhett Butler, whom she didn't love either, because he basically overwhelmed her with his looks, his money and his personality. Once she was married to him, she couldn't stand his strength of character and took every opportunity to hurt him in any way she could. Scarlett fought against everyone and everything and had nothing but contempt for gentle, sensitive or kind people whom she regarded as weak and useless. Just like Mother.

"Scarlett convinced herself that Ashley Wilkes was the one man she'd ever loved and that love, or the illusion of it, survived because she couldn't have him. Scarlett never stopped being convinced that Ashley loved her and believed that he'd married Melanie only because it had been arranged between their families. My mother also had her Ashley Wilkes. Despite his happy and successful marriage of more than forty years' duration to 'another woman,' Mother always contended that she had been his first choice and that she'd turned down his proposal of marriage because she was afraid of his strength. She believed, or suffered the delusion, that she had and always would love this man and that it was a cross she would always have to bear.

"At the end of *Gone With the Wind,* when Melanie dies in childbirth and Scarlett runs to Ashley to share their love freely at last, she finds him devastated by the loss of his wife, whom he loved more than life itself. It shatters Scarlett and she runs back to Rhett, but he's finally had enough of her cavalier treatment and walks out. When Scarlett pleads with him to stay and asks what she'll do now, Rhett exits with his famous line 'Frankly, my dear, I don't give a damn.'

"Unfortunately, I'm Mother's Rhett Butler but, unlike him, I still give a damn even though I have to walk out. After Rhett closed the door behind him, Scarlett cried for a while and then looked up bravely as she remembered her father's words that, no matter what else, she would always have her land, Tara. Tara would be there when all else failed and Scarlett decided to go back there and begin again. Mother's career is Tara. More often than I can count, she's said to the press, 'My work is all there is. In the final analysis, it's the only thing that never lets me down.'

"Most people's view, including mine, is that Scarlett got exactly what she deserved and brought all her misery on herself. Mother's interpretation is truly fascinating and tells it all. She sees Scarlett as the brave, bright woman who fought the good fight all her life and survived betrayal by everyone. Scarlett rose above them all and, when Rhett left her at the end, just as all men do when you need them the most, she overcame that too . . . she had the courage to begin again at Tara. Scarlett, to Mother, was the real winner and we should all be as great as Scarlett.

"Now . . . I realize this is all highly illuminating but doesn't change a thing. Our situation, regrettably, remains unaltered by the discovery of the missing piece of the puzzle. So . . . I've decided what I'm going to do. Are you ready? I'm going to *make* her listen to me . . . I'm going to write a book."

EPILOGUE

So here it is, Mother, the story of you and me, not as you would have it be but as it really was. You wanted me to be like you, a fighter, but I never wanted to fight. Fighting and grand drama have brought you some kind of satisfaction, I hesitate to say happiness, but they bring me misery. Love and laughter have brought me my happiness, but they bore you to tears. I let you have your way and tried to understand you for all those years because, for the most part, I loved and respected you. My husband clenched his teeth and stayed out of the way most of the time because he loved me and understood my dilemma. He also liked the real you, the Ruth Elizabeth you so seldom exposed to any of us. Ashley was able to cope, somehow, during *Family Reunion* and can now take care of himself. But you've gone one step too far; you've carried your fight to Justin, and he's too young to take care of himself. So just as *you* picked on *him* to compensate for what you saw as my weakness, *I* finally have to fight to prove my worth as his mother. Not with the Lilliputians as you would have me do, to stop them from devouring my soul, but with *you* to protect my child and make you realize you're wrong about everything except your career.

You've consistently refused to hear me. You tear up letters

you don't like without finishing them. You hang up the phone if you don't like the words you hear. You've used friends and lawyers to bring pressure to bear when you've wanted something I've been unwilling to give. You've played many roles during my life, some of them brilliantly, some of them basely, but you were only willing to be yourself for a couple of years some fifteen years ago.

Therefore, Mother, I'm bringing the fight to *your* doorstep; my word is pledged that it won't be fought on ours again. It seems to me that you have two choices. Neither of them is to say you forgive me for writing this book and only want me to love you.

You can go back to Tara, confident in the belief that you're in the right but forced to beat a strategic withdrawal. That's okay. It will permit me the privilege of remembering my mother with some love and much respect, and your grandchildren to recall the legend in years to come with the awe it deserves. While you're back at Tara, you might well, without the self-imposed distraction of trying to make me into something I'm not, find the time and inclination to plow some fertile ground and harvest another Oscar.

Or . . . you can hear, at long last, what I have been trying to tell you all along: Yours isn't the only way. It may work for you (though I don't really believe it has), but that's not my concern . . . it *doesn't* work for me. I have found true happiness by leading my life my way. I don't try to convince other people that mine is the only way and neither should you. If you wish to be part of my life, you must accept me as I am, and my family along with me.

It's your choice, Mother . . . go back to Tara or hear me at last. Regard this, Mother, as my cry in the wilderness, to prepare the way and make straight your path. There have been many miracles in my life lately and, if the one for which I now pray should be granted, you'll see that path. All that's asked is that Ruth Elizabeth, no roles and no fantasies, follow it to the door. The door will always be open to her.

My Mother's Keeper

B.D. Hyman

We know her as Queen Elizabeth I in *Elizabeth and Essex*, the betrayed woman in *All About Eve*, the lovelorn spinster in *Now, Voyager*. Few other actresses have achieved such memorable drama or kept audiences enthralled for more than five decades. She is, of course, the incomparable Bette Davis.

This is a spellbinding book about America's most revered actress by the only person who could write it— B. D. Hyman, who tells us what it's like to grow up the daughter of the world-famous star. We see Davis beset by private demons, struggling through her stormy marriage to Gary Merrill, obsessively attached to her

(continued on back flap)

William Morrow & Company, Inc.
105 Madison Avenue
New York, N.Y. 10016